Mitchell
Beazley
Pocket
Guides

WINES OF THE LOIRE, ALSACE AND THE RHÔNE

AND OTHER FRENCH REGIONAL WINES

Roger Voss

First published in Great Britain in 1983 as *The Mitchell Beazley Pocket Guide to French Regional Wines* by Roger Voss. This edition, revised, updated and expanded, published in 1998 by Reed Consumer Books Limited, 25 Victoria Street, London SW1H OEX

A CIP catalogue record for this book is available from the British Library.

ISBN 1 84000 016 3

Commissioning Editor: Sue Jamieson
Executive Art Editor: Fiona Knowles
Editor: Diane Pengelly
Design: Geoff Fennell
Production: Rachel Lynch
Index: Angie Hipkin

Typeset in Veljovic Book
Printed and bound in China

Contents

Introduction

I drank my first glass of wine in France. I was eight. I was staying with a family in a small, rather dilapidated château somewhere in the depths of Poitou. It was my hostess' birthday and a glass of something white (and watered) was thrust into my hand at the end of the meal. It was sweet, and I rather liked it: I asked for more. Perhaps luckily for my reputation as a guest, my request was received with a severe frown and a firm refusal.

I have no idea what that wine was – could it have been a Sauternes? But French wine has been a starting point – I almost wrote reference point – for most of my wine researches over the years. I am sure I am no different from most wine drinkers in that respect. We are still conditioned to start from the belief that French wine offers, if not always the finest quality, certainly the greatest variety of any wine-producing country.

This book is designed to set out that variety. From the frosty winters of the Loire and Alsace to the heat of Provence and Corsica, France's vineyards straddle the divide between cool-climate wines and those from hot, dry areas. With one style (Muscadet) influenced directly by the Atlantic, and others (from Provence, the Midi and Corsica) influenced by the benign Mediterranean, France can truly say that it offers a wine to suit all palates.

It was not so long ago, however, that for those outside the country, France stopped at Bordeaux, Burgundy and Champagne. These were – and still are – the classic areas of winemaking. That France also makes wines in other parts was known but little talked about, except among a few specialists and travellers. Gradually, the realisation dawned that France has more to offer than these few wine styles, great though they are.

One excellent reason for the discovery of France's other regions was the escalating price of wines from the classic areas. But I like to think that it was also because here was a wide and exciting range of tastes. And I am sure it was no coincidence that the gradual arrival of new technology in winemaking helped to launch wines that otherwise would have languished in their corners of France, unfairly dismissed as 'a little wine that won't travel'.

Some of these wines have gone on to achieve fame and fortune overseas. Take the classic pair from the Loire made from the Sauvignon Blanc grape: Sancerre and Pouilly-Fumé. Their style has been the role model for wines from vineyards as far apart as Washington State and New Zealand. The red wines of the Northern Rhône have become the model for a new generation of wine producers in California – known as the Rhône Rangers. Wines modelled on the Gewürztraminer of Alsace have turned up in Australia and New Zealand ... the list could go on.

There is one vital element in these French regional wines which – in French eyes at least – New World wines lack. That is the carefully observed relationship between grape variety, climate and soil, built up by empirical experimentation over centuries.

Traditionally, the French would no more think of planting Pinot Noir in Bordeaux than of planting Cabernet Sauvignon in Burgundy, although more recently, certainly in the south, growers are prepared to try more unorthodox combinations.

Typically of the French, this experimentation has had to be codified and legalised before it could be recognised. This is why a new category, called *vin de pays*, has been created to recognise not only traditions in areas not considered quite good enough for Appellation Contrôlée status, but also to allow space for 'foreign' grape varieties to infiltrate the wines.

Experimentation has begun not a moment too soon. France's wines may have a great tradition and a great reputation, but they are in the process of losing their pre-eminence in the wine world (not helped, it must be said, by a small harvest in '91). The New World and other European countries, Italy especially, are overtaking France in the quality stakes, as their growers experiment, absorb new ideas and move onwards – even if onwards also means a rediscovery of long-forgotten traditions.

France has been slow to catch on to the viticultural and vinicultural revolution, content to rely on its hitherto superior reputation and tradition. The experimentation in the Midi and the introduction of *vins de pays* as vehicles for this experimentation, is all new. The arrival of a new generation of growers and producers who have travelled the world, who have perhaps even studied in California or Australia, has brought the philosophy of tradition and the relationship of wine to its *terroir* into conjunction with the freer approach of the New World.

France may never regain its total dominance of wine – nor should it. What will keep it in the forefront of any wine drinker's mind is the diversity of its product. I hope this book offers a glimpse of that variety.

THE FOURTH EDITION

What a contrast a few years can make. When I wrote the introduction to the first edition of this book, back in 1987, France was on the point of experiencing one of the most exhilarating succession of vintages ever seen. 1988, '89 and '90 saw superb wines from all regions, wines which will be talked about long after most of them have been drunk.

This tremendous flowering of fine wines led French producers to believe that a golden age had arrived. And so it had. But the golden age was one which took in the whole world, one where France might play a lead part, but not *the* lead part.

By the time the second edition came out in 1992, that challenge was even more severe. It was compounded by the fact that after those three great vintages, France's vineyards had suffered terrible frost damage in 1991. The years of '92 and '93, while they brought quantity, never repeated the quality of '88, '89 or '90. By 1995 and the third edition, regions that were still relatively unknown back in 1987 were leading the way in showing that French wine can compete on a world stage. The *vins de pays* and Appellation Contrôlée wines of the south of

France, from Languedoc and Roussillon, represented the best
value the country could offer, made as they were with the latest
ideas in viticulture and winemaking, and using technology and
know-how inspired by the successes of Australia, California and
New Zealand among others.

Other regions in this book are finding that the world's
discovery that French wine doesn't stop at Bordeaux, Burgundy
and Champagne is to their advantage. The Rhône in particular is
riding high, the popularity of its wines encouraged by the fact
that they reflect popular tastes for fruit rather than too much
tannin, flavour rather than too much complexity. The quality of
the wines of the Loire has also risen enormously as producers
have not just invested in new technology but also shown
adaptability and a willingness to move away from time-honoured
traditions if they stand in the way of quality.

It is the amazing story of the south of France, the Languedoc,
with its varietally-labelled wines, that has been the continuing
success of the 1990s. Even the French, succoured from birth on
tales of Appellation Contrôlée wines, have succumbed to these
succulent newcomers: sales of *vin de pays* wines in French super-
markets have soared while those of AC wines have stagnated.

In the past few months, the realisation that the '96 harvest
was fabulous in regions such as the Loire (which badly needed
some happy news after the poor vintages of the early 1990s) and
in Alsace and parts of the Rhône, have, once again, given French
viticulturalists a boost.

But they do still suffer, against the onslaught of the New
World, from outdated regulations which make experimentation
and independence of thought very difficult. The rules which
govern French wine are designed to prevent fraud, rather than to
encourage new ideas or markets. It seems that, until the bureau-
cratic mentality is restrained, French regional wines will continue
to be at a disadvantage in the world market for wine.

France's Appellation System

Legally speaking, there are four categories of wine in France. At the top in quality and reputation is Appellation d'Origine Contrôlée, abbreviated to AOC or AC. Nearly 30 percent of all French wine comes into this category. It is a guarantee not only of origin, but also increasingly of minimum standards in the vineyard and cellar. An AC wine must come from a particular area, and from suitable vineyard sites in that area. It can be made only from a list of recommended grape varieties, planted to a certain density per hectare, and yield a specified amount (which can vary from harvest to harvest). The wine has to be vinified and matured in a certain way, and can be sold only after a certain time. The finished wine must have a minimum alcohol level, and pass a tasting test. The grower has to declare his production and stock each year on August 31.

The second category is Vins Delimités de Qualité Supérieure, or VDQS. This is found generally in smaller, out-of-the-way areas or in areas that are only just establishing their reputations. It is seen as a stepping stone to full AC status, and seems to be gradually disappearing. Only 1.3 percent of French wine falls into this category, whose requirements are the same as for AC.

The third category is relatively new. *Vin de pays* was created in 1973, and the late 1970s and 1980s saw a mushrooming of *vin de pays* regions. The idea was to give areas producing basic table wine a chance to improve quality, price and market. As with AC and VDQS wines, geographical area, grape varieties, yields, vineyard and winemaking requirements are specified, but they are less restricted. In addition, some *vins de pays* allow the use of non-local grape varieties – for example Cabernet Sauvignon or Chardonnay in the south of France – and it is these that often produce the most interesting wines. There are three *vin de pays* categories:

1 **Regional** *vins de pays*, covering huge areas of the country, certainly more than one French *département*;
2 **Departmental** *vins de pays*, covering all of one *département*;
3 **Zonal** *vins de pays*, covering smaller areas within a *département*. Often these can overlap with an AC or VDQS zone, but have different regulations, especially about permitted grape varieties.

Since, under European Community rules, the *vin de pays* is still only basic table wine, it will also be labelled 'Vin de Table de France'.

The fourth category is table wine (*vin ordinaire, vin de table*). This includes wine for distilling into brandy. It is sold by alcohol degree, and the rules stipulate that its origins cannot appear on any label, although it is likely that most comes from the Midi.

How to Use this Book

This book is a region-by-region guide to over 770 wine producers of Appellation Contrôlée (AC) wines, Vins Delimités de Qualité Supérieure (VDQS) and *vins de pays* in all the winegrowing regions of France apart from Bordeaux, Burgundy and Champagne (which are dealt with in separate Mitchell Beazley wine guides).

Each region is treated in the same way. There is an introduction, setting out the general styles and character of the wines from that region and describing the character of the countryside. This is followed by detailed notes on each of the AC, VDQS and *vin de pays* areas within the main region. These notes contain information on the colours of the wines made (red, rosé and white), whether sparkling wine is made, and the grape varieties permitted.

Producer entries follow. These are arranged alphabetically by producer within AC or VDQS areas. The AC and VDQS order follows that in the introduction to each section. Where a producer or *négociant* makes more than one AC or VDQS wine, he or she will be listed under the area in which their cellars are situated or where their principal vineyard holding is located.

Information contained in the producer entry is standardised as much as possible. The name of the producer is given first, followed by his or her address, including the Cedex code (it is essential to use this when writing to France). Details of the vineyards owned are set out next, followed by the production given in terms of 75-centilitre bottles. This figure refers only to wine bottled by the producer – any sold in bulk is not included. In addition, producers are codified by the type of business they operate (*see below*).

At the end of the entry, there are details of when the producer's tasting room is open. Often, the entry will indicate that appointments are preferred, but even when this is not stated, it is courteous to write to smaller producers in advance. Larger firms and cooperatives normally have tasting rooms that are open to the public.

Abbreviations

ha   hectares

VP-R a *vigneron proprietaire-récoltant*, a producer who makes wine only from his or her own land and does not buy in grapes or wine

N   *négociant*, or wine merchant, who buys in grapes or wine which is then sold under the firm's own name – a *négociant* may also own land, in which case the code will read VP-R and N

Coop cooperative of producers – this code is followed by the number of members in the cooperative

The Grape Varieties

A range of grape varieties makes up the bulk of the wine produced by each region, but each has also some unknowns or some that are not native. The following list shows in which AC and VDQS each grape variety is permitted.

RED

Abouriou *Southwest*: Côtes du Marmandais

Alicante *Provence*: Coteaux Varois

Aramon *Provence*: Coteaux Varois
Midi: Coteaux du Languedoc-Coteaux de Vérargues

Braquet *Provence*: Bellet

Cabernet Franc *Loire*: Bourgueil, Chinon, Coteaux du Loir, St-Nicolas de Bourgueil, Touraine, Touraine-Villages, Touraine-Mesland, Coteaux du Vendômois, Anjou, Saumur, Saumur-Champigny, Vin du Thouarsais, Coteaux d'Ancenis, Fiefs Vendéens
Midi: Côtes de la Malepère
Southwest: Béarn, Bergerac, Buzet, Côtes de Bergerac, Côtes de Duras, Côtes du Frontonnais, Côtes du Marmandais, Gaillac, Irouléguy, Madiran, Marcillac, Pécharmant, Côtes du Brulhois, Côtes de St-Mont, Tursan, Vin d'Entraygues et du Fel, Vin d'Estaing

Cabernet Sauvignon *Loire*: Bourgueil, Chinon, Touraine, Anjou, Saumur, Haut-Poitou, Vin du Thouarsais, Fiefs Vendéens
Provence: Coteaux d'Aix-en-Provence, Coteaux des Baux en Provence, Côtes de Provence, Coteaux Varois
Midi: Cabardès, Côtes de la Malepère
Southwest: Béarn, Bergerac, Buzet, Côtes de Bergerac, Côtes de Duras, Côtes du Frontonnais, Côtes du Marmandais, Gaillac, Irouléguy, Madiran, Marcillac, Pécharmant, Côtes du Brulhois, Côtes de St-Mont, Tursan, Vin d'Entraygues et du Fel, Vin d'Estaing

Calitor *Rhône*: Lirac
Provence: Bandol

Camarèse *Rhône*: Côtes du Rhône, Côtes du Ventoux

Carignan *Rhône*: Côtes du Rhône and -Villages, Coteaux du Tricastin
Provence: Bandol, Cassis, Coteaux d'Aix-en-Provence, Coteaux des Baux en Provence, Côtes Provence, Coteaux de Pierrevert, Coteaux Varois
Midi: Costières de Nîmes, Coteaux du Languedoc, Coteaux du Languedoc-Cabrières, Coteaux du Languedoc-La Clape, Coteaux du Languedoc-La Méjanelle, Coteaux du Languedoc-Coteaux de St-Christol, Coteaux du Languedoc-Coteaux de Vérargues, Coteaux du Languedoc-Montpeyroux, Coteaux du Languedoc-Pic-St-Loup, Coteaux du Languedoc-Quatourze, Coteaux du Languedoc-St-Drézéry, Coteaux du Languedoc-St-Georges d'Orques, Coteaux du Languedoc-St-Saturnin, Faugères, Minervois, St-Chinian, Corbières, Fitou, Cabardès, Collioure, Côtes du Roussillon, Côtes du Roussillon-Villages

Cinsaut *Rhône*: Côtes du Rhône, Côtes du Rhône-Villages, Châteauneuf-du-Pape, Coteaux du Tricastin, Côtes du Lubéron, Gigondas, Lirac, Tavel

Provence: Bandol, Bellet, Cassis, Coteaux d'Aix-en-Provence Coteaux des Baux en Provence, Côtes de Provence, Palette, Coteaux de Pierrevert, Coteaux Varois

Midi: Costières de Nîmes, Coteaux du Languedoc, Coteaux du Languedoc-Cabrières, Coteaux du Languedoc-La Clape, Coteaux du Languedoc-La Méjanelle, Coteaux du Languedoc-Coteaux de St-Christol, Coteaux du Languedoc-Montpeyroux, Coteaux du Languedoc-Pic-St-Loup, Coteaux du Languedoc Quatourze, Coteaux du Languedoc-St-Drézéry, Coteaux du Languedoc-St-Saturnin, Faugères, Minervois, Corbières, Fitou, Cabardès, Côtes de la Malepère, Collioure, Côtes du Roussillon, Côtes du Roussillon-Villages

Southwest: Côtes du Frontonnais

Counoise *Rhône*: Côtes du Rhône, Châteauneuf-du-Pape, Côtes du Ventoux

Provence: Coteaux d'Aix-en-Provence, Coteaux des Baux en Provence

Midi: Costières de Nîmes, Coteaux du Languedoc

Courbu Noir *Southwest*: Béarn, Béarn-Bellocq

Duras *Southwest*: Gaillac

Fer *Midi*: Cabardès

Southwest: Béarn, Bergerac, Côtes de Bergerac, Côtes du Marmandais, Gaillac, Irouléguy, Madiran, Marcillac, Tursan, Vin d'Entraygues et du Fel, Vin d'Estaing, Vin de Lavilledieu

Folle Noire *Provence*: Bellet

Gamay *Loire*: Châteaumeillant, Côtes d'Auvergne, Côtes du Forez, Côtes de Gien, Côtes Roannaises, St-Pourçain, Coteaux du Loir, Touraine, Touraine-Villages, Touraine-Mesland, Cheverny, Coteaux du Vendômois, Valençay, Anjou, Anjou Gamay, Saumur Mousseux, Haut-Poitou, Coteaux d'Ancenis, Fiefs Vendéens

Alsace: Côtes de Toul, Vin de Moselle

Savoie: Vin de Savoie, Vin de Bugey

Rhône: Coteaux du Lyonnais, Châtillon-en-Diois, Côtes du Lubéron, Côtes du Vivarais

Southwest: Côtes du Frontonnais, Marmandais, Gaillac, Marcillac, Vin d'Entraygues et du Fel, Vin d'Estaing, Vin de Lavilledieu

Grenache Noir *Rhône*: Côtes du Rhône, Côtes du Rhône-Villages, Châteauneuf-du-Pape, Coteaux du Tricastin, Côtes du Lubéron, Côtes du Ventoux, Gigondas, Lirac, Tavel, Rasteau VDN

Provence: Bandol, Bellet, Cassis, Coteaux d'Aix-en-Provence, Coteaux des Baux en Provence, Côtes de Provence, Palette, Coteaux de Pierrevert, Coteaux Varois

Midi: Costières de Nîmes, Coteaux du Languedoc, Coteaux du Languedoc-Cabrières, Coteaux du Languedoc-La Clape, Coteaux du Languedoc-Coteaux de St-Christol, Coteaux du

Languedoc-Coteaux de Vérargues, Coteaux du Languedoc-La Méjanelle, Coteaux du Languedoc-Montpeyroux, Coteaux du Languedoc-Pic-St-Loup, Coteaux du Languedoc-Quatourze, Coteaux du Languedoc-St-Drézéry, Coteaux du Languedoc-St-Saturnin, Faugères, Minervois, St-Chinian, Frontignan VDN, Corbières, Fitou, Cabardès, Côtes de la Malepère, Collioure, Côtes du Roussillon, Côtes du Roussillon-Villages, Banyuls VDN, Maury VDN, Rivesaltes VDN

Grolleau (Groslot) *Loire*: Coteaux du Loir, Rosé de Loire, Touraine, Touraine-Amboise, Touraine-Azay-le-Rideau, Anjou, Saumur Mousseux, Haut-Poitou

Jurançon Noir *Southwest*: Cahors, Gaillac, Marcillac, Vin d'Entraygues et du Fel, Vin d'Estaing, Vin de Lavilledieu

Ladoner Pelut *Midi*: Côtes du Roussillon and -Villages

Malbec (Cot or Auxerrois) *Loire*: Coteaux du Loir, Touraine, Touraine-Villages, Touraine-Mesland, Anjou, Saumur Mousseux
    Midi: Cabardès, Côtes de la Malepère
    Southwest: Bergerac, Buzet, Cahors, Côtes de Bergerac, Côtes de Duras, Côtes du Frontonnais, Côtes du Marmandais, Pécharmant, Côtes du Brulhois

Manseng Noir *Southwest*: Béarn, Béarn-Bellocq

Merlot *Midi*: Cabardès, Côtes de la Malepère
    Southwest: Bergerac, Buzet, Cahors, Côtes de Bergerac, Côtes de Duras, Côtes du Frontonnais, Côtes du Marmandais, Gaillac, Marcillac, Pécharmant, Côtes du Brulhois, Côtes de St-Mont, Vin d'Entraygues et du Fel, Vin d'Estaing

Mondeuse *Savoie*: Vin de Savoie, Vin de Bugey

Mourvèdre *Rhône*: Côtes du Rhône, Côtes du Rhône-Villages, Châteauneuf-du-Pape, Coteaux du Tricastin, Côtes du Lubéron, Côtes du Ventoux, Gigondas, Lirac, Tavel
    Provence: Bandol, Cassis, Coteaux d'Aix-en-Provence, Coteaux des Baux en Provence, Côtes de Provence, Palette, Coteaux Varois
    Midi: Costières de Nîmes, Coteaux du Languedoc, Coteaux du Languedoc-St-Saturnin, Minervois, Corbières, Cabardès, Collioure, Côtes du Roussillon, Côtes du Roussillon-Villages

Muscardin *Rhône*: Côtes du Rhône, Châteauneuf-du-Pape, Côtes du Ventoux

Négrette *Southwest*: Côtes du Frontonnais, Gaillac, Vin d'Entraygues et du Fel, Vin d'Estaing, Vin de Lavilledieu

Pineau d'Aunis *Loire*: Coteaux du Loir, Touraine, Coteaux du Vendômois, Anjou, Saumur, Saumur Mousseux, Fiefs Vendéens

Pinenc *Southwest*: Béarn

Pinot Meunier *Loire*: Vins de l'Orléanais, Touraine
    Alsace: Côtes de Toul

Pinot Noir *Loire*: Menetou-Salon, Reuilly, Sancerre, Côtes de Gien, St-Pourçain, Touraine, Coteaux du Vendômois, Saumur Mousseux, Vin du Haut-Poitou, Fiefs Vendéens
    Alsace: Alsace, Crémant d'Alsace, Côtes de Toul, Vin de Moselle
    Jura: Arbois, Arbois Pupillin, Côtes du Jura

    Savoie: Vin de Savoie, Vin de Bugey

    Rhône: Châtillon-en-Diois

    Southwest: Vin d'Entraygues et du Fel, Vin de l'Estaing

Portugais Bleu *Southwest*: Gaillac

Poulsard (Plousard) *Jura*: Arbois, Arbois Pupillin, Côtes du Jura, L'Étoile

    Bugey: Vin de Bugey

Syrah *Rhône*: Côtes du Rhône, Côtes du Rhône-Villages, Cornas, Côte Rôtie, Coteaux du Lyonnais, Crozes-Hermitage, Hermitage, St-Joseph, Châteauneuf-du-Pape, Châtillon-en-Diois, Coteaux du Tricastin, Côtes du Lubéron, Côtes du Ventoux, Gigondas, Lirac

    Provence: Bandol, Coteaux d'Aix-en-Provence, Coteaux des Baux en Provence, Côtes de Provence, Coteaux Varois

    Midi: Costières de Nîmes, Coteaux du Languedoc-Montpeyroux, Coteaux du Languedoc-St-Saturnin, Minervois, Corbières, Cabardès, Côtes de la Malepère, Collioure

Tannat *Southwest*: Béarn, Cahors, Irouléguy, Madiran, Côtes du Brulhois, Côtes de St-Mont, Tursan

Terret Noir *Rhône*: Côtes du Rhône, Châteauneuf-du-Pape, Côtes du Ventoux

    Midi: Costières de Nîmes, Coteaux du Languedoc, Coteaux du Languedoc-La Clape, Corbières

Tibouren *Provence*: Bandol, Côtes de Provence

Trousseau *Jura*: Arbois, Arbois Pupillin, Côtes du Jura

Vaccarèse *Rhône*: Côtes du Rhône, Châteauneuf-du-Pape, Côtes du Ventoux

WHITE

Aligoté *Savoie*: Vin de Savoie, Vin de Bugey

Altesse (Roussette) *Savoie*: Roussette de Savoie, Seyssel, Seyssel Mousseux, Vin de Savoie, Vin de Savoie Ayse Mousseux, Vin de Savoie Mousseux, Vin de Bugey, Vin de Bugey Mousseux

Baroque *Southwest*: Béarn, Béarn-Bellocq, Irouléguy, Tursan

Bourboulenc *Rhône*: Côtes du Rhône, Côtes du Rhône-Villages, Châteauneuf-du-Pape, Coteaux du Tricastin, Côtes du Lubéron, Côtes du Ventoux, Lirac, Tavel, Côtes du Vivarais

    Provence: Bandol, Bellet

    Midi: Costières de Nîmes, Coteaux du Languedoc, Coteaux du Languedoc-La Méjanelle, Coteaux du Languedoc-Pic-St-Loup, Coteaux du Languedoc-Quatourze, Corbières

Chardonnay *Loire*: St-Pourçain, Touraine, Cheverny, Coteaux du Vendômois, Valençay, Anjou, Saumur, Saumur Mousseux, Haut-Poitou, Fiefs Vendéens

    Alsace: Crémant d'Alsace

    Jura: Côtes du Jura, Côtes du Jura Mousseux, L'Étoile

    Savoie: Roussette de Savoie, Vin de Savoie, Vin de Bugey, Vin de Bugey Mousseux

    Rhône: Coteaux du Lyonnais, Châtillon-en-Diois, Côtes du Lubéron

    Provence: Bellet

    Midi: Blanquette de Limoux

Chasselas *Loire*: Pouilly-sur-Loire
   Alsace: Alsace
   Savoie: Crépy, Seyssel Mousseux, Vin de Savoie
Chenin Blanc (Pineau de la Loire) *Loire*: Coteaux du Loir,
   Jasnières, Montlouis, Touraine and -Villages, -Azay-le-Rideau,
   -Mesland, Vouvray, Cheverny, Coteaux du Vendômois, Anjou,
   Anjou Coteaux de la Loire, Anjou Mousseux, Bonnezeaux,
   Coteaux de l'Aubance, Coteaux du Layon and -Villages,
   Coteaux du Saumur, Quarts-de-Chaume, Saumur, Saumur
   Mousseux, Savennières, Haut-Poitou, Vin du Thouarsais,
   Coteaux d'Ancenis, Fiefs Vendéens
   Southwest: Bergerac Sec, Montravel, Saussignac, Vin
   d'Entraygues et du Fel, Vin d'Estaing
Clairette *Rhône*: Côtes du Rhône, Côtes du Rhône-Villages,
   Châteauneuf-du-Pape, Clairette de Die, Clairette de Die
   Mousseux, Côtes du Lubéron, Côtes du Ventoux, Lirac, Tavel,
   Côtes du Vivarais
   Provence: Bandol, Bellet, Cassis, Coteaux d'Aix-en-Provence,
   Coteaux des Baux en Provence, Côtes de Provence, Palette,
   Coteaux de Pierrevert, Coteaux Varois
   Midi: Clairette de Bellegarde, Costières de Nîmes, Clairette du
   Languedoc, Coteaux du Languedoc, Coteaux du Languedoc-
   La Clape, Coteaux du Languedoc-La Méjanelle, Coteaux du
   Languedoc-Picpoul de Pinet, Coteaux du Languedoc-
   Pic-St-Loup, Coteaux du Languedoc-Quatourze, Faugères,
   Blanquette de Limoux, Corbières
Courbu Blanc *Southwest*: Béarn, Irouléguy, Jurançon, Jurançon
   Sec, Pacherenc du Vic-Bilh
Gewürztraminer *Alsace*: Alsace, Alsace Grand Cru
Grenache Blanc *Rhône*: Côtes du Rhône, Châteauneuf-du-Pape,
   Côtes du Lubéron, Côtes du Ventoux, Côtes du Vivarais
   Provence: Cassis, Coteaux d'Aix-en-Provence, Coteaux des
   Baux en Provence, Palette, Coteaux Varois
   Midi: Costières de Nîmes, Banyuls VDN
Grenache Gris *Midi*: Banyuls VDN
Gros Plant (Folle Blanche) *Loire*: Gros Plant du Pays Nantais,
   Fiefs Vendéens
Jacquère *Savoie*: Vin de Savoie, Vin de Bugey, Vin de Bugey
   Mousseux
Jurançon Blanc *Southwest*: Côtes de St-Mont
Lauzat *Southwest*: Béarn, Irouléguy
Len de l'El *Southwest*: Gaillac, Gaillac Doux, Gaillac Mousseux,
   Gaillac Premières Côtes
Macabeo *Rhône*: Lirac
   Midi: Banyuls VDN, Rivesaltes VDN
Malvoisie (Pinot Beurot) *Loire*: Coteaux d'Ancenis
   Provence: Coteaux Varois
   Midi: Coteaux du Languedoc, Côtes du Roussillon, Banyuls
   VDN, Rivesaltes VDN
Manseng, Gros *Southwest*: Béarn, Béarn-Bellocq, Irouléguy,
   Jurançon, Jurançon Sec, Pacherenc du Vic-Bilh
Manseng, Petit *Southwest*: Béarn, Béarn-Bellocq, Irouléguy,

Jurançon, Jurançon Sec, Pacherenc du Vic-Bilh

Marsanne *Rhône*: Côtes du Rhône, Crozes-Hermitage, Hermitage, St-Péray, St-Péray Mousseux, Coteaux du Tricastin, Côtes du Lubéron, Côtes du Ventoux, Côtes du Vivarais
Provence: Cassis, Coteaux de Pierrevert

Mauzac Blanc *Midi*: Blanquette de Limoux
Southwest: Côtes de Duras, Gaillac, Gaillac Doux, Gaillac Mousseux, Gaillac Premières Côtes, Vin d'Entraygues et du Fel, Vin d'Estaing, Vin de Lavilledieu

Melon de Bourgogne (Muscadet) *Loire*: Muscadet des Coteaux de la Loire, Muscadet de Sèvre-et-Maine

Meslier *Southwest*: Côtes de St-Mont

Mondeuse Blanche *Savoie*: Roussette de Savoie, Vin de Bugey, Vin de Bugey Mousseux

Muscadelle *Southwest*: Bergerac Sec, Buzet, Côtes de Bergerac Moelleux, Côtes de Duras, Côtes de Montravel, Gaillac, Gaillac Doux, Gaillac Mousseux, Gaillac Premières Côtes, Haut Montravel, Monbazillac, Montravel, Rosette, Saussignac

Muscat Blanc à Petits Grains *Alsace*: Alsace, Alsace Grand Cru
Rhône: Clairette de Die Mousseux, Muscat de Beaumes-de-Venise
Midi: Muscat de Frontignan VDN, Muscat de Lunel VDN, Muscat de Mireval VDN, Muscat de St-Jean-de-Minervois VDN, Banyuls VDN, Muscat de Rivesaltes VDN

Muscat Ottonel *Alsace*: Alsace, Alsace Grand Cru

Ondenc *Southwest*: Bergerac Sec, Côtes de Duras, Gaillac, Gaillac Doux, Gaillac Mousseux, Gaillac Premières Côtes, Montravel, Saussignac

Picardan *Rhône*: Châteauneuf-du-Pape

Picpoul *Rhône*: Châteauneuf-du-Pape, Lirac, Tavel
Midi: Coteaux du Languedoc, Coteaux du Languedoc-La Méjanelle, Coteaux du Languedoc-Picpoul de Pinet, Coteaux du Languedoc-Pic-St-Loup, Coteaux du Languedoc-Quatourze, Corbières
Southwest: Côtes de St-Mont, Vin de Lavilledieu

Pineau Menu (Arbois) *Loire*: Touraine, Cheverny, Valençay

Pinot Auxerrois *Alsace*: Alsace, Crémant d'Alsace

Pinot Blanc (Klevner) *Alsace*: Alsace, Crémant d'Alsace, Vin de Moselle
Jura: Côtes du Jura, Côtes du Jura Mousseux

Riesling *Alsace*: Alsace, Alsace Grand Cru

Rolle *Provence*: Bellet, Côtes de Provence

Romorantin *Loire*: Cheverny, Cour Cheverny, Valençay

Roussanne *Rhône*: Côtes du Rhône, Côtes du Rhône-Villages, Crozes-Hermitage, St-Péray, St-Péray Mousseux, Châteauneuf-du-Pape, Côtes du Ventoux, Côtes du Vivarais
Provence: Bellet, Coteaux de Pierrevert

Ruffiac *Southwest*: Pacherenc du Vic-Bilh

Sauvignon Blanc *Loire*: Menetou-Salon, Pouilly-Fumé, Quincy, Reuilly, Sancerre, Côtes de Gien, Touraine, Cheverny, Valençay, Anjou, Saumur, Saumur Mousseux, Haut-Poitou, Fiefs Vendéens

Provence: Bandol, Cassis, Coteaux d'Aix-en-Provence, Coteaux des Baux en Provence

Southwest: Béarn, Bergerac Sec, Buzet, Côtes de Bergerac, Côtes de Bergerac Moelleux, Côtes de Duras, Côtes du Marmandais, Côtes de Montravel, Gaillac, Gaillac Mousseux, Gaillac Premières Côtes, Haut Montravel, Irouléguy, Monbazillac, Montravel, Pacherenc du Vic-Bilh, Rosette, Saussignac, Côtes de St-Mont

Savagnin (Gringet) *Jura*: Arbois, Arbois Mousseux, Arbois Pupillin, Château-Chalon, Côtes du Jura, L'Étoile

Savoie: Vin de Savoie Ayse Mousseux, Vin de Savoie Mousseux

Sémillon *Provence*: Coteaux d'Aix-en-Provence, Coteaux des Baux en Provence, Côtes de Provence

Southwest: Béarn, Bergerac Sec, Buzet, Côtes de Bergerac Moelleux, Côtes de Duras, Côtes du Marmandais, Côtes de Montravel, Gaillac, Gaillac Doux, Gaillac Mousseux, Gaillac Premières Côtes, Haut Montravel, Irouléguy, Monbazillac, Montravel, Pacherenc du Vic-Bilh, Rosette, Saussignac

Sylvaner *Alsace*: Alsace, Vin de Moselle

Terret Blanc *Midi*: Coteaux du Languedoc-Picpoul de Pinet

Tokay-Pinot Gris *Loire*: Reuilly, Touraine

Alsace: Alsace, Alsace Grand Cru, Vin de Moselle

Savoie: Vin de Bugey

Tressalier *Loire*: St-Pourçain

Ugni Blanc *Rhône*: Côtes du Rhône, Côtes du Lubéron, Côtes du Vivarais

Provence: Bandol, Cassis, Coteaux d'Aix-en-Provence, Coteaux des Baux en Provence, Côtes de Provence, Palette, Coteaux Varois

Midi: Costières de Nîmes

Southwest: Côtes de Duras, Côtes du Marmandais, Montravel

Viognier *Rhône*: Château-Grillet, Condrieu, Côte Rôtie

The Loire

In its unhurried 1,021-kilometre meander through France, the River Loire passes through the most quintessentially French countryside. Leaving the mountainous Ardèche region, the river runs alongside woods and open fields, great châteaux and historic towns, travelling its tree-lined route across an undulating landscape that is devoted mostly to agriculture – much of it to the growth of vines.

Sunlight is filtered through the trees that line the river, the waters reflecting the rays and tingeing the air with softness.

For the first part of its course the river runs north, parallel to the Saône and the Burgundy vineyards, which are only a few miles east. Almost halfway along its journey, in a huge arc, it turns west towards the Atlantic.

The largest Loire vineyards are almost entirely in the second half of the river's course. Well to the south, on a level with the Beaujolais, are the small VDQS areas of Côtes Roannaises, Côtes du Forez and Côtes d'Auvergne and, a few miles north, St-Pourçain-sur-Sioule. But the first major wine areas appear just before the river turns to the west, at Sancerre and Pouilly-sur-Loire. Nearby but set away from the river are the wine districts of Reuilly, Quincy and Menetou-Salon. A little further north of Pouilly there is a small vineyard area at Gien.

At the top of the river's arc, to the west, the historic cathedral city of Orléans is the centre of a minor area of light-red, white and rosé wine production. From here the river runs westward, passing the châteaux of Touraine. South of Blois, the vineyards of Cheverny produce white wines. This district is on the edge of the main Touraine wine-producing area, which has a number of smaller but nonetheless famous appellations: Vouvray and Montlouis, Chinon and Bourgueil, and towns such as Amboise and Mesland that are *crus* within the general Touraine area.

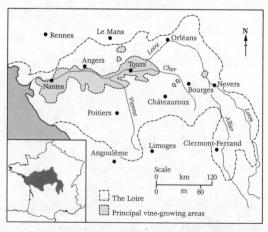

Scale
0   km   120
0   m   60
☐☐ The Loire
▨ Principal vine-growing areas

Away to the north are the outlying vineyards of Vendôme, Coteaux du Loir and Jasnières, while to the south are the vineyards of Valençay and Haut-Poitou.

Touraine – centred around the cathedral city of Tours – is at the transitional point of the Loire vineyards. Here the Sauvignon Blanc of Sancerre and Pouilly-Fumé meets the Chenin Blanc of Anjou; the Pinot Noir and Gamay of Burgundy meet the Cabernets of Bordeaux.

It is the Chenin Blanc and the Cabernets that take over in the neighbouring province of Anjou. The Chenin makes a whole range of whites, from piercingly acid and dry, still and sparkling, to lusciously sweet. The Cabernet Franc is joined by the Groslot to produce rosés: on its own it makes reds. Then, as the river continues westward, nearing its mouth, there is an abrupt change. The Chenin Blanc is replaced by the Melon de Bourgogne and the vineyards of Muscadet stretch out to the Atlantic horizon.

Small pockets of Malvoisie produce a sweet white wine at Ancenis and the Gros Plant makes a white that can make lemon juice taste soft.

While there is great variety in the wines of the Loire there is also, not unnaturally, a common thread. These are northern vineyards. The growing season is long and comparatively cool. This gives Loire wines their general character of intense fruit flavours and often piercing acidity. They are cool wines in climate and also in taste.

A few years ago, Loire wines were relatively unknown. Some have been discovered now but others are still waiting. Sancerre and Pouilly-Fumé and the wines of Muscadet were the classic discoveries and, suddenly fashionable, their price shot up. Often the price rises have been unreasonable: these are, after all, still country wines, which never reach the peaks of quality attained in Bordeaux and Burgundy.

While some wines have become fashionable, others – potentially greater – are only just getting the recognition they deserve. Anjou makes some of the world's great sweet wines in the small areas of Quarts de Chaume and Bonnezeaux, but they are still more written about than drunk. They are the equals of Sauternes, German *Trockenbeerenauslesen* or late-harvest wines, and their prices are still low. The dry whites of Savennières, produced not far away, are finally being appreciated.

The reds of Chinon and Bourgueil and Saumur-Champigny are also attracting the attention they deserve. While suffering from their northerly situation, in good years these vineyards can produce smooth, rich wines, much more generous and rewarding than the light reds of Sancerre that command such absurd prices.

And finally, there are the tiny VDQS areas, hanging like forgotten fruit from the branches and tributaries of the Loire. Many of these areas were devastated by the phylloxera epidemic and it is only the committed work of only a few dedicated growers that keeps them alive. Others – like Haut-Poitou – have been discovered as a result of the fact that the winemakers have adapted to compete in the commercial wine world.

The Appellations

There are currently 61 entries on the full list of Loire AC and VDQS areas. The list is arranged here as it is in the producers' directory that follows.

UPPER LOIRE AC

Blanc Fumé de Pouilly *See* Pouilly-Fumé

Menetou-Salon White, red and rosé wines, made on 196 hectares of chalky soil west of Sancerre. Whites from Sauvignon; rosés and reds from Pinot Noir grapes. The whites can match the average Sancerre in quality, reds and rosés can often be fuller.

Pouilly-Fumé White wines made from Sauvignon around the village of Pouilly-sur-Loire on 750 hectares of calciferous (*marne argileuse*) and flint (*silex*) soils. There are no reds or rosés produced under this appellation. The wines tend to be fuller, higher in alcohol, richer and longer lasting than white Sancerre, but sometimes lack the initial crisp fruit.

Pouilly-sur-Loire White wine made in the same area as Pouilly-Fumé, but from the Chasselas grape. There is a small but stable production.

Quincy White wine from the Sauvignon grape. The 119 hectares of gravelly soil lie along what was once the bed of the River Cher. The wine can be attractively soft and round while retaining the gooseberry acidity of the Sauvignon grape.

Reuilly White from Sauvignon Blanc and red and rosé from Pinot Gris and Pinot Noir grows on 74 hectares of chalk soil. The white wine is light and fresh, the rosé (especially from the Pinot Gris) very attractive, and the red light and fruity.

Sancerre White from Sauvignon, red and rosé from Pinot Noir. About 2,000 hectares. This is the most important appellation in terms of production in the Upper Loire. The soil – a mixture of calciferous and gravel (*caillottes*), flint (*silex*) and the heavier *marne argileuse* – produces three distinct styles of wine. While many are blended, wines from Chavignol and Bué reflect the qualities of the *caillottes* soil. Those from Verdigny have more of the character of the heavier *marne argileuse*. Around the town of Sancerre, flint soil predominates. The whites have the classic Sauvignon taste of gooseberries and grapefruit and are immediately attractive. Some fine barrel-aged reds are made, but on the whole these and the rosés tend to be overrated.

UPPER LOIRE VDQS

Châteaumeillant Red and rosé from Gamay, south of Sancerre.

Côtes d'Auvergne Gamay and Pinot Noir red and rosé, with a little white from Chardonnay, from near Clermont-Ferrand in the Puy de Dôme.

Côtes du Forez Gamay red from near St-Étienne, almost at the source of the Loire.

Côtes de Gien or **Coteaux du Giennois** Area centred around Cosne, north of Sancerre and Pouilly-sur-Loire. Red and rosé from Pinot Noir and Gamay, white from Sauvignon Blanc and Chenin Blanc.

Côtes Roannaises Gamay red, further down river from Côtes du Forez. Due west of Beaujolais.

St-Pourçain On the River Allier, north of the Côtes d'Auvergne. Whites from Tressalier, Chardonnay, Sauvignon Blanc, Aligoté and St-Pierre Doré; reds and rosés from Gamay and Pinot Noir.

TOURAINE AC

Bourgueil Red and rosé wines made mainly from the Cabernet Franc with a little Cabernet Sauvignon, in a district at the western end of Touraine on the north bank of the Loire. There are about 1,136 hectares under vine on three different soil types running in bands parallel to the Loire: gravelly soil (the least important) near the Loire; a higher level called *la terrasse* made of sand and gravel soil (the most important); and *les coteaux* at a higher level. Bourgueil is one of the few Loire Valley reds that needs time to develop. Five or six years is a minimum. Vintages: '85, '88, '89, '90, '93, '95, '96.

Cheverny AC created in 1992 with 337 hectares of vines. White, red and rosé wines from a district southwest of Blois on the south bank of the Loire. Whites come from Chenin Blanc, Sauvignon Blanc, Chardonnay, Menu Pineau and Romorantin grapes. Red comes mainly from Gamay, as does the rosé. *See also* Cour Cheverny.

Chinon This district lies due south of Bourgueil, between the Loire and Vienne rivers. There are nearly 1,800 hectares and, like Bourgueil, there are three soil types moving away from the Vienne River: the gravel nearest to the river; clay and gravel on *les plateaux*; and clay and lime form *les coteaux* which produces the best wines. More immediately attractive than Bourgueil, Chinon wines tend to mature more quickly, although given careful ageing in old barrels they can last for some years. Vintages: '85, '88, '89, '90, '93, '95, '96.

Coteaux du Loir 'Le Loir' is a tributary, via the River Sarthe, of the main river, 'La Loire'. Le Loir runs northwest from Angers past Vendôme. The tiny Coteaux du Loir vineyards (just 37 hectares) lie 24 kilometres north of Tours. Red wines are made from Cabernet Franc, Pineau d'Aunis, Gamay and Cot; rosés from Groslot and whites from Pineau de la Loire (or Chenin Blanc).

Cour Cheverny This, a small portion of the AC of Cheverny, is regarded as a separate appellation devoted to the production of white wine from the Romorantin grape.

Crémant de Loire A general Loire-wide AC for white and rosé made in small quantities in Touraine and Anjou (including Saumur). The rules are stricter than they are for the sparkling wines of Saumur – yields must be lower, for example – and quality can be high. Permitted grape varieties include Pinot Noir and Chardonnay, although Cabernet Franc and Chenin Blanc are also used.

Jasnières White wine made from Pineau de la Loire in two communes: Lhomme and Ruillé-sur-Loir in the Coteaux du Loir AC. This rare dry wine is produced from 31 hectares.

Montlouis The twin vineyard of Vouvray (*see below*) on the Loire's southern bank east of Tours, on the tongue of land between the Loire and the Cher. Wines come from the communes of Montlouis-sur-Loire, Lissault and St-Martin-le-Beau. Chalk underlies a sandy top-soil. Only white wines are produced from the Chenin Blanc. Most of the still wines are dry, less full-bodied but softer than Vouvray and more attractive when young. In very good years, *demi-sec* and *moelleux* (sweet) wines can be made. Vineyard area is around 250 hectares.

Montlouis Pétillant and Mousseux Slightly sparkling (*pétillant*) and full-pressure classic-method sparkling wines (*mousseux*) are made from the same vineyards as still Montlouis. Generally made in cooler years when the grapes are greener.

Rosé de Loire Dry rosé which can be made in Touraine, Anjou and Saumur, but comes mainly from Touraine. Groslot and the two Cabernets (a minimum of 30 percent Cabernet – higher proportion than in Rosé d'Anjou) are used.

St-Nicolas-de-Bourgueil A 788-hectare commune west of the main Bourgueil vineyard making a red from Cabernet Franc. It is a lighter colour than Bourgueil, ages more quickly and can be drunk slightly chilled. Vintages: '88, '89, '90, '93, '95, '96.

Touraine A catch-all AC for the whole Touraine region. It covers 5,600 hectares – about one-third of the vineyard area in the province (the other two-thirds are in smaller, more precise ACs). Red, rosé and white, still and sparkling wines are made from a variety of grapes. The reds are made from Cabernet Franc, Cabernet Sauvignon, Gamay and Malbec, or from Pinot Gris, Pinot Meunier and Pinot Noir. Rosés from the red grapes or from Groslot or Pineau d'Aunis. Whites from Chardonnay, Chenin Blanc, Pineau Menu and Sauvignon. Gamay and Sauvignon are the most widely planted grapes.

Touraine Pétillant and Mousseux Slightly sparkling (*pétillant*) and full-pressure classic-method sparkling (*mousseux*) wines made all over the Touraine AC area.

Touraine-Villages Three smaller districts have the right to add their name to the general Touraine AC. Touraine-Amboise is on the Loire due east of Tours and makes reds from Gamay, Malbec (Cot) and both Cabernets; rosé from Gamay and Cabernet Franc, and a little dry white from Chenin Blanc and Sauvignon Blanc (216 hectares). Touraine-Azay-le-Rideau, to the southwest of Tours, makes dry and semi-sweet white from the Chenin Blanc and rosé from Groslot (Grolleau) and red grapes (43 hectares). Touraine-Mesland produces red from Gamay, the Cabernets and Malbec (Cot), smaller amounts of white from Chenin Blanc and Sauvignon Blanc (209 hectares). On the whole, the reds are better than the whites in Mesland and Amboise: Mesland especially makes some fine long-lasting wines from Cabernet Franc. Azay-le-Rideau is better at producing whites than rosés.

Vouvray White wine made on the north bank of the Loire, just east of Tours. The vineyards are on the plateau above the river on chalk soil. The cliffs facing the river and the small side valleys are riddled with caves and cellars – some people still live in troglodyte houses half built into the cliff. There are three styles of still Vouvray: dry, semi-dry (*demi-sec*) and sweet (*moelleux*). The only grape is Chenin Blanc (Pineau de la Loire). The sweeter wines – and some of the better dry ones – can age seemingly forever. They can be luscious but have the hard edge of acidity that Chenin provides and that gives them long life. At its best (from top estates), this is one of the finest Loire wines. A decreasing amount of inferior Vouvray is coming from *négociants* whose premises are elsewhere. Vintages (for sweet): '76, '83, '85, '88, '89, '90, '93, '95, '96.

Vouvray Mousseux and Pétillant The full-pressure classic-method sparkling Vouvray is normally dry but sometimes produces semi-sweet or even sweet. It must always be white. Vintages (for dry): '87, '92, '94.

TOURAINE VDQS

Coteaux du Vendômois Just to the east of the Coteaux du Loir AC is this larger (94-hectare) area, around the town of Vendôme on the Loir. Red (from Cabernet Franc, Gamay and Pinot Noir), rosé (from Pineau d'Aunis and Gamay), and white (from Chenin Blanc and Chardonnay) are made.

Vin de l'Orléanais Vineyards around the city of Orléans make up this, the most northerly Loire vineyard region. Red, white and rosé wines are made. The largest production is of rosé from Pinot Meunier grapes.

Valençay Mainly red Gamay-based wine from a small area to the south of the Cher in southeast Touraine. Some rosé is also made from Gamay, while increasing quantities of white come from Pineau Menu, Chardonnay or Sauvignon Blanc. A little Romorantin is also planted.

ANJOU AC

Anjou The general AC for those of the region's vineyards that are not covered by more precise appellations. White, red and rosé are produced under this name. There are around 2,300 hectares making wine – 15 percent red, 55 percent rosé, 30 percent white. Reds are made from Gamay (the wine is called Anjou Gamay) and Cabernets Franc and Sauvignon (the wine is called Anjou). Rosé (which is semi-sweet) is made mainly from Groslot (Grolleau), with some Cabernet Franc, Cabernet Sauvignon, Gamay, Pineau d'Aunis and Malbec. White is mainly from Chenin Blanc (Pineau de la Loire) with some Chardonnay or Sauvignon Blanc. The style of white ranges from dry to sweet.

Anjou Coteaux de la Loire White wines from the area just south of Angers. Can be dry or semi-sweet. The grape used is the Chenin Blanc (Pineau de la Loire).

Anjou Gamay Red wines from the general Anjou AC made from the Gamay grape.

Anjou Pétillant and Mousseux Semi-sparkling (*pétillant*) and full-pressure classic-method sparkling wines made in the general Anjou AC area. They can be from Chenin Blanc or from red grapes (pressed to make white). Only very small quantities of wine are produced.

Anjou-Villages This appellation covers 46 villages within the main Anjou appellation area. It can be used only for red wines made from Cabernet Franc and Cabernet Sauvignon. The quality is higher than it is for Anjou Rouge.

Bonnezeaux One of the two great sweet white wine appellations (*see also* Quarts de Chaume). The small vineyard area, 85 hectares of clay and limestone soil, is in the commune of Thouarcé, part of the larger Coteaux du Layon AC (*see below*). Grapes should ideally be left to develop noble rot – certainly they need to be harvested late to give the required sweetness and intensity, and the wine can be made only in good years (the better producers sell it as Coteaux du Layon in poor years). Vintages: '76, '82, '83, '85, '89, '90, '95, '96.

Cabernet d'Anjou A rosé wine made throughout the Anjou AC area from Cabernet grapes. It is usually sweet. The wine can be attractive when properly made (without too much sulphur) but can also tend to become cloying.

Cabernet de Saumur Rosés from the Saumur AC area, normally semi-sweet and made from the two Cabernet grapes. There is a small production of wines which tend to be better than ordinary Cabernet d'Anjou.

Coteaux de l'Aubance A white wine area to the east of Coteaux du Layon, due south of Angers on the River Aubance. The delimited area is large but production is small as only about 65 hectares make the wine. Normally a medium-sweet white made from ripe Chenin Blanc grapes which have been fermented slowly. In good years sweet wines can be made. Good examples can age well, although they are not too harsh when young.

Coteaux du Layon The modest River Layon runs southwest to northeast towards the Loire, making a wide valley. On the southwest facing slopes are around 1,400 hectares of Chenin Blanc producing sweet white wines from very ripe grapes, some with noble rot. Coteaux du Layon is the general AC and there are smaller ACs with an even higher quality which are enclaves in the area (Quarts de Chaume, Bonnezeaux). The wines represent remarkable value.

Coteaux du Layon-Villages Seven communes are allowed to add their name to the main Coteaux du Layon AC. Their wines are generally better with higher alcohol and there are lower yields too in one commune (Chaume). The communes are: Beaulieu-sur-Layon, Chaume, Faye d'Anjou, Rablay-sur-Layon, St-Aubin-de-Luigné, Rochefort-sur-Loire, St-Lambert-du-Lattay.

Coteaux de Saumur Semi-sweet wine from Chenin Blanc, made in tiny quantities in the Saumur AC area. It has similar qualities to some Vouvray or Montlouis: a rich, full-bodied, slightly honeyed flavour, balanced by a touch of bitter acidity.

Crémant de Loire *See* Touraine.

Quarts-de-Chaume Along with Bonnezeaux (*see* page 22), this is one of the two great sweet wine appellations of Anjou. The vineyard area covers 28 hectares on four fingers of hilly land which stretch towards the Layon Valley in the centre of the Coteaux du Layon AC area. The higher plateau behind protects the vineyards from winds. The wine is sweet, made from late-harvested grapes, in good years infected with noble rot, but always picked as ripe as possible. The wine tastes surprisingly fresh in its youth (rather like young Sauternes) but after between three and ten years becomes quiescent. It is at its greatest between ten and 20 years – but fine wines will last longer. Good Quarts de Chaume ranks with Sauternes and German *Trockenbeerenauslesen* as one of the world's great sweet wines. Vintages: '71, '76, '81, '82, '83, '85, '88, '89, '90, '95, '96; older vintages if you can find them.

Rosé d'Anjou Medium-sweet rosé wine made anywhere in the general Anjou region (*see under* general Anjou AC).

Rosé d'Anjou Pétillant Rarely found semi-sparkling medium-sweet Rosé d'Anjou.

Saumur White and red still wines from 38 communes around Saumur. The bone-dry white is made from Chenin Blanc with up to 20 percent Chardonnay or Sauvignon Blanc and is normally rather tart and acid. The red comes mainly from Cabernet Franc with Cabernet Sauvignon and Pineau d'Aunis.

Saumur-Champigny A red wine, also from Saumur, but from seven communes in the best part of the area for reds on a plateau above the Loire. A finer wine than ordinary red Saumur, it is in great demand and prices can be too high. Like Chinon and Bourgueil it has characteristic bitter cherry and vanilla flavours. Vintages: '89, '90, '93, '95, '96.

Saumur Pétillant and Mousseux While only small quantities of the *pétillant* are made, the Saumur Mousseux is, in France, the second sparkling wine to champagne and around 12 million bottles a year are produced. Made in the same way as champagne (by the classic method), much of the production is now linked to champagne companies. Chenin Blanc, Chardonnay and Sauvignon Blanc are the white grape varieties used; the two Cabernets, Gamay, Groslot, Malbec, Pineau d'Aunis and Pinot Noir are the red grapes (which are pressed in the same way as white). The soil is generally chalk. Most Saumur is made by big *négociant* houses and, like champagne, blending ensures continuity of their house style. While not an exciting wine, Saumur is reliable and easy to drink and is much cheaper than champagne. There is also rosé *mousseux* wine made from a combination of red grapes. The wine is now marketed as Saumur d'Origine.

Savennières From a small area (only about 69 hectares) on the north bank of the Loire west of Angers, opposite Rochefort-sur-Loire and Coteaux du Layon. The wine can be sweet or dry (now normally dry) and is made from Chenin Blanc. Grapes are picked very ripe and fermented dry, giving high alcohol. In the rare good years, the wine is superb, combining a dry palate with a peaches-and-cream bouquet. Like many great Chenin Blanc wines, they age well. Vintages: '76, '78, '82, '83, '85, '88, '89, '90, '95, '96.

Savennières-Coulée-de-Serrant The Coulée-de-Serrant vineyard is the heart of Savennières with seven hectares making fine dry white wines with an immensely long life. Vintages: '76, '78, '82, '83, '85, '88, '89, '90, '93, '95, '96 (as for Savennières); older wines will probably survive better.

Savennières-Roches-aux-Moines The second great Savennières vineyard with 17 hectares under production. The wines tend to be lighter than Coulée-de-Serrant. Vintages: '76, '78, '82, '83, '85, '88, '89, '90, '95, '96 (as for Savennières).

ANJOU VDQS

Haut-Poitou While this area is not in Anjou, it is normally linked in for convenience. It is an isolated pocket of wine-making away from the main Loire area, near Vienne in the *département* of Deux-Sèvres to the south. Nothing would be known about Haut-Poitou were it not for the cooperative, which is making delightful varietal wines from Chardonnay and Sauvignon – Sauvignon being the more successful variety here. Chenin Blanc is also permitted for whites. Reds and rosés are made from Gamay, Pinot Noir, Cabernet Sauvignon and Grolleau (Groslot). The wines are fresh and fruity and should be drunk young.

Vin du Thouarsais Red, rosé and dry white wines from the Deux-Sèvres *département*, south of Angers and west of Poitiers. The red and rosé are produced from Cabernet Franc and Cabernet Sauvignon; the white, which is normally medium-dry, from Chenin Blanc. These wines should be drunk young.

WESTERN LOIRE AC

Muscadet This is the basic AC for the white wines of what is called the Pays Nantais – the region south of the city of Nantes, almost at the mouth of the Loire. Simple Muscadet made from the Muscadet grape (also called Melon de Bourgogne) comes mainly from the southwest part of the area. The straight Muscadet very rarely reaches the character or the freshness and fruit of a Muscadet from one of the superior appellations – and it is normally worth paying the extra to buy the better wine. The wines are never bottled *sur lie* (*see under* Muscadet de Sèvre-et-Maine).

Muscadet des Coteaux de la Loire A small area of 450 hectares on chalky soil along the banks of the Loire east of Nantes in the same area as the Coteaux d'Ancenis. The different soil produces a fuller, somewhat coarse wine, which rarely leaves its native area.

Muscadet Côtes de Grand Lieu Wines produced from the area around the low-lying Lac du Grand Lieu were given their own appellation with the '94 vintage. These wines can be bottled *sur lie* (*see under* Muscadet de Sèvre-et-Maine).

Muscadet de Sèvre-et-Maine This is the biggest Muscadet area by far, covering 9,700 hectares south of Nantes. The best vineyards are generally agreed to be in St-Fiacre and Vallet, but much of the production is bought by *négociants*, either local or from Saumur and points west. The area has been vastly expanded to take in what used to be simple Muscadet vineyard – not altogether surprising considering the difference in the prices the wines could command.

Superior Muscadet de Sèvre-et-Maine is described as being bottled *sur lie*, that is straight from the unracked, unfiltered cask or tank, giving a slight 'prickle' and extra freshness to the taste. Under new regulations with the '94 vintage, this bottling now has to be effected in the place where the wine was made ('*mis en bouteille au château*' or '*au domaine*' confirms that this has happened). In the past the wine was sometimes taken off the lees and transferred elsewhere for bottling, and a little carbon dioxide added to give the prickle.

Muscadet has been an immense success story. From humble origins as the local wine for Breton seafood, it has conquered the world as an easy-to-drink dry white that is sufficiently anonymous to suit most occasions. No Muscadet can, or should, be pretentious: the character of the Melon de Bourgogne grape cannot take it.

WESTERN LOIRE VDQS

Coteaux d'Ancenis White, rosé and red wines made in the same area as Muscadet Coteaux de la Loire AC. Only a little white is made from the Chenin Blanc (Pineau de la Loire) and Malvoisie (Pinot-Beurot) which makes both dry and sweet wines. Gamay and Cabernet Franc produce the red and rosé. There is a small production from 214 hectares. All Coteaux d'Ancenis wines have to carry the name of the grape variety on the label: Pineau de la Loire, Chenin Blanc, Malvoisie, Pinot-Beurot, Gamay or Cabernet.

Gros Plant or Gros Plant du Pays Nantais This is an extremely dry white wine from the lesser grape of the Muscadet area. The Gros Plant (or Folle Blanche) grape covers 3,000 hectares, mostly in the same area as the simple Muscadet, but also in Sèvre-et-Maine. It is more acid than Muscadet and not a wine to drink by itself, but it goes well with shellfish. It can be bottled *sur lie*. A little sparkling wine is also made.

Fiefs Vendéens Red, dry white and rosé wines from the Vendée, south of the Pays Nantais. Red and rosé from Cabernet Franc, Cabernet Sauvignon, Gamay, Pinot Noir and Pineau d'Aunis. Whites from Chenin Blanc, Chardonnay, Gros Plant and Sauvignon. Only a little white is made. These are simple wines for drinking young.

LOIRE VINS DE PAYS
Regional *vin de pays*
Vin de Pays du Jardin de la France While covering the whole of the Loire Valley, the Vin de Pays du Jardin de la France

region is actually centred on the Touraine area. Production is of white wines from the Sauvignon and Chardonnay grapes (30 percent), and red wines mainly from the Gamay (60 percent). A small amount of rosé is also made. The total production is considerable, and mostly of single-variety wines.

Other regional *vins de pays*:

Vin de Pays des Comtes Rhodaniens (*see* The Rhône)

Vin de Pays du Puy-de-Dôme

Departmental *vins de pays*

Vin de Pays de l'Indre-et-Loire Wines from the Tours region; principally whites from the local Touraine grapes, with a smaller proportion of reds. Production is limited by the greater success of the Vin de Pays du Jardin de la France.

Vin de Pays du Loir-et-Cher From around Blois and Vendôme, the wines of this region are made from Pinot Noir and Pineau Menu (or Arbois), for the reds and whites respectively. Much of the *vin de pays* here goes into Vin de Pays du Jardin de la France.

Vin de Pays du Maine-et-Loire This *vin de pays* covers the area of Anjou and Saumur. Ninety percent of the production is of red and rosé wines from the Gamay, Cabernet Franc, Cabernet Sauvignon and Grolleau grape varieties. Small quantities of white wine are made from Sauvignon Blanc, Chenin Blanc, Pinot Blanc and Grolleau Gris.

Other departmental *vins de pays*:

Vin de Pays du Cher

Vin de Pays des Deux-Sèvres

Vin de Pays de Loire-Atlantique

Vin de Pays du Loiret

Vin de Pays de la Nièvre

Vin de Pays de la Sarthe

Vin de Pays de la Vendée

Vin de Pays de la Vienne

Zonal *vins de pays*

Vin de Pays des Marches de Bretagne A zone to the east of Nantes in the Muscadet region, making white wine from the Muscadet and Folle Blanche, and reds from the unusual Abouriou grape which originally came from Gascony.

Vin de Pays de Retz Produced south of the Loire, in the region between Nantes and the Atlantic. Mainly red and rosé wines. A particular speciality of Vin de Pays de Retz is a rosé made from Grolleau.

Vin de Pays d'Urfé A wide area in the Loire *département*, near the source of the river. The grape varieties used are Chardonnay, Gamay and Pinot Noir, with some Aligoté and Viognier. Production is small.

Other zonal *vins de pays*:

Vin de Pays du Bourbonnais

Vin de Pays des Coteaux Charitois

Vin de Pays des Coteaux du Cher et de l'Arnon

Upper Loire Producers

MENETOU-SALON AC

Domaine Chavet et Fils
GAEC des Brangèrs, 18510 Menetou-Salon.
Vineyards owned: Menetou-Salon: Sauvignon Blanc 7.5ha,
Pinot Noir 7.8ha. 120,000 bottles. VP-R
The red wine is a well balanced product, made half from grapes that have been pressed and half from macerated grapes, with some ageing in wood. The whites are very fresh and full of grape fruit. A small amount of attractive, lively rosé wine is also made. The firm goes back to the 18th century, but recent changes have meant that it has been able to keep pace with new developments in vinification techniques, especially for white wines.
Open: Mon–Sun 7.15am–noon, 1.15–7pm.

Clément Père et Fils (Domaine de Châtenoy)
18510 Menetou-Salon.
Vineyards owned: 40ha. 450,000 bottles. VP-R
A family firm dating back to 1560. The red is more interesting than the white – vinified traditionally and aged for up to a year in new barrels, giving a wine that needs time to mature, with a life of anything from ten to 12 years. *Open: Mon–Sat 9am–noon, 2–6pm.*

Domaine Henry Pellé et Fils
Morogues, 18220 Aix-d'Angillon. Vineyards owned: Sauvignon
Blanc 30ha, Pinot Noir 7ha. 312,000 bottles. VP-R
The tragic death of Eric Pellé in 1995 has cast a shadow over this firm, but it remains one of the best producers in Menetou-Salon. It also owns vineyards in the Sancerre appellation. Most of the production is of a very fine white. A red and rosé are also made. The red is sometimes aged for a year in wood. The village name of Morogues is used as a brand name.
Open: Mon–Sat 9am–noon, 1–6pm.

Les Chais du Val du Loire
34 Route de Bourges, 18510 Menetou-Salon. Vineyards owned:
Menetou-Salon 22ha, Quincy 15ha, Reuilly 7ha. VP-R
For the area, this is a considerable estate, making wine in three neighbouring appellations: Menetou-Salon, Reuilly and Quincy. A red, rosé and white Menetou, red and white Reuilly, and a classic white Quincy are made. The best wine is probably the white Menetou, Domaine Louis Jouannin.
Open: Mon–Fri 8am–5.30pm; Sat (summer only) 10am–noon, 2–6pm.

POUILLY-FUMÉ AC, POUILLY-SUR-LOIRE AC

Michel Bailly
Les Berthiers, Les Loges, 58150 Pouilly-sur-Loire. Vineyards
owned: 13ha. VP-R
This small estate is the result of a division of land between the

sons of Maurice Bailly: Jean-Louis and Michel. Michel makes very good wine from land in the Champ de Gris, Les Griottes and Les Perriers. *Open: Appointments preferred.*

Bernard Blanchet
Les Berthiers, St-Andelain, 58150 Pouilly-sur-Loire.
Vineyards owned: 5ha. VP-R
M Blanchet's house is close to the main N7 road and his cellars are in newly excavated underground workings. He produces Pouilly-Fumé, and a Pouilly-sur-Loire which is bottled early and untreated, giving it extra flavour. *Open: By appointment only.*

Patrick Coulbois
Les Berthiers, 58150 St-Andelain.
Vineyards owned: 8.4ha. 38,000 bottles. VP-R
Patrick has broken away from his father, Gérard, and set up on his own. Relations are amicable, however, and he sends his Chasselas back to make sparkling wine under the Pouilly-sur-Loire appellation. Patrick's still Pouilly-Fumé, made in cellars beneath a modern bungalow, is full and traditional in style, and an assembly from all his vineyards. *Open: Mon–Sat 8am–6pm.*

Didier Dagueneau
Les Berthiers, 58150 Pouilly-sur-Loire.
Vineyards owned: Les Berthiers 11ha. 5,300 bottles. VP-R
One of the most original and innovative producers of Pouilly-Fumé, who has been influenced by developments among the younger generation of Burgundy winemakers. Fermentation now takes place in small new-oak barrels, using specially selected yeasts. Some of this wine is later blended with wine fermented in stainless steel. Much of the land is on high-quality flinty *silex* soil, and this name is used on his finest wine. All his wines age well and should not be drunk too young. *Open: By appointment only.*

Jean-Claude Dagueneau
58150 Pouilly-sur-Loire. VP-R
Largest of the three Dagueneau firms in Les Berthiers, bearing the name of Domaine des Berthiers. Serge, Jean-Claude's cousin, has premises next door, while his son Didier (*see above*) works down the road. Wines include a top Cuvée d'Eve from old vines.

Paul Figeat
Les Loges, 58150 Pouilly-sur-Loire. Vineyards owned: 8ha. VP-R
This is a traditional firm making wines that need some ageing in bottle. The family has been in business for at least 200 years. A small proportion of Pouilly-sur-Loire is also made.

Denis Gaudry
Tracy-sur-Loire, 58150 Pouilly-sur-Loire. VP-R
One of many historic family firms in Pouilly-sur-Loire. Premises are in the Boisgibault, with vineyards in Tracy-sur-Loire. The wine is exported and sold within France, and also sold to *négociants*.

Domaine de Maltaverne
58150 Tracy, Pouilly-sur-Loire.
Vineyards owned: 16ha. 60,000 bottles VP-R
A small vineyard situated on particularly chalky soil, once part of
the estate of the Château de Tracy (*see* page 30), which makes
attractive wines designed for relatively early drinking.
Open: Mon–Sun during working hours.

Domaine Masson-Blondelet
1 Rue de Paris, 58150 Pouilly-sur-Loire. Vineyards owned:
Pouilly 13ha, Sancerre 3ha. 80,000 bottles. VP-R
Modern cellars and vinification produce some very reliable wines
and one or two fine ones. The best from Masson-Blondelet are
from the Les Bascoins vineyard in Pouilly, and there is a top *cuvée*
from old vines called Tradition Cullus. Red and white Sancerre are
also made here. *Open: Mon–Sun 8am–noon, 2-6.30pm.*

Château de Nozet
58150 Pouilly-sur-Loire.
Vineyards owned: 52ha. 1.5 million bottles. VP-R and N
The largest producer in Pouilly-sur-Loire, Patrick de Ladoucette
owns a magnificent 19th-century château in the centre of his
vineyard on high ground above the village of Pouilly-sur-Loire.
He buys in much of his needs, reserving his own estate for top
wines like Baron de L (made only in good years). He also owns
the Sancerre firm of Comte Lafond, and has other interests
elsewhere on the Loire and in Chablis. The quality is fair, even
if the wines from this estate are not the most exciting Pouilly-
Fumés. *Open: By appointment only.*

Roger Pabiot
Tracy-sur-Loire, 58150 Pouilly-sur-Loire. VP-R
Wines are sold here under two labels: Les Champs de la Croix and
Les Girannes, depending on the market. Vines are on pebble soil
in Tracy-sur-Loire, and M Pabiot uses a harvesting machine. A
tiny proportion of Pouilly-sur-Loire is made.
Open: By appointment only.

Les Caves de Pouilly-sur-Loire
39 Avenue de la Tuilerie, 58150 Pouilly-sur-Loire.
Vineyards owned: 200ha. Coop (130 members).
The only cooperative in Pouilly makes both Pouilly-Fumé and
Pouilly-sur-Loire, as well as having an interest in the Coteaux du
Giennois just to the north. The top *cuvée* is Tinelum, made from
old vines. *Open: Mon–Sun 8am–noon, 2-6pm; Sun (during summer)*
10am–12.30pm, 2.30–6pm.

Michel Redde et Fils
La Moynerie, 58150 Pouilly-sur-Loire.
Vineyards owned: Pouilly 34.5ha. 250,000 bottles. VP-R
One of the larger estates in Pouilly run by the sixth generation of
the Redde family. Wines made are mostly Pouilly-Fumé with a

little Pouilly-sur-Loire, mainly from flinty soil which gives them ageing potential. The finest wine is Cuvée Majorum, made only in better years (the last two were '90 and '96). All the wine is made in stainless steel and bottled as quickly as possible.
Open: Mon–Sun 9am–7pm.

Domaines Guy Saget
58150 Pouilly-sur-Loire.
Vineyards owned: Pouilly 35ha, Touraine Mesland 45ha,
Montlouis 10ha, Anjou 80ha. 1.2 million bottles. VP-R and N
An old-established family firm which has expanded into a *négociant* business from vineyard holdings. The wines are made by cool temperature-controlled vinification which gives them good fruit but not too much acidity. The vineyard holdings are in Chantalouettes, Les Loges, Les Bascoins and Château de la Roche for Pouilly; Clos du Roy for Sancerre. The wines are generally soft and very accessible. The *négociant* business includes wines from Touraine and Anjou and there are also vineyards in Touraine, in Montlouis and in the Coteaux du Layon in Anjou.
Open: Mon–Sun 8am–noon, 2–6pm.

Château de Tracy
Tracy-sur-Loire, 58150 Pouilly-sur-Loire. Vineyards owned:
Tracy and Les Loges 24ha. 80,000 bottles. VP-R
A traditional family firm, owned by the Comte d'Estutt d'Assay and run by his two sons. The estate has been in the family since the 16th century. The wines produced here are full of character and mature relatively quickly. *Open: By appointment only.*

QUINCY AC

Claude Houssier
Domaine du Pressoir, 18120 Quincy.
Vineyards owned: 12.5ha. 40,000 bottles. VP-R
Mainly white Quincy is produced, with a little red Vin de Pays du Cher. The white wines are made naturally dry, without chaptalisation, and are designed to age well over a period of four or five years. Sold locally and in Paris. *Open: Mon–Sun 8am–noon, 2–7pm.*

Domaine de la Maison Blanche
18120 Quincy. VP-R
One of the most important producers of Quincy, making good quality wines, which are – for Quincy – widely distributed.
Open: By appointment only.

Jean Mardon
40 Route de Reuilly, 18120 Quincy.
Vineyards owned: 12ha. 88,000 bottles. VP-R
One of the producers making attractive Quincy. His vineyards are on the banks of the River Cher just outside the village of Quincy, as are his new cellars. He also makes Vin de Pays du Cher red and rosé. *Open: Mon–Sat 9am–noon, 1.30–7pm.*

Domaine Meunier
18120 Quincy. Vineyards owned: 10ha. 40,000 bottles. VP-R
A small estate. The wines are available through a pleasant restaurant and shop which the family owns on the Route de Vierzon, just outside Quincy. Only one wine is made, a Quincy, which is made in the traditional way. *Open: "Every day, all day".*

REUILLY AC

Gérard Bigonneau
La Chagnat, Brinay, 18120 Preuilly.
Vineyards owned 6.5ha. VP-R
A small producer making particularly attractive white Reuilly as well as a little red and rosé. The red is partly aged in wood, but the white and rosé are made in stainless steel and bottled quickly for freshness. *Open: 8am–8pm, appointments preferred.*

Domaine Desroches
13 Route de Charost, 18120 Preuilly. 42,000 bottles. VP-R
Mainly white, but also red and rosé Reuilly are made by Domaine Desroches. The firm is one of a group of six producers in Reuilly who have come together to share equipment, as a result of which it can afford new stainless-steel vinification. The resulting wines – the whites in particular – are delightfully fresh.
Open: By appointment only.

Claude Lafond
Le Bois St-Denis, 36260 Reuilly.
Vineyards owned: Reuilly: Sauvignon Blanc 7.4ha, Pinot Gris 2.75ha, Pinot Noir 3.2ha. 100,000 bottles. VP-R
This grower makes a very dry white Reuilly from the vineyard of La Raie; a rare rosé from Pinot Gris grown in La Grande Pièce vineyard; and a light, fresh red from Pinot Noir in Les Grands Vignes. A certain amount of rosé and red wine is matured in wood. Claude Lafond is one of the more dynamic producers in the Reuilly area as well as being chairman of the local Syndicat Vinicole. *Open: Mon–Sun 8am–7pm.*

Alain Mabillot
Ste-Lizaigne, 36260 Reuilly. Vineyards owned: 4ha. VP-R
From his small vineyard, Monsieur Mabillot makes an attractive white Reuilly, which is produced in stainless steel. He also makes small quantities of a light, fresh red.

Jean-Michel Sorbe
9 Route de Boisgisson, 18120 Preuilly. Vineyards owned:
Reuilly 6ha, Quincy 1.8ha. 39,000 bottles. VP-R
One of the best producers both in Reuilly and in Quincy, Monsieur Sorbe makes very fresh whites and a comparatively rich red. A new cellar and temperature-control equipment help him in making his wines as clean and fresh as possible.
Open: By appointment only.

SANCERRE AC

Pierre Archambault
Caves du Clos la Perrière, Verdigny, 18300 Sancerre.
Vineyards owned: Verdigny (Sancerre): Sauvignon 51ha, Pinot
Noir 6ha. 800,000 bottles. VP-R and N
This *vigneron* and *négociant* makes a wide range of single-vineyard Sancerre, producing red, rosé and white wines from his own vineyard and from bought-in grapes. His finest wine is the very dry white Carte d'Or la Perrière. The white wines are made in stainless steel, but wood is used to age the reds. A small amount of his Pouilly-Fumé La Loge aux Moines is also made from bought-in grapes. *Open: Mon–Fri 2.30–6pm; holidays (April–Sept) 2.30–7pm. Appointments necessary for groups.*

Bernard Bailly-Reverdy et Fils
Bué, 18300 Sancerre. Vineyards owned: Sancerre: Sauvignon
10ha, Pinot Noir 7ha. 75,000 bottles. VP-R
Red wines are a speciality with this firm and are aged partly in new wood, giving a surprisingly spicy, rich result, which is sold two years after the vintage. The white wine, Clos du Chêne Marchand, is fermented slowly at a controlled temperature, giving considerable flavour and fruit. Other wines are sold as Domaine de la Mercy-Dieu. *Open: By appointment only.*

Bernard Balland et Fils
Bué, 18300 Sancerre. Vineyards owned: Sancerre: Sauvignon
15.5ha, Pinot Noir 4.5ha. 118,000 bottles. VP-R
An old-established firm (1650) with new ideas. Treatment of the wine is kept to a minimum with modern equipment. Two whites, Le Grand Chemarin and Le Clos d'Ervocs, are bottled separately; a red, Les Marnes, is in a modern style. The whites are fresh and very fragrant, the reds are now being aged in new wood and are much richer than they used to be. *Open: By appointment only.*

Philippe de Benoist
Domaine du Nozay, Sancerre.
The owner of this estate is related to Aubert de Villaine, co-owner of Domaine de la Romanée-Conti in Burgundy. The style of the Sancerre is elegant and light. The domaine was set up in 1970.

Domaine Henri Bourgeois
Chavignol, 18300 Sancerre.
Vineyards owned: Sancerre: Sauvignon 39ha, Pinot Noir 7ha,
Pouilly-Fumé 3.6ha. 350,000 bottles. VP-R
A sizeable firm whose cellars stretch down the main street of Chavignol and include an ultra-modern fermentation and bottling area. A wide range of wines is produced; the top Sancerre comes from Les Monts Damnés vineyard in Chavignol. There is also a wood-fermented Sancerre, Cuvée Étienne Henri. La Bourgeois comes from flint soil in St-Satur. Bourgeois also owns Domaine Laporte (*see page 34*). *Open: Mon–Sun 9am– noon, 2–6.30pm.*

Roger Champault (Domaine de Colombier)
Crézancy en Sancerre, 18300 Sancerre.
Vineyards owned: Sancerre: Sauvignon 9ha, Pinot Noir 4.5ha,
Menetou-Salon: 0.5ha. 115,000 bottles. VP-R
An old-established vineyard which has been in the Champault
family for generations. It produces traditional wines which see
some wood before bottling. Domaine de Colombier is the main
vineyard, but the family also owns land in Clos du Roy, Moulin à
Vent and Côte de Champtin (all in Crézancy).
Open: Mon–Sat 8am–noon, 1–6pm.

Lucien Crochet
Place de l'Église, Bué, 18300 Sancerre. Vineyards owned: Bué,
Crézancy, Sancerre: Sauvignon 24ha, Pinot Noir 8ha. VP-R
A family firm with holdings in some of the best Sancerre
vineyards: Chêne Marchand and Grand Chemarin for white; Clos
du Roy for red. About 40 percent of production is from bought-in
grapes and must, 60 percent is from the firm's own vineyards.
The quality of the wines is now extremely high (thanks partly to
a huge space-age cellar which has been carved out of the sur-
rounding hillside; the single-vineyard Cuvée Chêne from the
Chêne Marchand vineyard has great character.
Open: Mon–Sat 9am–noon, 2–6pm.

Vincent Delaporte
Chavignol, 18300 Sancerre. Vineyards owned: Chavignol and
Sancerre: Sauvignon 15ha, Pinot Noir 4ha. 80,000 bottles. VP-R
A top-quality producer, especially for his whites from Chavignol,
which age unusually well for Sancerre. One of his best wines
comes from the Clos Beaujeu. The reds tend to be quite tannic
when young, and benefit from some ageing. White wines are
produced in modern stainless steel, the reds are aged in wood.
Open: By appointment only.

Fournier Père et Fils
Verdigny, 18300 Sancerre. Vineyards owned: Sancerre 13.5ha,
Menetou-Salon 6.5ha. 480,000 bottles. VP-R
Cave des Chaumières is the brand name for the estate white, red
and rosé Sancerre made by this firm of growers and *négociants*.
Only stainless steel is used in the cellar; the wines are light, fruity
and immediately attractive. Red and white wines are also made
from a new vineyard in Menetou-Salon. Sauvignon grapes are used
to make Vin de Pays du Jardin de la France.
Open: Appointments preferred.

Gitton Père et Fils
Chemin de Lavaud, Ménétréol, 18300 Sancerre.
Vineyards owned: Sancerre: Sauvignon 18.7ha, Pinot Noir
1.6ha. Pouilly-sur-Loire: Sauvignon 9ha. 300,000 bottles. VP-R
One of the larger landowners in the area, from holdings built up
since World War II. The firm specialises in separate bottlings for
different holdings. Fruit from young vines is vinified in stainless

steel, that from old vines in wood. There are ten Sancerres (including two reds) and five Pouilly-Fumés. A red and a white wine are also being made in the Côtes de Gien. The wines retain the characteristics of the different vineyards to a considerable degree. *Open: Mon–Fri 8am–noon, 2–6pm.*

Pascal Jolivet
Route de Chavignol, 18300 Sancerre.
Vineyards owned: Sancerre 9ha, Pouilly-Fumé 1.7ha. VP-R
A modern company making a wide range of wines, particularly in Sancerre, although some would argue that the wines from Pouilly are even better. The firm has expanded rapidly and is now buying vineyards as well as constructing a new cellar. The Sancerres include wines from the Chêne Marchand and Clos du Roy vineyards. *Open: By appointment only.*

Domaine Laporte
Cave de la Cresle, 18300 St-Satur. Vineyards owned: Sauvignon 14ha, Pinot Noir 2ha. 140,000 bottles. VP-R
Although owned by the Bourgeois family (*see* page 32), this domaine is run separately from a modern winery that would not look out of place in California. The wine style is very fruity and open. The labels can be fairly gaudy. Domaine du Rochoy and Les Duchesses are the best Sancerres; some Pouilly-Fumé is also made. *Open: Mon–Fri 8am–noon, 2–6pm.*

Alphonse Mellot
18300 Sancerre. Vineyards owned: Sauvignon 38ha, Pinot Noir 7ha. 270,000 bottles. VP-R and N
One of the largest firms in Sancerre, acting both as grower and *négociant*. The top wine is Domaine de la Moussière, from what is agreed to be the largest single vineyard in Sancerre. Mellot also makes wines in Menetou-Salon, Quincy and Reuilly and in Pouilly-Fumé. *Open: Mon–Sat 8am–1pm, 2–6pm.*

Joseph Mellot
Route de Ménétréol, 18300 Sancerre.
Vineyards owned: 40ha. VP-R and N
The Mellot family is dominant in Sancerre and Joseph Mellot's firm is a *négociant*, making wines from Menetou-Salon, Quincy, Reuilly and the Coteaux du Giennois, as well as from its own vineyards in Sancerre. *Open: Mon–Fri 8am–noon, 2–6pm.*

Paul Millérioux
Champtin, 18300 Crézancy-en-Sancerre.
Vineyards owned: 16ha. 100,000 bottles. VP-R
A top-class producer whose Clos du Roy white has a surprising ability (for a Sancerre) to age. Monsieur Millérioux's vineyards are ideally situated in the northern slopes of Sancerre facing south and southwest. His red Sancerre, Côte de Champtin, also has good ageing ability. Both red and white mature for a while in wood. *Open: Appointments preferred.*

Roger Neveu (Domaine du Colombier)
18300 Verdigny-en-Sancerre. Vineyards owned: Sancerre:
Sauvignon 8ha, Pinot Noir 2ha. 55,000 bottles. VP-R
Established in the 18th century, this family firm is run by the
father and his two sons. The white is Clos des Bouffants, the red
Domaine du Colombier. The white is quite delicate in style. As
with many producers in Sancerre, old and new techniques are
used in the winery. *Open: Mon–Fri, during working hours.*

Clos de la Poussie
Bué, 18300 Sancerre.
This magnificent amphitheatre of vines which closes the valley
of Bué is now producing the sort of quality that its spectacular
situation suggests. The wines are light in style, emphasising
elegance. The cellars are housed in a building that looks something like a Swiss chalet. *Open: By appointment only.*

Paul Prieur et Fils
Verdigny, 18300 Sancerre. Vineyards owned: Sancerre:
Sauvignon 7ha, Pinot Noir 5ha. 100,000 bottles. VP-R
A family firm which owns one part of the best Sancerre vineyards, Les Monts Damnés, giving a particularly elegant wine from
chalky soil. The red and rosé come from the gravelly Pichon
vineyard in Verdigny and great emphasis is placed on the red,
which the firm exported to England in the last century. I prefer
the white. *Open: By appointment only.*

Jean Reverdy et Fils (Domaine des Villots)
Verdigny, 18300 Sancerre. Vineyards owned: Sancerre:
Sauvignon 8ha, Pinot Noir 3.5ha. 93,000 bottles. VP-R
This family firm was established in 1646. Today it owns the whole
of the Clos de la Reine Blanche vineyard at Verdigny. The white
wines age attractively and their smooth fruit can certainly sustain
four or five years' cellaring. The red also gives plenty of fruit and
surprising colour. *Open: By appointment only.*

Domaine Jean-Max Roger
Bué, 18300 Sancerre. Vineyards owned: Sancerre: Sauvignon
10.4ha, Pinot Noir 2.6ha. Menetou-Salon: Sauvignon 4ha.
200,000 bottles. VP-R and N
Forty percent of the production from this firm is from grapes and
wines that are bought in. Principal holdings in Sancerre are in Le
Grand Chemarin and Le Chêne Marchand. In Menetou-Salon, the
small holding is at Morogues in Le Petit Clos. Quality is average,
with Le Grand Chemarin the best Sancerre, but the Menetou-
Salon is probably the most attractive white wine.
Open: By appointment only.

Château de Sancerre
18300 Sancerre.
Vineyards owned: Sauvignon 19ha. 150,000 bottles. VP-R
The old château at Sancerre is currently owned by the company

that produces the famous Grand Marnier liqueur. Here a white Sancerre is made, using mainly stainless steel, with 20 percent of the wine matured briefly in wood. The style is clean and modern with few pretensions.

Domaine Thomas et Fils
Chaudoux, Verdigny, 18300 Sancerre. Vineyards owned: Sauvignon 6.8ha, Pinot Noir 1.2ha. 60,000 bottles. VP-R
The best wine from this house is the white Clos de la Crèle, while the Clos Terres Blanches is flintier and more austere. The '83 red, aged in wood, was mellow and soft and had good colour. White wines, made in stainless steel at a low temperature, are bottled immediately. *Open: By appointment only.*

Domaine Vacheron
1 Rue du Puits Poulton, 18300 Sancerre. Vineyards owned: Sauvignon 23ha, Pinot Noir 11ha. 130,000 bottles. VP-R
Top-quality wines from the centre of Sancerre, one of the most popular visits for tourists. Wines can be tasted at le Grenier à Sel in the town during the summer months. The reds are the stars with this firm, although the whites are also of high quality. The reds can age remarkably – a '75 was still tasting too young at 11 years old. Some red is aged in new wood and all is kept in small barrels for a year. *Open: Mon-Sun 10am-12.30pm, 2.30-7pm; by appointment for groups.*

André Vatan
Chaudoux, Verdigny, 18300 Sancerre. Vineyards owned: Sauvignon 7.6ha, Pinot Noir 2.1ha. 87,000 bottles. VP-R
Monsieur Vatan makes both white and red wines using modern stainless-steel equipment, with some wood-ageing for six months for the reds. His wines are full of life and fruit and he has obviously learned much from his father, Jean Vatan, with whom he has also worked. *Open: By appointment only.*

CHÂTEAUMEILLANT VDQS

Centre Coopératif des Vins de Châteaumeillant
18370 Châteaumeillant. Vineyards owned: 32ha. 300,000 bottles. Coop (50 members).
By far the largest producer in this small VDQS zone, the cooperative makes pleasant light red, a better rosé, and a *vin gris* which it regards as its best wine. A white Vin de Pays du Cher from Sauvignon Blanc and Chardonnay is also made.
Open: Mon-Sat 8am-noon, 1.30-5.30pm.

Maurice Landoix
Domaine de Feuillat, 18370 Châteaumeillant. Vineyards owned: 8.5ha. VP-R
Produces red and rosé Châteaumeillant, operating from premises in the town. The red wine, from Gamay, is aged in wood, but vinified in stainless steel. *Open: By appointment only.*

CÔTES D'AUVERGNE VDQS

Michel et Roland Rougeyron
27 Rue de la Crouzette, 63119 Châteaugay.
Vineyards owned: 15ha. 100,000 bottles. VP-R
One of the few producers in the Côtes d'Auvergne with stainless steel. The family believe it is the oldest wine family in the region, and makes three wines under the brand name of Bousset d'Or – a red, a rosé and a white. *Open: Appointments preferred.*

Caves St-Verny
Route d'Issoire, 63960 Veyre-Monton.
The regional cooperative of the Côtes d'Auvergne. Its wines have vastly improved since the installation of stainless steel for the '93 harvest. A shop provides a good source for tasting the local wines.

CÔTES DU FOREZ VDQS

Les Vignerons Foreziens
Trelins, 42130 Boen-sur-Lignon.
Vineyards owned: Côtes du Forez 200ha, Vin de Pays d'Urfé 100ha. 800,000 bottles. Coop (250 members).
This acclaimed cooperative dominates the tiny Côtes du Forez VDQS region. The red, mainly from Gamay, is made using some carbonic maceration in a sub-Beaujolais style, to be drunk young and chilled. The two top wines are a Cuvée de Prestige and the explosively named Cuvée Volcanique. A small amount of rosé is produced from Pinot Noir, some of it medium-dry.
Open: By appointment only.

COTEAUX DU GIENNOIS VDQS

Alain Paulat
Villemoison, St-Père, 58200 Cosne-sur-Loire.
Vineyards owned: Villemoison 5.5ha. 33,000 bottles. VP-R
Monsieur Paulat practises organic farming and winemaking on his small holding, while using modern equipment in his cellars. He makes a light, fresh white from Sauvignon Blanc and a rosé from Pinot Noir and Gamay (80 percent). The red Réserve Traditionnelle is a more serious affair, made from Pinot Noir and aged for up to 18 months in large barrels. It needs at least four to five years to mature. If any wines are to ensure the survival of this small appellation, they are from this domaine.
Open: Mon-Sun 8am-noon, 3-7pm.

Jean Poupat et Fils
47 Rue Georges Clemenceau, 45500 Gien.
Vineyards owned: Gien 7ha. 35,000 bottles. VP-R
A Gamay-based red is the main production here, with small amounts of rosé and white. The white, from Sauvignon, is the best of the three and has something of the character of Sancerre in its crispness and liveliness. *Open: By appointment only.*

CÔTES ROANNAISES VDQS

Pierre Gaume
Les Gillets, 42155 Lentigny.
Vineyards owned: 4ha. 22,000 bottles. VP-R
Simple Gamay wines are made using both stainless steel and
wood. Monsieur Gaume makes a red and rosé from the VDQS
Côtes Roannaises and also a Gamay rosé and a Chardonnay Vin
de Pays d'Urfé. His wines are lively, with plenty of cherried fruit.
Open: By appointment only.

Maurice Lutz (Domaine de Pavillon)
42820 Ambierle.
Vineyards owned: Côtes Roannaises 5ha. 28,000 bottles. VP-R
A Gamay wine, made using semi-carbonic maceration techniques
to give plenty of strawberry fruit flavour and colour, is the bulk of
Monsieur Lutz's production. He makes a little soft, fruity rosé,
also from Gamay. *Open: Mon–Sun.*

ST-POURÇAIN VDQS

Cave Nebout
Route de Montluçon. 03500 St-Pourçain-sur-Sioule.
Vineyards owned: 16ha. 70,000 bottles. VP-R
A small producer operating from attractive old cellars which
nevertheless have stainless-steel equipment. The Nebouts are
particularly proud of their red from Gamay and Pinot Noir.
Open: Mon–Sat 8am–8pm; Sun by appointment.

Ray Père et Fils
Saulcet, 08600 St-Pourçain-sur-Sioule. Vineyards owned:
Saulcet 8ha (red and white). 65,000 bottles. VP-R
One of the best St-Pourçain producers, concentrating on a Pinot
Noir/Gamay red which takes two or three years' ageing. The
white is soft with a high Chardonnay content (50 percent) and a
touch of Sauvignon to balance the rather bland Tressalier. The
rosé, from Gamay, is in a very fresh style and needs to be drunk
young. Modern winemaking techniques are used in the cellars.
Open: By appointment only.

Union des Vignerons
Quai de la Ronde, 03500 St-Pourçain-sur-Sioule. Vineyards
owned: 300ha of Gamay, Pinot Noir, Chardonnay, Sauvignon,
Tressalier. 1.5 million bottles. Coop (200 members).
This is by far the biggest production unit in St-Pourçain and,
luckily, methods are good and the wines reliable. The bulk of
them are red, made from Gamay and a little Pinot Noir. Rosés
include a *vin gris* from Gamay. Standard whites are made using
the local Tressalier grape, but the top-quality wine is made from
Sauvignon and Chardonnay (50:50). A classic-method sparkling
wine, Anne de Bourbon, is also made.
Open: Mon–Fri 8am–noon, 2–4pm; appointments preferred.

Touraine Producers

BOURGUEIL AC, CHINON AC, ST-NICOLAS-DE-BOURGUEIL AC

Maison Audebert et Fils
20 Avenue Jean Causeret, 37140 Bourgueil. Vineyards owned: Bourgueil 28ha, St-Nicolas 5ha, Chinon 4ha. VP-R and N
Large producer specialising, both as Bourgueil grower and *négociant*, with smaller amounts of Chinon. As well as buying grapes, it owns some good vineyards in Bourgueil: Domaine du Grand Clos, Vignoble des Marquises and, in St-Nicolas, Vignoble de la Contrie. The newly acquired Chinon vineyard is Les Perruches (Savigny-en-Véron). All these are bottled as single-vineyard wines. Most wines spend a period in wood.
Open: Mon–Fri 8am–7pm.

Bernard Baudry
37500 Cravant-Les-Coteaux.
Bernard Baudry is the best Chinon producer among a number of Baudrys in Cravant-les-Coteaux. He has vineyards by the river, for faster-maturing wines, and on the *coteaux*, for wines which need time to mature. His *lieux-dits* – named vineyard sites, whose wines are bottled separately – include Grezeaux and Haies Martels. All his wines spend some time in wood. *Open: By appointment only.*

Caslot-Galbrun
La Hurolaie, Benais, 37140 Bourgueil.
Vineyards owned: 23ha. 97,000 bottles. VP-R
A long-established producer whose wines have considerable depth and quality. Although fermentation is now in stainless steel, all the wines see some wood. They always seem to need some years before being attractively drinkable; in their youth they have deep colour and a fair amount of stalky tannin.
Open: Mon–Sat 10am–noon, 2.30–7pm.

Christophe Chasle
37130 St-Patrice. Vineyards owned: 7ha, 42,000 bottles. VP-R
A producer of charming Bourgueil wines from the far eastern end of the appellation. His cellars, carved out of rock, have yielded some fascinating Gallo-Roman pieces. His wines are designed both for early drinking and for ageing. *Lieux-dits* include Les Gravois and Rochecot. *Open: By appointment only.*

Couly-Dutheil
12 Rue Diderot, 37502 Chinon.
Vineyards owned: Chinon 70ha. 400,000 bottles. VP-R and N
Mainly modern-style wines, from the flat plain of Chinon, sold under the names Domaine de Turpenay and Domaine René Couly. But there are quantities of finer wines for ageing from Clos de l'Écho and Clos de l'Olive on the higher plateau vineyards. Vinification techniques are modern here, and the only traditional

sights are the 11th-century *caves*. Bertrand Couly is in charge of vinification and local wine consultant Jacques Puisais is employed. The firm acts as *négociant* for other Touraine red and white wines and Saumur-Champigny.

Open: 8am–noon, 2–5.30pm; also tastings at Clos de l'Écho vineyard.

Domaine Dozon
Le Rouilly, 37500 Ligré.
Vineyards owned: Chinon 22ha. 133,000 bottles. VP-R
The Domaine's 13-hectare Clos du Saut au Loup vineyards are south of the Vienne, across the river from Chinon. Chinon white and Chinon rosé are made there, as well as the main domaine wine, Clos du Saut au Loup, which comes from old vines. The best can spend up to a year in wood. *Open: Mon–Sat 9am–6pm.*

Pierre-Jacques Druet
Le Pied Fourrier, 37140 Bourgueil. VP-R
One of the innovative younger producers, trained in Bordeaux, making wines that emphasise fruit rather than tannin, and yet age well. He makes wines from three *lieux-dits*: the lightest is Beaunais. Of medium weight and longevity is Le Grand Mont, while the biggest wine is Vaumoreau. *Open: By appointment only.*

Domaine des Forges
Place de Tilleuls, 37140 Restigné.
Vineyards owned: Bourgueil 18ha. 100,000 bottles. VP-R
Serious Bourgueil made by Jean-Yves Billet and aged in wood for up to one year. There are three different *cuvées*: Cuvée du Domaine, Cuvée Les Bézards and Cuvée Vieilles Vignes. Stainless steel is used for vinification, and the wines are aged in wood. *Open: By appointment only.*

Château de la Grille
37502 Chinon. Vineyards owned: 20ha. 100,000 bottles. VP-R
One of the showpiece estates of Chinon, owned by the champagne house of Gosset and arranged with the same elegance. The wine is bottled in copies of antique bottles, and is aged partly in new oak. The château itself was built in the 15th and 16th centuries – mainly the latter – and bristles with a large number of small turrets. *Open: Mon–Sat 9am–noon, 1.30–6pm.*

Jean Jacques Jamet (Domaine du Fondis)
Le Fondis, St-Nicolas-de-Bourgueil, 37340 Bourgueil.
Vineyards owned: 12ha. 40,000 bottles. VP-R
This company, in operation since 1970, makes wines that can be drunk young and fresh. A small quantity of Cabernet Sauvignon tends to give the wine some body and tannin. *Open: Mon–Fri.*

Charles Joguet
Sazilly, 37220 L'Île Bouchard.
Vineyards owned: 15.5ha. 98,000 bottles.
The major producer in the village of Sazilly (Chinon AC), Charles

Joguet is very much the Renaissance man: a practising artist, poet
and sculptor as well as a wine producer. He sells wines under four
different names: Cuvée du Clos de la Cure, Clos du Chêne Vert,
Clos de l'Haute Olive and Les Varennes du Grand Clos. There is
also a wine from old vines called Clos de la Dioterie. Monsieur
Joguet's wines are of the highest quality.
Open: By appointment only.

Lamé-Delille Boucard
*37140 Ingrandes de Touraine. Vineyards owned: Bourgueil
31ha, Touraine 1.5ha. 150,000 bottles.*
A traditional firm using wood for vinification and giving Bourgueil
up to three years in wood. It has been experimenting with new
clones of Cabernet Franc to improve quality at the expense of
yield (a rare phenomenon and one to applaud). A small amount
of Bourgueil rosé is made from Cabernet Sauvignon, and a Rosé
de Touraine is made from Grolleau and Gamay. A red Vin de Pays
du Jardin de la France is also produced. The brand name is
Domaine des Chesnaies.
Open: Mon–Fri 9–11.30am, 2–5pm; Sat 9–11.30am.

Château de Ligré
Route de Champigny-sur-Veude. 37500 Ligré.
Vineyards owned: Chinon 32ha. 220,000 bottles. VP-R
White, rosé and (principally) red Chinon are made at this estate
which is based around a 19th-century manor house across the
River Vienne from Chinon. Pierre Ferrand vinifies in wood and
then keeps the red wine in barrels for up to two years.
Open: Mon–Fri 9am–12.30pm, 2–6pm.

Pascal et Alain Lorieux
*64 Avenue St-Vincent, 37140 St-Nicolas-de-Bourgueil. Vineyards
owned: St-Nicolas 9.5ha, Chinon 5ha. 85,000 bottles. VP-R*
Hardly the most romantic of cellars – a converted garage – but
Pascal Lorieux makes some high-quality St-Nicolas. His brother,
Alain, has land in Chinon, and they use the same vinification
facilities, although Alain also has a cellar in Cravant-les-Coteaux
in Chinon. The best St-Nicolas, les Mauguerets la Contrie, is a
blend of grapes grown on two *lieux-dits*.
Open: By appointment only.

Jean-Claude Mabileau (Domaine du Bourg)
La Jarnoterie, St-Nicolas-de-Bourgueil, 37140 Bourgueil.
Vineyards owned: St-Nicolas 15ha. 107,000 bottles. VP-R
Monsieur Mabileau makes a light red from vineyards on the St-
Nicolas *coteaux*, using carbonic maceration techniques (as in
Beaujolais) and vinifying in cement tanks, subsequently maturing
the wines in oak for a short period. Although they can be drunk
young, he maintains that his wines will age for anything up
to 30 years and has old vintages in his spectacular tufa cellars that
date back as far as 1893 to prove his point.
Open: By appointment only.

Marc Mureau
37140 Bourgueil.

M Mureau has five sons in wine production in Bourgueil. Marc himself makes wines that have remarkable ageing ability. The cellars, in a former quarry, provide perfect conditions for maturing in bottle. A large proportion of wines is exported elsewhere in Europe and to the US.

Plouzeau et Fils (Château de la Bonnelière)
37500 Chinon. Vineyards owned: Touraine 20ha, Chinon 3ha. 900,000 bottles. VP-R and N

The biggest firm in Chinon, making wines from all over Touraine and Anjou. Its vineyards (once owned by the Duc de Richelieu) produce Sauvignon de Touraine and Cabernet de Touraine, plus a small quantity of an early-drinking Chinon. Other wines handled are Saumur-Champigny, Cabernet d'Anjou, Vouvray, Saumur and Coteaux du Layon, but there are few exciting products. *Open: Mon–Fri 9am–noon, 2–6pm. Appointments necessary for groups.*

Domaine du Roncée
Panzoult, 37220 Île-Bouchard.
Vineyards owned: Chinon 23ha. 173,000 bottles. VP-R

A considerable holding, established in 1964, making light, soft reds and rosés, most of which are for early drinking. Some, from older vines in Le Clos des Marronniers and Le Clos des Folies, are aged in wood for a short period to give greater longevity and some depth. *Open: By appointment only.*

Gérard Spelty
17 Rue Principale, 37500 Cravant-les-Coteaux.
Vineyards owned: Chinon 15ha. VP-R

One of the most interesting and exciting Chinon producers, making two *cuvées*: Domaine du Carroi Portier, which is designed for earlier drinking, and Clos de Neuilly, a selection from old vines, aged for 18 months in wood and intended for longer maturation. *Open: Mon–Fri 9am–noon, 2–6pm.*

Joel Taluau
Chevrette, St-Nicolas-de-Bourgueil, 37140 Bourgueil. Vineyards owned: St-Nicolas 15ha, Bourgueil 2ha. 110,000 bottles.

M Taluau has set up in business separately from his father, Albert. He goes against tradition in St-Nicolas by not using wood for ageing. He bottles wines under three labels: Jeunes Vignes from young vines, Domaine de la Chevrette and Vieilles Vignes from old vines. *Open: Mon–Sat 8am–noon, 2–6pm.*

CHEVERNY AC, COUR CHEVERNY AC

Bernard et François Cazin
Le Petit Chambord, 41700 Cheverny.
Vineyards owned: Cheverny 10.5ha, Cour Cheverny 3.5ha, Crémant de Loire 1.5ha. 80,000 bottles. VP-R

The bulk of production is of a fruity carbonic-maceration Gamay, but there is also a small quantity of the rare white from the Romorantin grape under the Cour Cheverny AC. Look also for the well-made classic-method sparkling wine from Chardonnay. Other wines made include still whites from Sauvignon Blanc and Chardonnay, and a rosé and red from Pinot Noir.
Open: By appointment only.

Patrice Hahusseau
38 Rue de la Chaumette, 41500 Muides-sur-Loire.
Vineyards owned: Cheverny 7.5ha. VP-R
Red, white and rosé Cheverny are made, along with some sparkling Crémant de Loire, from Chardonnay. *Open: By appointment.*

Domaine des Huards
Les Huards, 41700 Cour Cheverny. Vineyards owned: Cheverny 18ha, Cour Cheverny 7ha. 130,000 bottles. VP-R
Romorantin Cour Cheverny Cuvée François 1er is the star wine at this estate, which has been in the Gendrier family since 1846. It also makes white, red and rosé Cheverny, and some sparkling wine from Chardonnay. *Open: 9am–1pm, 2–7pm, by appointment.*

Domaine Sauger Père et Fils
41700 Cheverny.
A wide range of wines is produced from this 17-hectare vineyard. Chardonnay and Sauvignon are used for the white wines; Gamay, Cot, Cabernet Franc for the reds, and Pineau d'Aunis for the rosés. There is also a vintage-dated sparkling wine, made for the first time in '89, from Chardonnay.

Philippe Tessier
41700 Cour Cheverny. Vineyards owned: Cheverny 10ha, Cour Cheverny 2ha. 80,000 bottles.
The third generation to run the family vineyard, Monsieur Tessier is full of ideas and enthusiasm. He is particularly keen on Romorantin, which makes a wine that can age well. He is better at whites than reds, and his Sauvignons show good, grassy freshness. *Open: 9am–noon, 2.30–7pm.*

JASNIÈRES AC, COTEAUX DU LOIR AC

Joel Gigou
72340 La Charte-sur-Loir.
In the Domaine de la Charrière, Monsieur Gigou makes a typical Chenin wine, muted when young and needing some years to open out. Bottled under the name Cuvée Clos St-Jacques.

Jean-Baptiste Pinon
12 Promenade du Tertre, 41800 Montoire-sur-le-Loir.
Vineyards owned: Jasnières 4.5ha, Coteaux du Vendômois 1ha, Vouvray 1ha. 25,000 bottles. VP-R
This may be a small holding of Jasnières but it represents about a

tenth of the appellation total. The wine is dry, almost harsh when young, and matures slowly. The small portion of Coteaux du Vendômois produces a red from Gamay and Pineau d'Aunis and a little medium-dry Vouvray. *Open: By appointment only.*

TOURAINE AC

Jacques Bonnigal

17 Rue d'Enfer, Limeray, 37530 Amboise.
Vineyards owned: Limeray 10ha. 40,000 bottles. VP-R

M Bonnigal's traditional techniques produce an excellent red, Touraine-Amboise Cuvée François I (a Gamay, Cot [Malbec] and Cabernet Franc blend) which needs three or four years to achieve maturity; an average Sauvignon and a honeyed medium-sweet still white from Chenin Blanc. A small proportion of this production is of a classic-method sparkling wine from Chenin. He has planted Chardonnay which has improved quality considerably. *Open: Mon–Fri 8am–7pm; appointments necessary for groups.*

Bougrier

41400 St-Georges-sur-Cher. VP-R and N

The family-owned vineyard of Domaine Guenault produces a wide range of AC Touraine wines: Sauvignon Blanc, Cabernet Franc, Gamay and Chenin Blanc. The bulk of production, however, is from the *négociant* side of the business.

Clos de la Briderie

7 Quai des Violettes, 37400 Amboise.
Vineyards owned: Mesland 9ha. 68,000 bottles. VP-R

Touraine Mesland and Crémant de Loire sparkling wine are the two wines produced here. Everything, even with the reds, is designed for freshness and fruit, and stainless steel and early bottling are both employed. The vineyard is cultivated using the biodynamic system, eschewing fertilisers and following the rhythm of the seasons. *Open: Mon–Sat 8am–noon, 2–6pm.*

Philippe Brossillon

Domaine de Lusqueneau, Mesland, 41150 Onzain.
Vineyards owned: Mesland 18ha, Mouteaux 10ha, Onzain 2ha.
150,000 bottles. VP-R

A 200-year-old family firm which relies on traditional practices apart from mechanical harvesting. The Domaine de Lusqueneau lies in the Touraine-Mesland appellation area and produces mostly red wine, with small amounts of rosé and white and two sparklers – a rosé and a white. Some of the reds (90 percent Gamay and ten percent Cot and Cabernet) are now aged in wood, giving them extra longevity. *Open: Appointments preferred.*

Paul Buisse

69 Route de Vierzon, 41420 Montrichard.
Vineyards owned: 14ha. 1.6 million bottles. VP-R and N

One of Montrichard's two major *négociants* (Monmousseau [*see* page 47] is the other). Its small domaine, Paul Buisse, produces Sauvignon, Gamay, Cabernet Franc and Pineau d'Aunis, But the bulk of production is from bought-in grapes and wine. Wines produced include Touraine, Bourgueil, Chinon, Vouvray, Saumur and Sancerre, with three levels of quality: Cuvée Prestige, Cuvée Selection Paul Buisse and two special selections of a Chinon and a Sauvignon Blanc. *Open: By appointment only.*

Pierre Chainier (Château de la Roche)

Chargé, 37530 Amboise. Vineyards owned: Chargé 30ha, Pocé 35ha. 8 million bottles. VP-R and N

Besides owning two estates in the Amboise district, this firm runs a big *négociant* business, buying in 80 percent of its requirements. A full range of Touraine wines is made, of which the Touraine-Amboise from the Château de Pocé is the best. Also made is Vin de Pays du Jardin de la France, the general Loire *vin de pays*. Another name used is Philippe de Guerois.

Château de Chenonceaux

37150 Chenonceaux. Vineyards owned: 30ha. VP-R

One of the few great Touraine châteaux to produce wine from its own vineyard, and very good it is too. An ultra-modern *chai* is situated in the farm buildings of the château, where it makes two ranges of wine, both appellation Touraine: Les Dômes de Chenonceaux, named after the distinctive domes on the roof of the château and, the top *cuvée*, Château de Chenonceaux. Reds and whites are made. Please note that the wine cannot be bought at the château. *Open: By appointment only.*

Confrérie des Vignerons de Oisly et Thésée

Oisly, 41700 Contres. Vineyards owned: 275ha. 3.5 million bottles. Coop (60 members).

This is generally regarded as the best cooperative on the Loire, and one of the best in France. It was established in 1961 in an attempt to improve the quality of the Touraine wines. Strict quality control is practised, and any below-standard grapes are sold off. The wines – especially the Gamay de Touraine, Cabernet de Touraine and white Sauvignon de Touraine – are top-quality examples of what Touraine can produce given a little more commitment. Vinification is mainly in stainless steel, but some reds do spend time in wood. Blended wines carry the brand name Baronnie d'Aignan. A creamy white sparkling Crémant de Loire is made using Pinot Noir, Cabernet Franc and Chenin Blanc. *Open: By appointment only.*

Jacques Delaunay (Domaine des Sablons)

40 Rue de la Liberté, 41110 Pouillé. Vineyards owned: 15.5ha. VP-R

On well-drained soil on the left bank of the Cher, Monsieur Delaunay makes good examples of Touraine generic wines: Cabernet and Gamay for reds, Pineau d'Aunis for rosé and Sauvignon Blanc for whites. He also makes a sparkling Blanc de Blancs Touraine. *Open: Mon-Sat 8am-noon, 2-7pm.*

Clos de la Dorée

Le Vau, 37320 Esvres.

Vineyards owned: 12ha. 60,000 bottles. VP-R

M Rousseau has revived a Touraine tradition by making a light rosé, or *gris de gris*, called Noble Joué, a blend of Pinot Meunier, Pinot Gris and Pinot Noir. He has grouped a few producers together to bring back to life this deliciously fresh wine, once made in vineyards on the edge of Tours which were engulfed by the city's expanding suburbs. *Open: Mon–Sat 8am–12.30pm, 2–7pm.*

Domaine Dutertre

20/21 Rue d'Enfer, 37530 Limeray. Touraine Amboise 30ha. 100,000 bottles. VP-R

Most of the wines produced by this firm come under the Touraine Amboise AC, although there is also a sparkling Touraine Crémant. The style for the whites and rosés – made using the full range of Loire grapes – is modern, clean and fresh. Reds, however, are made traditionally and see some time in wood, which gives them good ageing potential. Cot, Cabernet Franc and Gamay are used in the blend. *Open: By appointment only.*

Domaine de la Gabillière

13 Route de Blere, 37400 Amboise. Vineyards owned: Touraine-Amboise and Touraine 15ha. 60,000 bottles. VP-R

The domaine, set around an 18th-century château, is one of the French Ministry of Agriculture's viticultural training schools. A red and white are made in the Touraine-Amboise AC area, the red produced mainly from Gamay and Malbec with a little Cabernet Franc, the white from Chenin Blanc. A classic-method sparkling Crémant de Loire is made from Chenin and Chardonnay, and a sparkling Touraine from ten percent Chenin. All the wines are (as expected) extremely correct. *Open: By appointment only.*

Vincent Girault (Clos Château Gaillard)

41150 Mesland.

Vineyards owned: Mesland 30ha. 60,000 bottles. VP-R

Red wines of the Touraine-Mesland AC are the speciality of this house. The best red is Vieilles Vignes Tradition, a blend of Gamay, Cabernet Franc and Malbec; 100 percent Gamay wines tend to be rather short and light, although well made. His other important production is of white Touraine-Mesland from Chenin Blanc. One of Monsieur Girault's stars is his dry Crémant de Loire, Les Doucinières, full of soft, smooth Chenin fruit.

Open: 9am–noon, 2–6pm, by appointment only.

Lucien Launay

Ange, 41400 Montrichard.

Vineyards owned: Ange 10ha. 80,000 bottles. VP-R

A full range of Touraine wines is made by this firm, most from Cabernet Franc and Gamay. Other grape varieties are Pineau d'Aunis and Sauvignon. Monsieur Launay also makes sparkling wines by the classic method. *Open: Mon–Sun.*

Henry Marionnet (Domaine de la Charmoise)
Soings, 41230 Mur-de-Sologne.
Vineyards owned: Soings 50ha. 400,000 bottles. VP-R
Gamay and Sauvignon are the two principal varieties on this large estate, which makes a red from Gamay and a still white. A rosé is blended from Pineau d'Aunis, Cot and Cabernet Franc. The approach is modern, everything is done in stainless steel, and the Gamay is treated to carbonic maceration to bring out the colour.
Open: Mon–Fri 8.30–noon, 1.30–5.30pm; Sat by appointment only.

Christian Mauduit (Domaine de la Mechimière)
Le Mechimière, Mareuil-sur-Cher, 41110 St-Aignan.
Vineyards owned: 20ha. 147,000 bottles. VP-R
Sauvignon Blanc wines retain the largest production and are the most successful, but there are also reds made from Gamay and Cabernet, a rosé from Pineau d'Aunis and a sparkling wine based on Chenin Blanc. *Open: Mon–Sat 9–7pm; Sun morning only.*

J-M Monmousseau
41400 Montrichard.
Vineyards owned: 40ha. 320,000 bottles. VP-R and N
Most of the production from this firm (now owned by the Fourcroy family, makers of Mandovine Napoleon liqueur) is of sparkling wine made by the classic method. The brand names used include Brut de Mosny, JM Rosé and the top *cuvée* JM93. Wines are aged in chalk cellars dug out of cliffs above the River Cher at Montrichard.
Open: During working hours (by appointment at the weekend).

Château de Nitray
37270 Athée-sur-Cher.
Vineyards owned: 15ha. 80,000 bottles. VP-R
Under the ownership of Hubert de l'Espinay and Alexandre Scriabine, this estate specialises in a sparkling *brut* – a blend of Chenin Blanc and Chardonnay, under the name Comte Hubert de l'Espinay – as well as making still Touraine wines from Chenin and Sauvignon Blanc. No reds are produced.
Open: June 15–Sept 15; other times by appointment.

Domaine Octavie
Oisly 41700. Vineyards owned: 19ha. 143,000 bottles. VP-R
Good quality red from Gamay and Cabernet Franc and white from Sauvignon Blanc are made at this family-owned firm in Oisly. Vinification in stainless steel and only minimal ageing gives the wines maximum freshness. *Open: Mon–Sun 8am–8pm.*

Gaston Pavy
La Basse-Chevrière, Saché, 37190 Azay-le-Rideau.
Vineyards owned: 3ha. 13,500 bottles. VP-R
The top name in the Touraine-Azay-le-Rideau AC which has been operating since 1890. Monsieur Pavy makes only two wines: a white from Chenin Blanc that can be dry but is also lusciously sweet in good years, and a rosé made in tiny quantities from a

blend of Grolleau, Cot and Cabernet Sauvignon, which ages well.
Both wines are matured in wood for two to three months and this
brings out considerable depths – especially in the whites.
Open: By appointment only.

Pibaleau Père et Fils
Luré, 37190 Azay-le-Rideau.
Vineyards owned: Azay-le-Rideau 7.8ha. 45,000 bottles.
This relatively young firm has adopted traditional winemaking
techniques such as vinification in wood. This approach in the
cellar benefits the white and rosé as much as the red wine: the
white, especially, needs some ageing, being characteristically acid
in youth and developing honeyed depths in older vintages. A
small amount of classic-method white and rosé sparkling wine is
also made at this domaine.
Open: Mon–Sun 8am–noon, 2–7pm.

Jacky Preys
*Le Bois Pontois, 41130 Meusnes. Vineyards owned: Touraine
58ha, Valençay 10ha, Vin de Pays 4ha. 600,000 bottles. VP-R*
With vineyard holdings in the Touraine AC and Valençay, this
dynamic grower produces a full range of wines using Sauvignon
and Pinot Blanc for white; Gamay, Cabernet Franc and Cot for red
and rosé. The firm also makes a Crémant de Loire. Pinot Noir and
Chardonnay have been planted.
Open: Appointments preferred.

VOUVRAY AC, MONTLOUIS AC

Domaine Daniel Allias
Le Petit Mont, Vouvray. Vineyards owned: 10ha.
As with many Vouvray producers, Monsieur Allias' cellars are
carved out underneath his vines. The vineyard – Le Clos du Petit
Mont – is at the highest point of the Vallée Coquette. In good years
he makes *moelleux* wines which age superbly, while the bulk of
production is of dry and sparkling wines. The present owners of
the vineyard are the fourth generation to own that land.

Domaine des Aubuisières
37210 Vouvray. Vineyards owned: 20ha. 100,000 bottles. VP-R
Bernard Fouquet is producer of two styles of wine, expressing the
two different soils in his vineyard. He makes a faster maturing
wine from the limestone soil, and a wine which ages better from
the flint soil. The wines are matured in wood, and the different
cuvées include: Vouvray Sec, Cuvée Victor and Cuvée Cyrielle.
Open: Mon–Sat 9am–noon, 2–6.30pm.

Benoit Gautier
Domaine de la Chataigneraie, 37210 Rochecorbon.
Vineyards owned: 12ha. 60,000 bottles. VP-R
Two ranges of wine are made by this producer: a Cuvée Domaine,
which is aged only in stainless steel, and a Cuvée Clos Château

Chevrier, which sees some wood-ageing. New planting of part of the vineyard in 1992 are beginning to yield good results.
Open: By appointment only.

Berger Frères
135 Rue de Chenonceaux, St-Martin-le-Beau, 37270 Montlouis.
Vineyards owned: St-Martin 20ha. 100,000 bottles. VP-R
A well-run, modern firm which makes some attractive wines. The *demi-sec* Montlouis is particularly good in better years, and the *pétillant* is lighter than the same style of wine in Vouvray. A Crémant de Loire is made from Chenin Blanc, as well as a Chardonnay and Cabernet Franc which is aged for two to three years in bottle before being released. *Open: Appointments preferred.*

Domaine Bourillon-d'Orléans
4 Rue du Chalateau, 37210 Rochecorbon.
Vineyards owned: 18ha. 120,000 bottles. VP-R
One of the dynamic new generation of Vouvray producers, Frédéric Bourillon makes a full range of wines, depending on the quality of the vintage. He has built a new cellar, full of stainless steel, which was first used for the '92 harvest.
Open: Appointment preferred.

Marc Brédif
Rochecorbon, 37210 Vouvray. 250,000 bottles. N
This is purely a *négociant* firm, but has the distinction of being responsible for much of the history of Vouvray: it was first to develop sparkling Vouvray wines. It is now owned by the de Ladoucette family of Pouilly-Fumé fame. The firm's cellars in Rochecorbon are quite spectacular. *Open: Appointments preferred.*

Catherine et Didier Champalou
7 Rue du Grand Ormeau, 37210 Vouvray.
Vineyards owned: 12ha. 55,000 bottles. VP-R
The Champalous made their first wine in '85, having studied at the viticultural school at Montreuil-Bellay. The firm believes in a style called Sec Tendre, slightly drier than *demi-sec* and slightly sweeter than *sec*. In most years, this is the still wine made; only in special years is a sweet *moelleux* wine produced. *Open: Appointments preferred.*

G Delétang et Fils
St-Martin-le-Beau, 37270 Montlouis. Vineyards owned:
Montlouis 12ha, Touraine 6ha. 100,000 bottles. VP-R
The cellars of Monsieur Delétang in the centre of St-Martin-le-Beau are filled with old bottles of wine gathering cobwebs. But modern techniques have been applied to fermentation. His still Montlouis can be dry or sweet, depending on the quality of the vintage. The sparkling wine is aged for two years in bottle before sale and is slightly full and off-dry. He also makes Touraine AC wines from Sauvignon, Cabernet Franc, Gamay and Grolleau.
Open: Mon–Sat 10am–noon, 3–6pm.

Philippe Foreau (Domaine du Clos Naudin)
37210 Vouvray.
Vineyards owned: Vouvray 12ha. 50,000 bottles. VP-R
One of the top Vouvray producers, now in its third generation, making still and sparkling wines. All the still wines are fermented and aged in wood, the classic-method sparkling wine in stainless steel. The still wine is aged for a considerable time – especially the sweet wine, which is made only in good years. The results are well worth the wait. *Open: By appointment only.*

Domaine Freslier
37210 Vouvray.
Vineyards owned: 10ha. 40,000 bottles. VP-R
A small, traditional producer, making still and sparkling Vouvray using wood for fermentation. The vineyard, known as the Quarts de Moncontour, is near the Château Moncontour, one of the top sites of Vouvray. The Fresliers make a little of the rare Vouvray *pétillant. Open: Mon–Sat 8am–noon, 2–7pm; Sun 9am–noon.*

Sylvain Gaudron
59 Rue Veuve, Vernou, 37210 Vouvray. Vineyards owned: Vernou, Noizay, Chançay 14ha. 60,000 bottles.
Typical Vouvray cellars, carved out of rock in the 14th century. Monsieur Gaudron is a traditionalist who vinifies at least part of his wine in wood. He makes all styles of Vouvray – from dry through to classic-method sparkling. Gaudron's '89 and '90 sweet wines will be classics in about 15 years' time.
Open: Mon–Sat 8am– noon, 2–7pm.

Gaston Huët
Domaine du Haut-Lieu, 37210 Vouvray.
Vineyards owned: Vouvray 32ha. 130,000 bottles. VP-R
Monsieur Huët is a great propagandist for the wines of Vouvray. Luckily he is also one of the best producers in the area, making wines from some of the very finest sites – Le Haut-Lieu, Le Clos du Bourg and Le Mont – which are vinified and sold individually. Huët uses a judicious mix of traditional techniques and modern stainless-steel equipment, but his finest wines are all matured in small wood casks. Under the influence of his son-in-law Noël Pinguet, who is now involved in the business, the Huët vineyards are run under strict biodynamic principles. The extensive cellars, carved out of the tufa rock of Vouvray, are crammed with half a million bottles, and some of the sweet still wines are of remarkable antiquity. Monsieur Huët also makes sparkling and *pétillant* medium-dry wines. He makes very little dry wine, believing that Vouvray's vocation is as a sweet wine.
Open: Mon–Fri 9am–noon, 2–6pm.

Jean-Pierre Laisement
15 La Vallée Coquette, 37210 Vouvray.
Vineyards owned: 12.6ha. VP-R
First established in 1983, Monsieur Laisement's small vineyard

produces great still and sparkling Vouvray. A new tasting room has been installed in his 400-year-old cellars and adds to the welcome he offers his visitors. Some wood maturation is used.
Open: Mon–Sun 8am–noon, 1.30–8pm.

Château Moncontour
Rochecorbon, 37210 Vouvray. Vineyards owned: 108ha.
Now one of the largest estates in Vouvray, Château Moncontour has (under the château) an enormous and expensive cellar, which is designed specifically for the production of sparkling Vouvray. Both the sparkling wine and the still wines are of good quality, the sparkling wine being a particularly enjoyable drink.
Open: By appointment only.

Dominique Moyer
2 Rue de la Croise des Granges, Husseau, 37270 Montlouis.
Vineyards owned: Husseau 12ha. 40,000 bottles. VP-R
The Moyer family has been in the wine business since 1830 and some of its vines have been around since the 1920s, giving wines with great intensity. Great care is taken in picking to the extent that pickers go through the vineyard a number of times selecting only the those grapes that are ready, in order to ensure that the fruit is as ripe as possible: although this is the old tradition in Montlouis, it is so labour-intensive – and therefore costly – it is now carried out only in a few of the best properties. Virtually all the production is of dry or medium-dry still wines – the medium-dry wines coming from the oldest vines. Fifteen percent of production is of classic-method sparkling or *pétillant* wine. The family home is a hunting lodge dating from 1620.
Open: By appointment only.

Prince Poniatowski
Le Clos Baudoin, Vallée de Nouys, 37210 Vouvray.
Vineyards owned: Le Clos Baudoin 3.8ha, Aigle Blanc 18.3ha.
150,000 bottles. VP-R
Prince Poniatowski is from an ancient Polish family that has lived in France for many years – the Vouvray estate has been in the family for 70 years. The wines produced tend to be on the dry side, are of great elegance and finesse, with intense fruit flavours and take some time to mature. Clos Baudoin is one of the best sites in Vouvray, situated on the top of a sheltered valley, facing south. Aigle Blanc is a brand for both still and sparkling wines – more sparkling wine is made in cooler years. The Poniatowski house, like so many in Vouvray, is half carved out of the rock.
Open: By appointment only.

Cave des Producteurs de Vouvray
38 La Vallée Coquette, 37210 Vouvray.
Vineyards owned: 200ha. Coop (50 members).
The better of the two cooperatives in Vouvray, making a standard range of wines. The sparkling wine is good.
Open: *Mon–Sun 9am–noon, 2–6.30pm.*

Domaine de la Saboterie

37210 Rochecorbon. Vineyards owned: 8ha. VP-R

A small estate set up in 1987, generally making one style of wine: a *sec* (still dry). Only in '89 and '90 did the owner, Christian Chaussard, produce sweet wines. *Open: By appointment only.*

Domaine de la Taille aux Loups

15 Rue des Aitres, 37270 Montlouis.

Vineyards owned: 7.5ha. 25,000 bottles. VP-R

This may be a small and young estate, having made its first wine in 1989, but by using organic farming methods, cutting yields and fermenting the juice in small *barriques* purchased from Château d'Yquem in Sauternes, Jacky Blot has made quite an impression in Montlouis. *Open: Appointments preferred.*

Domaine du Viking

Melotin, 37380 Reugny. Vineyards owned: 11ha. 50,000 bottles.

Sparkling and still Vouvray are made here by Lionel Gauthier-Lhomme. The sparkling is aged in bottle for three years before release, while the still wines spend some time maturing in large barrels. *Open: By appointment only.*

VIN DE L'ORLÉANNAIS VDQS

Clos St-Fiacre

560 Rue St-Fiacre, 45370 Mareau-aux-Près.

Vineyards owned: 18.5ha. VP-R

One of the more important private estates in this small VDQS area. Daniel Montigny produces a full range of wines – a white from Chardonnay, a rosé from Pinot Gris, and reds from Pinot Meunier and Pinot Noir as well as Cabernet Franc. He also makes a Sauvignon Blanc Vin de Pays du Jardin de la France. In 1990, he opened a small museum of vines and wines.

Open: Mon, Tues, Thurs: 5.30–9.30pm; Sat all day; Sun morning.

Les Vignerons de la Grand'Maison

550 Route des Muids, 45370 Mareau-aux-Près.

Vineyards owned: 100ha. Coop (70 members).

Almost all Vin de l'Orléannais production goes through this well-run cooperative. A handful of private estates manages the rest. A full range of wines is made as well as a *vin de pays* from Gamay. *Open: Mon–Sat 9am–noon, 2–5.30pm.*

VALENÇAY VDQS

Les Vignerons Réunis

Fontguenaud, 36600 Valençay.

Vineyards owned: 74ha. 100,000 bottles. Coop (70 members).

Some pleasant Valençay is produced at this cooperative, the best being the red: a blend of Gamay, Cot and Pinot Noir. Vin *de pays* from Chardonnay and a sparkling wine from Pineau Menu and Chardonnay are also made. *Open: Mon–Sat 8am–noon, 2–6pm.*

COTEAUX DU VENDÔMOIS VDQS

Maison Patrice Colin
5 La Gaudetterie, 41100 Thoré-la-Rochette.
Vineyards owned: 14ha. 120,000 bottles.

One of the 15 growers in this out-of-the-way area in the valley of the River Loir, which is a tributary of the Loire. Patrice Colin makes excellent crisp rosé from Pineau d'Aunis, a Chenin Blanc fermented in wood, and a surprisingly colourful red from a blend of Gamay, Pinot Noir and Pineau d'Aunis.

Open: Mon–Sat 8am–noon, 2–7pm; a charge is made.

Anjou Producers

ANJOU AC

Domaine de Bablut
49320 Brissac-Quincé.
Vineyards owned: 85ha. 530,000 bottles. VP-R

The Daviau family makes a wide range of Anjou wines: red, white and rosé as well as Anjou-Villages, sweet Coteaux de l'Aubance and *vins de pays* from Sauvignon Blanc and Chardonnay. The wines are labelled under two names: Domaine de Bablut and Château de Brissac, whose vineyard is the Daviaus' own. Records of the family in the region exist from 1546.

Open: Mon–Sat 9am–noon, 2–6pm.

Bonnin et Fils
Domaine la Croix des Loges, 49540 Martigné-Briand.
Vineyards owned: Anjou 30ha. 200,000 bottles. VP-R

Modern techniques dominate at this large estate which covers mainly wines from the AC Anjou, but also produces a small quantity of fine sweet white Bonnezeaux. The Anjou Rouge from Cabernet Franc is a well-made wine with plenty of youthful raspberry fruit, but it also has some ageing potential. Other wines include Anjou Rosé, Cabernet Rosé, a medium-dry Anjou Blanc and Rosé de Loire. Some sparkling Saumur is also made. *Open: Appointments preferred.*

Brault Père et Fils
Domaine de Ste-Anne, Ste-Anne, 49320 Brissac-Quincé.
Vineyards owned: Anjou 48ha. 140,000 bottles. VP-R

This estate has adopted the high-vine training of the Lenz Moser method for the most part and although yields (which are supposed to be higher under this Austrian system than with conventional vine training) are controlled by the AC laws, the quality of the fruit is certainly good. This quality is clear in the well-made wines which cover the full range of Anjou ACs, including some Coteaux du Layon and Coteaux de l'Aubance. Just under half the production is bottled, the remainder being sold in bulk to *négociants*. The best wines tend to be the reds.

Open: Appointments preferred.

Les Caves de la Loire
49320 Brissac. Vineyards owned: 2,000ha. 4 million bottles.
Coop (500 members).
One of the largest cooperatives on the Loire, Les Caves de la Loire
has made a name for itself in supplying reliable, well-made wines
on an own-label basis. In an ultra-modern winery the full range of
Anjou wines is made: Anjou Rouge, Anjou Blanc, Rosé d'Anjou,
Cabernet d'Anjou, Rosé de Loire. The firm also makes sparkling
Crémant de Loire, Saumur Mousseux and some good-quality
sweet Coteaux du Layon. *Open: By appointment only.*

Jean Douet (Château des Rochettes)
Concourson-sur-Layon, 49700 Doué-la-Fontaine. Vineyards
owned: Anjou and Coteaux du Layon 25ha. 80,000 bottles. VP-R
A long-established family firm which makes the full range of
Anjou wines, plus some Coteaux du Layon made from old vines.
The company tends to use a mixture of traditional techniques for
the reds (with wood-ageing) and temperature-controlled fermen-
tation for other wines. The bulk of the production is of Anjou red.
Open: Appointments preferred.

Domaine Gaudard
Chaudefonds-sur-Layon, 49290 Chalonnes-sur-Loire.
Vineyards owned: 15.1ha. 100,000 bottles. VP-R
The firm has been expanding plantings of the noble varieties –
Chardonnay and Cabernet Franc – on this estate and cutting back
on the local Grolleau and Chenin. The Chardonnay is used as a
cépage améliorateur in a classic-method Anjou sparkler. Cabernet
Franc goes into the Anjou Rouge, a well-made, long-lasting wine.
Other wines include the range of Anjou wines, plus some Coteaux
du Layon. *Open: Mon–Fri 8am–5pm.*

Guy Gousset (Clos de l'Aiglerie)
St-Aubin-de-Luigné, 49190 Rochefort-sur-Loire.
Vineyards owned: 12ha. 60,000 bottles. VP-R
Monsieur Gousset makes a range of wines: Anjou Rouge and Rosé
from Cabernet Franc, sweet Coteaux du Layon, and some Vin de
Pays de Maine-et-Loire. Techniques are traditional – fermentation
is in wood for all wines. Quality is reliable, with a few pleasant
surprises, especially in the reds. *Open: During working hours.*

Yves Leduc (Château Montbenault)
Faye d'Anjou, 49380 Thouarcé.
Vineyards owned: Anjou 20ha. 35,000 bottles. VP-R
Monsieur Leduc specialises in the sweet wines of the Coteaux du
Layon Faye AC. These wines are made cleanly, using stainless
steel for vinification, and tend not to last as long as some other
sweet wines of the area. Part of his Coteaux du Layon from the
Clos Poirier Bourgeau vineyard is vinified and bottled separately.
Anjou Rouge and Blanc, Rosé d'Anjou, Cabernet d'Anjou, Rosé de
Loire and a classic-method sparkling Anjou are also made.
Open: Mon–Sat 9am–noon, 2–5pm.

Vins Mottron

Rue d'Anjou, 49540 Martigné-Briand.
Vineyards owned: Anjou 25ha. 1 million bottles. VP-R and N
One of the largest Anjou *négociants*. From its own vineyards it makes red and rosé wines in the modern winery, using the Cabernet d'Anjou, Rosé d'Anjou and Anjou Rouge ACs, plus Vin de Pays du Jardin de la France. It also produces Muscadet, Saumur, Chinon, Bourgueil, Touraine, Sancerre and Pouilly-Fumé. Brands include Caves de Bel Air, Caves de Petit Colombier, Pierre Frain, Louis Bret and Roger Lefèvre. *Open: By appointment only.*

Château de Passavant

49560 Passavant-sur-Loire. VP-R
The château at Passavant dates back to the 12th century and is now occupied by the David family which produces a large range of Anjou wines, including Anjou-Villages. The firm regards this, its wines from Coteaux du Layon and its Crémant de Loire sparkling as its best wines. *Open: By appointment only.*

Domaine Richou

Chauvigné, Mozé-sur-Louet, 49190 Rochefort-sur-Loire.
Vineyards owned: Anjou 28ha. 90,000 bottles. VP-R
The white Anjou Blanc is the star from this old-established firm. This blend of Chenin (80 percent) and Chardonnay (20 percent) makes a dry, full-of-fruit, clean wine, best drunk in the year following the vintage. The firm also makes a Cuvée de Printemps from young vines – a red of blended Cabernets which is designed to be drunk early. From old vines, Anjou Rouge and Cabernet d'Anjou are made, plus some sweet Coteaux de l'Aubance. *Open: By appointment only.*

Les Vins Touchais

49700 Doué-la-Fontaine. Vineyards owned: 16ha. VP-R and N
One of the remarkable discoveries of the 1980s was the vast quantity of old wines held in the cellars of Touchais in Doué-la-Fontaine. Most of the wines were of Coteaux du Layon and Anjou, and all were sweet. They came from the family vineyards, Les Vignobles Touchais. There is also a *négociant* business which deals in Anjou Rosé and other local wines.

COTEAUX DU LAYON AC, QUARTS DE CHAUME AC, BONNEZEAUX AC

Domaine des Baumard

8 Rue de l'Abbaye, 49190 Rochefort-sur-Loire.
Vineyards owned: Quarts de Chaume 6ha, Savennières 15ha, Coteaux du Layon 1ha, Anjou 12ha. 200,000 bottles. VP-R
Quarts de Chaume and Savennières are the top two wines from this producer, but the quality throughout the range is high. Jean Baumard, now joined by his son Florent, make some of the best and most consistent wines in the region. The Quarts de Chaume has the characteristic intensity of this great sweet wine and

develops beautifully after ten years in bottle. The Savennières (the company owns part of the Clos du Papillon), on the other hand, is a faster developer than Savennières from other producers and is very drinkable after four to five years. Clos de Ste-Catherine Coteaux du Layon is a lovely combination and contrast of intensity and lightness. Other wines made are a Crémant de Loire from Chardonnay and a red Anjou, Logis de la Giraudière, from Cabernet Franc. *Open: Appointments preferred.*

Domaine Beaujeau

Champ-sur-Layon, 49380 Thouarcé. Vineyards owned: 10ha.
From cellars near the church of Champ-sur-Layon, the Beaujeau family makes long-lived Coteaux du Layon.

Château de Breuil

Le Breuil, 49750 Beaulieu-sur-Layon.
Vineyards owned: 34ha. 200,000 bottles. VP-R
Making an enormous range of wines, Marc Morgat sees his finest as the Anjou-Villages and, above all, the Coteaux du Layon. He has links with the École Supérieure d'Agriculture et Viticulture at Angers and so has experimental plantings of Pinot Noir, Pinot Blanc, Chardonnay, Sauvignon Blanc, Cabernet Franc and Cot. Some of these go into his *vin de pays*. *Open: Appointments preferred.*

Jean-Pierre Chéné

Impasse de Jardins, Beaulieu-sur-Layon, 49190 Rochefort-sur-Loire. Vineyards owned: 21ha.
A family vineyard in Beaulieu-sur-Layon produces red wines from Cabernet Franc as well as Coteaux du Layon Beaulieu. There are also named vineyards: Clos du Paradis Terrestre, Clos des Mulonnières and Clos des Ontinières. The firm uses a long, slow fermentation process to achieve maximum fruit.

Domaine des Épinaudières

St-Foy, 49750 St-Lambert-du-Lattay.
Vineyards owned: 28.5ha. VP-R
The Fardeau family makes wines under a number of appellations: Coteaux de Layon, Anjou Blanc, Anjou Mousseux and Cabernet d'Anjou, and also makes a red Anjou-Villages and a white *vin de pays* from Sauvignon Blanc. From this large range, it considers its Coteaux du Layon (which ages well) to be the best wine.
Open: Appointments preferred.

Château de Fesles

49380 Thouarcé. Vineyards owned: 33ha. 400,000 bottles. VP-R
Although this Bonnezeaux estate has undergone changes in ownership, the winemaking is still overseen by previous owner Jacques Boivin. The sweet wine is probably Bonnezeaux' finest, but it also makes a range of Anjou wines and *vins de pays*. The château is in a prominent position looking down the Bonnezeaux vineyards to the River Layon, and the cellars and tasting room are in first-class order. *Open: Mon–Sat 9am–12.30pm, 2–6.30pm.*

Domaine des Forges
Les Barres, 49190 St-Aubin-de-Luigné.
Vineyards owned: 32ha. 52,000 bottles. VP-R
This traditional domaine produces some excellent Coteaux du Layon St-Aubin and Chaume as well as Anjou Rouge, rosé, and some *vin de pays* from Chardonnay and Sauvignon Blanc. The firm has recently opened a tasting room.
Open: Mon–Sat 9am–noon, 1–7pm.

Château de Fresne
49380 Faye d'Anjou.
Vineyards owned: 72ha. 470,000 bottles. VP-R
A large producer (for Anjou), its main wines are Anjou red and Coteaux du Layon-Faye-d'Anjou, though a *vin de pays* and some rosé is also made. The estate is the result of a union between two families, Robin and Bretault. It has recently had an underground ageing cellar excavated as the need to stock bottles is increasing.
Open: Beginning June–end Feb Mon–Sat 8am–noon, 2–7pm; March–May open every day.

Vignobles Laffourcade (Château de Suronde)
49190 Rochefort-sur-Loire. Vineyards owned: Quarts de Chaume 20ha. 60,000 bottles. VP-R
The largest producer in the Quarts de Chaume. Fine examples of this superb sweet wine are produced by its being fermented in stainless steel before being matured in wood. Do not expect to enjoy the wine before ten years, but then savour every mouthful. Names used are Château de Suronde and Château de l'Écharderie.
Open: By appointment only.

Jacques Lalanne (Château de Belle Rive)
49190 Rochefort-sur-Loire. Vineyards owned: Quarts de Chaume 17ha. 20,000 bottles. VP-R
Expense is no object in the vineyard: picking is effected over a number of weeks in a series of passes, gathering only the ripest, most nobly-rotten grapes each time. Fermentation takes place in large barrels and bottling in the spring after the vintage. Quarts de Chaume matures in bottle, taking upwards of ten years to do so. The rewards are there for those willing to wait. Quarts de Chaume is the only wine made. *Open: By appointment only.*

Vignoble Lecointre
Château la Tomaze, 49380 Champ-sur-Layon.
Vineyards owned: 40ha. 320,000 bottles. VP-R
Monsieur Lecointre makes two ranges of wine. One is called La Pierre Blanche and consists of *vin de pays*, Anjou white and red and a Coteaux du Layon. His domaine wines, under the name Château la Tomaze, are made up of an Anjou-Villages and a Coteaux du Layon-Rablay-sur-Layon. The Anjou-Villages is matured in wood. He regards his Coteaux du Layon-Rablay-sur-Layon Cuvée de Lys as his finest wine.
Open: 9am–7pm (appointments preferred).

Domaine de la Motte

31 Avenue d'Angers, 49190 Rochefort-sur-Loire.
Vineyards owned: Rochefort 18ha. 100,000 bottles. VP-R
While Rosé d'Anjou dominates Monsieur Sorin's production, he
also makes an excellent Coteaux du Layon-Rochefort from a
south-facing slope. Apart from these, he makes the usual range of
Anjou wines, including an Anjou *sec* Clos des Belles Mères from
Chardonnay and an Anjou *mousseux* from Chenin Blanc.
Open: 9am–noon, 2–6pm, preferably by appointment.

Domaine Ogereau

44 Rue de la Belle-Angevine, 49750 St-Lambert-du-Lattay.
Vineyards owned: 21ha. 130,000 bottles. VP-R
Coteaux du Layon St-Lambert is the top wine from this estate,
while smaller quantities of red Anjou and Anjou-Villages are also
made. Vincent Ogereau is the fourth generation of the family to
make wine at the estate. *Open: Appointments preferred.*

Domaine du Pithon

3 Chemin du Moulin, 49750 St-Lambert-du-Lattay.
Vineyards owned: 5ha. 12,000 bottles.
A tiny production, of which the most important is Coteaux du
Layon, including a luscious botrytised wine made from
individually picked berries. The wine is aged in *barriques* and is
exceptional. *Open: By appointment only.*

Château de Plaisance

Chaume, 49190 Rochefort-sur-Loire.
Vineyards owned: 35ha. 80,000 bottles. VP-R
By far the largest part of Henri Rochais' production is of Coteaux
du Layon-Chaume, aged in wood, which seems to win plenty of
gold medals. His other wines include Savennières, Anjou-Villages
and red Anjou, as well as some sparkling Anjou Mousseux and
Crémant de Loire. *Open: Mon–Sat 9am–noon, 2–6pm.*

Domaine de Terrebrune

Place de Champ de Foire, 49380 Thouarcé.
Vineyards owned: 89ha. 400,000 bottles. VP-R
This estate is an amalgamation of the domaines of a number of
producers: René Renou, Patrice Laurendeau and Alain Bouteau. It
makes some fine Bonnezeaux, but concentrates its efforts equally
on other wines: Anjou Rouge, Rosé d'Anjou, Rosé de Loire and
Coteaux du Layon. *Open: Mon–Fri 8am–12.30pm, 1.30–5.30pm; Sat
9am–noon, 2–5.30pm.*

Pierre-Yves Tijou (Domaine de la Soucherie)

Beaulieu-sur-Layon, 49750 Rochefort-sur-Loire.
Vineyards owned: 35ha. 200,000 bottles. VP-R
A large landowner in an area of small holdings, the bulk of
Monsieur Tijou's wine is of Coteaux du Layon and Coteaux du
Layon-Chaume. He tends not to use wood for his white wines,
preferring to make a wine that is fresher and quicker to mature

than some of the sweet wines of the area. He also makes the full range of Anjou AC wines, including a superior Crémant de la Soucherie. *Open: By appointment only.*

SAUMUR AC, SAUMUR-CHAMPIGNY AC

Ackerman-Laurance
St-Hilaire-St-Florent, 49400 Saumur.
Vineyards owned: 52ha. 6 million bottles. VP-R and N
A *négociant* and producer specialising in sparkling wines. The oldest producer of Saumur, and still one of the largest. The bulk of production is of average-quality sparkling white and rosé Saumur, all made in stainless steel, but in a range of qualities, including the top Cuvée Privilège and Cuvée Privée. The firm also makes considerable quantities of very good Crémant de Loire. *Open: Mon–Fri 9.30am–noon, 2.30–5pm. Appointments necessary for groups.*

Bouvet-Ladubay
St-Hilaire-St-Florent, 49400 Saumur.
Vineyards owned: none. 1.6 million bottles. N
Producers of some of the best sparkling Saumur, the firm has contracts with 150 growers in the Saumur region, from which it draws all its wine requirements. It makes two qualities of Saumur – a standard range and the Excellence range, which includes the Crémant Brut Saphir and the vintage Crémant d'Or. More recently a partly wood-matured sparkling wine, Trésor, has been introduced, which most would regard as the finest sparkling Saumur. Other wines in the portfolio include white, red and rosé *brut* sparkling wine using the general Anjou AC. Overall, the standard is high. The firm is part of the Taittinger Champagne group. *Open: Mon–Sun 9am–noon, 2–6.30pm.*

Domaine Vinicole de Chaintres
Dampierre-sur-Loire, 49400 Saumur.
Vineyards owned: Saumur 66ha. 120,000 bottles. VP-R
The Château de Chaintres is a red wine estate, producing wine for the firm's classic Saumur-Champigny. Methods are traditional and wood is used for maturation, giving wines with some lasting power and extra tannin. The style seems to have become lighter in recent years, probably because stainless steel is being used as well. Owner Bernard de Tigny also makes a white Saumur Blanc. *Open: Mon–Fri 9am–noon, 2–6pm.*

Clos des Cordeliers
49400 Champigny. Vineyards owned: 16.5ha. 80,000 bottles. VP-R
The Ratron family make only Saumur-Champigny at the estate. A Cuvée Prestige is made as well as a standard *cuvée*. *Open: Mon–Sat 8am–noon, 2–6.30pm.*

Claude Daheuiller
28 Rue du Ruau, Varrains, 49400 Saumur.
Vineyards owned: Saumur 23ha. 130,000 bottles. VP-R

The main production here is of a good Saumur-Champigny made from the estate of Domaine des Varinelles. Half the wine is made in wood, the other half in stainless steel, then the two are blended, giving some firmness and structure but allowing for early drinking and plenty of instant fruit. A still white Saumur is also made, a little sparkling Saumur Brut and small quantities of Sauvignon and Rosé de Loire. *Open: By appointment only.*

Denis Duveau

27 Rue de la Mairie, Varrains, 49400 Saumur. Vineyards owned: Saumur-Champigny 10ha. 50,000 bottles. VP-R
Producer of one of the more intense, rich Saumur-Champignys, principally because at least 20 percent of the wine comes from old vines. Vinification and maturation are all in wood. The family has been on the land for four generations and produces only the one wine. *Open: By appointment only.*

Domaine Filliatreau

Chaintres, Dampierre-sur-Loire, 49400 Saumur.
Vineyards owned: 30ha.
This is the largest producer of Saumur-Champigny, which is made in a modern manner with controlled fermentation at 24°C (low for red wines). Some of the *cuvées* see wood: Vieilles Vignes and Lena Filliatreau for example; while the Jeunes Vignes is bottled straight from the tank. The wines are excellent examples of the appellation and have done much to promote its virtues.

Foucault et Fils (Clos Rougeard)

Chacé, 49400 Saumur. Vineyards owned: 8ha.
The Foucault brothers are the latest in the family's many generations of wine producers in Saumur-Champigny. They make different *cuvées* of Saumur-Champigny: Clos Rougeard, Cuvée Les Poyeux and Cuvée Le Bourg, of which the Le Bourg, kept in new wood, is designed for ageing. Some wine is matured in casks which originate from Château Margaux in Bordeaux.
Open: By appointment only.

Gratien, Meyer, Seydoux

Château de Beaulieu, Route de Chinon, 49400 Saumur.
Vineyards owned: Saumur 20ha. 2.5 million bottles. VP-R and N
Gratien & Meyer is the brand name for a range of sparkling Saumur wines – *brut*, *demi-sec* and rosé. The firm also makes a red sparkling wine from 100 percent Cabernet Franc. The quality is very reliable (they consider that "behind the *mousse* there should be a pleasant wine") and the wines are widely distributed throughout the world. The firm owns the champagne house of Alfred Gratien. *Open: Mon–Sat 9am–noon, 2–6pm.*

Yves Lambert

Le Bourg, 49260 St-Just-sur-Dive.
Vineyards owned: 28ha. 270,000 bottles. VP-R
Producing both Saumur-Champigny and Saumur Blanc, Monsieur

Lambert has a typically mixed – and expanding – estate. His Saumur-Champigny is aged for between six months and two years, depending on the year. He also makes a Crémant de Loire and a red sparkling wine from Cabernet Franc.

Open: By appointment only.

Langlois-Chateau

BP6, 3 Rue Léopold Palustre, St-Hilaire-St-Florent, 49400 Saumur. Vineyards owned: Saumur 27ha, Sancerre 15ha. 200,000 bottles. VP-R and N

One of the famous names in sparkling Crémant de Loire, Langlois-Chateau also produces red and white still wines from the same AC and Sancerre red and white wines from the estate at Château Fontaine-Audon. Production is quite modern in approach: stainless steel is used. The firm is owned by the Champagne house of Bollinger.

Open: Summer only, Mon–Fri 10.30am–12.30pm, 3–6.30pm.

Sylvain Mainfray

Rue Jean Jaurès, 49400 Saumur. 360,000 bottles. N

A firm of *négociants* that sells wines from Anjou, Saumur and Touraine. Unusually, the wines are bottled by the growers themselves, rather than the *élevage* and bottling being effected at a central cellar. This certainly enhances the individual characteristics of each wine.

Régis Neau

4 Rue de la Paleine, 49260 St-Cyr-en-Bourg. 200,000 bottles. VP-R

A good-sized producer, making red Saumur-Champigny, some Saumur Blanc – one of the better examples from the appellation – and sparkling Crémant de Loire. A cellar built in 1988 has brought up-to-date a family business that has been making wine here for seven generations.

Open: Mon–Fri 8am–noon, 2–6pm; and Sat morning.

De Neuville

St-Hilaire-St-Florent, 49400 Saumur. Vineyards owned: 40ha.

Producers of sparkling Saumur, partly from its own vineyards and partly from purchased grapes. Quality is reliable.

Édouard Pisani-Ferry (Château de Targé)

49730 Parnay. Vineyards owned: Saumur-Champigny 23ha. 140,000 bottles. VP-R

The château has been in the family since 1655, but methods are entirely modern, with stainless steel and temperature control used for fermentation. The production is of Saumur-Champigny, which is matured for six months in wood. The blend includes ten percent Cabernet Sauvignon to top up the Cabernet Franc. The resulting wine is very enjoyable as early as the second year after vintage but will mature for several more years, particularly when from a ripe vintage.

Open: Mon–Fri 8am–noon, 2–6pm; Sat closes at 4pm.

Rémy-Pannier
St-Hilaire-St-Florent, 49400 Saumur.
Vineyards owned: none. 15 million bottles. N
Probably the largest *négociant* in the Loire Valley, buying in all its requirements. It makes wines from virtually every appellation in the Loire, all to a standard, if uninspiring, quality. The Saumur wines are probably the best of the range. Marketing techniques are highly sophisticated.

Domaine de la Renière
49260 Le Puy-Notre-Dame.
Vineyards owned: 17ha. 93,000 bottles. VP-R
René Hugues-Gay is producer of some of the best Saumur red and white at his estate, which has been in the family since 1536. All the first sons have been called René, hence the punning name of the estate, Renière. The firm makes two red wines: a Vieilles Vignes and a Cuvée Prestige. *Open: By appointment only.*

Philippe et Georges Vatan (Château du Hureau)
Dampière-sur-Loire, 49400 Saumur.
Vineyards owned: 18ha. 110,000 bottles. VP-R
Based at the Château de Hureau, the Vatan family has been producing wine for three generations. It makes a red Saumur-Champigny, which in good years can age remarkably well, and some Saumur Blanc, as well as tiny quantities of a rare sweet Coteaux de Saumur – when the weather permits.
Open: Appointments preferred.

SAVENNIÈRES AC, COULÉE DE SERRANT AC, ROCHES-AUX-MOINES AC

Domaine du Closel
49170 Savennières. Vineyards owned: Savennières 12ha, Anjou 3ha. 87,000 bottles. VP-R
Madame de Jessey makes a classic dry white Savennières, vinified and matured in wood and needing several years before it is ready to drink. This is probably the truest Savennières, sometimes lacking the intensity of Coulée de Serrant, but with what the French call *nervosité* and poised balance. Madame de Jessey also makes red Anjou wine from Cabernets Sauvignon and Franc, again matured in wood. *Open: Mon–Sat 9am–noon, 2–7pm.*

Vignoble de la Coulée de Serrant
Château de la Roche-aux-Moines, 49170 Savennières.
Vineyards owned: Savennières-Coulée de Serrant 7ha,
Savennières-Roche-aux-Moines 3.5ha, Savennières 3.5ha,
Cabernet Rouge 1ha. 20,000 bottles.
Low yields, intense fruit, high quality and a strong adherence to biodynamic theories of viticulture are the reasons for the low production at this famous estate. Madame Joly and her son Nicolas, who is in charge of production, are among the few owners in France who control an entire appellation (AC Coulée

de Serrant); the other well-known example is the Château Grillet AC on the Rhône. Coulée de Serrant is an ancient monastic vineyard and Roche-aux-Moines was first planted in the 12th century. Wines are treated as naturally as possible with few chemicals. They are vinified in wood and bottled with the minimum of filtration. Despite their dryness, these Savennières wines need a minimum of five years' maturation in bottle before drinking, and survive seemingly for ever. The risks are high: for three years in the 1970s production was well below normal and in '72 nothing was made at all. Demand, however, is enormous and prices have followed it upwards. Madame Joly also makes a Coteaux de Loire Rouge from Cabernet Franc and Cabernet Sauvignon – with the same extreme care. *Open: Mon–Sat 8.30am–noon, 2–5.30pm; there is a charge for the visit.*

Château d'Épiré
Épiré, 49170 Savennières. Vineyards owned: Savennières 9ha, Anjou 1ha. 60,000 bottles. VP-R
The Savennières is not really drinkable for ten to 12 years, and will last for up to 30, sometimes even more. Here, as in the vineyards at other Savennières producers, pickers need to pass through the vineyard two or three times to pick the grapes at their ripest – even though a dry wine is being made. Vinification and maturation of the wines is all in wood. Small quantities of Anjou Rouge and Rosé de Loire are also made – probably to help with cash flow. *Open: Appointments preferred.*

Domaine aux Moines
La-Roche-aux-Moines, 49170 Savennières.
Vineyards owned: 8ha. 35,000 bottles. VP-R
Madame Laroche makes only Savennières Roche-aux-Moines from her small vineyard which has magnificent views onto the Loire. These are lighter than some Savennières, but seem to age just as well. The wine spends a short time in wood.
Open: Mon–Sun 10am–noon, 2–7pm.

Pierre et Yves Soulez (Château de Chamboureau)
49170 Savennières. Vineyards owned: Savennières 16ha, Savennières Roche-aux-Moines 8ha, Quarts de Chaume 2ha, Anjou 2.5ha. 100,000 bottles. VP-R
One of the most technically advanced of the Anjou producers, who yet contrives to make a Savennières that really needs time in bottle. Most of the production is of Savennières and the three sections of the estate are bottled separately: Domaine de la Bizolière, Clos du Papillon and Château de Chamboureau. Of the three, I prefer Clos du Papillon, of which the Soulez family own two hectares. A small amount of the superior Savennières-Roche-aux-Moines is also produced, under the Château de Chamboureau name. The other wines include a sweet Quarts de Chaume as well as red Anjou which, unusually, includes a high proportion of Cabernet Sauvignon.
Open: Mon–Sat 10am–noon, 1–6pm.

HAUT-POITOU VDQS

Cave Coopérative du Haut-Poitou
32 Rue Alphonse Plault, 86170 Neuville de Poitou.
Vineyards owned: 808ha. 3.2 million bottles.
Coop (625 members).
This cooperative has revived the fortunes of the Haut-Poitou by making a very good range of single varietal wines. The best are from Chardonnay and Sauvignon Blanc, but they also make reds from Cabernet Franc and Gamay. Also produced are classic-method sparkling wines from Chardonnay and a sparkling rosé called Diane de Poitiers. All the wines are made by modern techniques, using stainless steel. *Open: By appointment only.*

Western Loire Producers

MUSCADET ACS, GROS PLANT VDQS

Aubert Frères
49270 La Varenne. Vineyards owned: Muscadet 59ha, Anjou 13ha. 7 million bottles. VP-R and N
One of the major *négociants* of the Muscadet/Anjou area, although the main vineyard holdings are in Muscadet. The range of wines includes lesser appellations such as Coteaux d'Ancenis, but the firm's interests cover the whole Loire: from Sancerre and Pouilly-Fumé in the east to Vin de Pays de Maine-et-Loire and Muscadet in the west. It also produces wines from further afield: Côtes de Provence, Côtes de Duras and Côtes du Rhône. The techniques are modern and the cellars well run. *Open: By appointment only.*

Jérome et André Batard
La Bigotière, 44690 Maisdon-sur-Sèvre.
Vineyards owned: Muscadet de Sèvre-et-Maine: Domaine le Rossignol 15ha. 50,000 bottles. VP-R
Nine-tenths of production is of Muscadet de Sèvre-et-Maine, with a small amount of Gros Plant. The vineyard has been run by the family for many generations, and now modern techniques, stainless steel and temperature control are used. There is a *cuvée de prestige*, Carte Noire. *Open: Appointments preferred.*

Auguste Bonhomme
1 Rue de la Roche, 44190 Gorges.
Vineyards owned: Muscadet 27ha. 180,000 bottles. VP-R and N
Fief de la Brie and Domaine du Haut Bancherau are the two estate-bottled wines from this *négociant*. Eighty percent of sales come from wine which is bought in from the area. A smaller amount of Gros Plant is also sold. Techniques are fairly traditional. *Open: Mon–Fri 8am–noon, 2–6pm.*

Guy Bossard (Domaine de l'Écu)
La Bretonnière, 44930 Le Landreau.
Vineyards owned: 18ha. 129,000 bottles. VP-R

Monsieur Bossard has made a considerable name for himself with his entirely organic Muscadet, which regularly shows well at tastings and which demonstrates the high quality of wines bottled from the lees. The wines have the additional quality – not normally associated with Muscadet – of ageing well.

Open: 9am–noon, 2–5.30pm (appointments preferred).

Jean Bouyer
49 Rue d'Anjou, La Charouillère, 44330 Vallet.
Vineyards owned: 11.5ha. 20,000 bottles. VP-R

Domaine de la Pingossière and Domaine du Clos Julienne are the two names used by this young producer. Monsieur Bouyer makes Muscadet de Sèvre-et-Maine, plus a little Gros Plant du Pays Nantais and Gamay-based Vin de Pays des Marches de Bretagne. Fifty percent of production is sold to *négociants*.

Open: Appointments preferred.

André-Michel Brégeon
Les Guisseaux-Gorges, 44190 Clisson.
Vineyards owned: 7.5ha. 48,000 bottles. VP-R

Traditional techniques (including a short period of wood maturation) are used here and the wines are bottled at the estate *sur lie*. This gives a fuller style and also an attractive prickle on the palate. Monsieur Brégeon's Gros Plant is a very good example. He also makes a small quantity of Vin de Pays des Marches de Bretagne from Cabernet Franc and Cabernet Sauvignon.

Open: Mon–Fri 10am–7pm.

Robert Brosseau (Domaine des Mortiers Gobin)
44690 La Haye-Fouassière.
Vineyards owned: 8ha. 30,000 bottles. VP-R

The wines sold as Domaine des Mortiers Gobin are bottled *sur lie* and methods are traditional, with some wood maturation before bottling. Monsieur Brosseau's family has owned the land 'forever'.

Open: Mon–Sun 8am–7pm; closed July 15 to Aug 20.

Le Cellier des Ducs
Rue de Sèvre-et-Maine, 44450 La Chapelle-Basse-Mer.
1 million bottles.

This is a large-scale *négociant* with a range of Pays Nantais wines. A number of them come from Muscadet de Sèvre-et-Maine estates: Domaines de Bigotière and des Morines, and Châteaux de la Bigotière and de Richebourg. *Open: By appointment only.*

Guy Charpentier
Les Noues, 44430 Le Loroux-Bottereau.
Vineyards owned: 12ha. 40,000 bottles. VP-R

Three-quarters of production here is of Muscadet de Sèvre-et-Maine, with smaller amounts of Gros Plant and Vin de Pays du Jardin de la France (from Gamay), plus Vin de Pays des Marches de Bretagne (from Cabernet Franc). Vineyard holdings are in four communes: Le Loroux-Bottereau, Le Landreau, La Chapelle-

Heulin and La Chapelle-Basse-Mer. Monsieur Charpentier also makes a classic-method sparkling wine called La Belle Folie.
Open: By appointment only.

Ets Chéreau-Carré
Château de Chasseloir, St-Fiacre-sur-Maine,
44690 La Haie-Fouassière. Vineyards owned: 79ha.
505,000 bottles. VP-R and N

The Chéreau family is one of the biggest landowners in Muscadet de Sèvre-et-Maine, with five estates on some of the best vineyard land in the area. Château de Chasseloir (17 hectares) is the centre of operations. The other estates are: Château du Coing (30 hectares), La Bournaire (five hectares), Moulin de la Gravelle (12 hectares), and Château de l'Oiselinière de la Ramée at Vertou (ten hectares). Each estate makes a straight Muscadet de Sèvre-et-Maine and a *cuvée de prestige*, but all are bottled *sur lie* at the individual estate and sold under the estate name. The quality of the wines is high, although Château de Chasseloir is generally regarded as the best. *Open: Mon–Fri 8am–noon, 2–6pm; contact Madame Véronique Günther-Chéreau.*

Bruno Cormerais
La Chambaudière, 44190 St-Lumine-de-Clisson.
Vineyards owned: 12ha. 50,000 bottles. VP-R

A dynamic man, Monsieur Cormerais believes Muscadet is a wine that can be drunk young but can also age. He has old vines from which he makes a Cuvée Prestige that is fermented in old barrels. *Open: Appointments preferred.*

Donatien Bahuaud
La Loge, La Chapelle-Heulin, 44330 Vallet.
Vineyards owned: 18ha. 412,000 bottles. VP-R and N

Two main brands come from this firm. Le Master de Donatien is the *négociant* brand, launched with the '84 vintage. This is sold in a specially designed, painted bottle. Quality is reliable if unexciting. More interesting is the estate-bottled Château de la Cassemichère which is bottled *sur lie* and has some wood maturation. The firm has undertaken extensive marketing for its wines and has gained widespread publicity. A good Chardonnay *vin de table*, called Le Chouan, is also made.
Open: By appointment only.

Domaine des Dorices
La Touché, 44330 Vallet.
Vineyards owned: 31ha. 200,000 bottles. VP-R

The Boullault family has run this ancient vineyard since the 1930s, making their wines without using chemicals in the winery. They are particularly proud of their Domaine des Dorices which, unusually for Muscadet, needs two years' ageing. They also make a younger style Muscadet, Château la Touché, plus a Gros Plant and a classic-method sparkling wine called Leconte. Quality is high here. *Open: By appointment only.*

Joseph Drouard
La Hallopière, 44690 Monnières.
Vineyards owned: 13ha. 80,000 bottles. VP-R
As serious a producer as it is possible to find with Muscadet, making wine traditionally and bottling *sur lie* at the domaine. The wine is full-bodied and needs a little time in bottle. Monsieur Drouard allows no other wines to distract him.
Open: By appointment only.

Drouet Frères
8 Boulevard de Luxembourg, 44330 Vallet.
Vineyards owned: 26ha. 156,000 bottles. VP-R
Two styles of Muscadet, both bottled *sur lie*, are made here. The larger production is of Domaine du Landreau-Village, a modern style of wine. The smaller production is of Domaine de la Sensive, which the producer describes as the top *cuvée*.
Open: Mon-Fri 8.30-11.30am, 3-6pm.

R E Dugast
Domaine des Moulins, Monnières, 44690 La Haie-Fouassière.
Vineyards owned: 9ha.
A small estate which makes Muscadet *sur lie* under the names Domaine des Moulins and Cuvée des Grands Quarterons and also some sparkling wines from Gros Plant which, according to the producer, need to be drunk very cold.

Gabare de Sèvre
Le Pé de Sèvre, Le Pallet, 44330 Vallet.
Vineyards owned: 80ha. 160,000 bottles. VP-R
This group of nine small landowners was set up in 1982 and already it has become a powerful force in the Pays Nantais region. Each member of the group vinifies and bottles his own wine; the group then sells it on. The 70 percent of wine not sold in bottles goes to *négociants*. The bulk of production is of Muscadet, which is sold under the Gabare de Sèvre label; the remainder comes from Gros Plant. The name Gabare refers to the barges which used to transport wine along the River Sèvre.
Open: By appointment only.

Château de la Galissonière
Le Pallet, 44330 Vallet.
Vineyards owned: 33ha. 270,000 bottles. VP-R
The estate consists of two properties, Château de la Galissonière and Château de la Jannière, both of which produce lively, fresh Muscadet of good quality. The family of Pierre Lusseaud, the owner, has been at the estate since 1912.

Modern techniques are very much to the fore here, cool fermenting and stainless steel allowing the production of wine that is delicious in the summer following the vintage. Monsieur Lusseaud also makes Gros Plant du Pays Nantais and Vin de Pays des Marches de Bretagne from Cabernet Franc and Chardonnay.
Open: Mon-Fri 8am-7pm.

Château de Goulaine
44115 Haute-Goulaine.
Vineyards owned: 25ha. 160,000 bottles. VP-R and N
The château of Goulaine dates from the 15th century and the
estate has been in the family for 1,000 years. The wine continues
to set a good example to the neighbours. Much of it is of a modern
style, which needs early drinking, but the Cuvée du Millénaire,
made from old vines, repays a couple of years' keeping. Gros
Plant is also produced.
Open: Mon–Fri 9am–noon, 2–6pm; the winery by appointment only.

Guilbaud Frères
Les Lilas, Mouzillon, 44330 Vallet.
Vineyards owned: 16.5ha. 2.5 million bottles. VP-R and N
About five percent of production here is from three estates owned
by this large *négociant* firm. It bottles Domaine de la Pingossière,
Domaine de la Moutonnière and Clos du Pont separately. Other
Muscadet de Sèvre-et-Maine goes under a variety of brand names:
Le Soleil Nantais, Cuvée Grand Or and Cuvée du Lion. Wines tend
to a soft style. *Open: By appointment only.*

Domaine La Haute Févrie
La Févrie, Maisdon-sur-Sèvre, 44690 La Haie-Fouassière.
Vineyards owned: 18ha. 70,000 bottles. VP-R
Three generations of the Branger family have worked this land in
Maisdon-sur-Sèvre. The firm now employs modern techniques of
temperature control in the winery but continues to bottle its
wines *sur lie* to protect the wine's 'gaiety and youth'. The result is
a classic Muscadet which can take some bottle-ageing.
Open: Mon–Sat 8am–12.30pm, 2–7pm.

Domaine de la Hautière
44690 St-Fiacre-sur-Maine.
Vineyards owned: 10ha. 90,000 bottles. VP-R and N
The Thébaud family have run this small *négociant* business and
farm for many generations and today buys in 50 percent of its
stock as grapes from vineyards owned by other members of the
family. It makes one estate wine, Domaine de la Hautière, bottled
sur lie in the March following vintage. It also makes a *négociant*
Muscadet, Les Doyennes, and a Gros Plant.
Open: Appointments preferred.

Domaine de la Louvetries (Pierre et Joseph Landron)
Les Brandières, 44690 La Haie-Fouassière.
Vineyards owned: 22ha.
The vineyards of this estate are on a well-sited slope, Coteaux du
Breil, on schist soil, which gives the wines an ability to age. The
basic *cuvée*, Domaine de la Louvetries, however, is designed for
fresh, early drinking. The firm makes a *prestige cuvée*, which is
sold in a satinised bottle, and two *cuvées* (Cuvée Concours and
Hermine d'Or) which are blends assembled after critical blind
tastings by other growers.

Luneau-Papin (Domaine Pierre de la Grange)

44430 Le Landreau. Vineyards owned: 30ha. 150,000 bottles. VP-R
The Muscadet here is bottled *sur lie*. The style is quite traditional (the family have been *vignerons* since 1680) and tends to fullness. The firm also makes a small quantity of Gros Plant, bottling the different sections of the vineyard separately and labelling them accordingly: Clos des Allées, les Pierres Blanches.
Open: By appointment only.

Château de la Mercredière

Le Pallet, 44330 Vallet.
Vineyards owned: 36ha. 220,000 bottles. VP-R
The vineyard surrounds a beautiful 14th-century château on the banks of the River Sèvre. The winemaking, however, is modern, with stainless steel and bottling under inert gas. The wine is smooth, not too acid, and has plenty of fruit. It responds well to a little ageing. *Open: Mon–Fri 9am–noon, 2–6pm.*

Louis Métaireau

La Fevrie, 44690 Maisdon-sur-Sèvre.
Vineyards owned: 107ha. 210,000 bottles. Group of producers.
Louis Métaireau has organised a group of nine producers who pool resources and make *cuvées* which are sold under Monsieur Métaireau's name. The wines are selected jointly, but bottled *sur lie* at each producer's own cellars. The group also owns one vineyard, the Grand Mouton, as a joint venture. The success of this enterprise lies in the high quality of the wines.
Open: By appointment only.

Château la Noë

44330 Vallet. Vineyards owned: 32ha. 200,000 bottles. VP-R
The Comte de Malestroit, whose family property this is, produces a classic Muscadet: unusually full-bodied and intended for some ageing. The estate, set around a classical mansion, has been in the same family since 1740. *Open: By appointment only.*

Château de l'Oiselinière Gorges

44190 Clisson. Vineyards owned: 30ha. 140,000 bottles. VP-R
The heart of the estate is a 19th-century Italianate villa, but the Aulanier family has owned the land since 1765. It is divided into four parcels, mainly producing Muscadet de Sèvre-et-Maine. There is also some Gros Plant. The winemaking is a mixture of traditional and modern. *Open: 9.30am–noon, 2–6pm.*

Château de la Ragotière

La Regrippière, 44330 Vallet.
Vineyards owned: 59ha. 400,000 bottles. VP-R
The château is an old property, with a 14th-century chapel, but the present owners, the Couillaud family, have been in charge since 1979. Winemaking techniques are moving away from the traditional towards stainless steel. The Muscadet de Sèvre-et-Maine is clean and penetrating, with citrus undertones: it can be

very attractive when drunk young. The firm also makes a Gros
Plant wine and a Vin de Pays du Jardin de la France from
Chardonnay.
Open: Mon–Fri 8am–noon, 2–6pm; Sat by appointment only.

Clos des Rosiers
44330 Vallet. Vineyards owned: 13ha. 70,000 bottles. VP-R
This traditional producer uses some wood for maturation, making
a fragrant wine with plenty of fruit which takes some ageing. About
two-thirds of the production is of Muscadet de Sèvre-et-Maine, the
rest is of Gros Plant. The vineyard's title, Clos des Rosiers, is used
as a brand name. *Open: By appointment only.*

Marcel Sautejeau (Domaine de l'Hyvernière)
Le Pallet, 44330 La Chapelle-Heulin.
Vineyards owned: 45ha. 300,000 bottles. VP-R and N
In its winemaking capacity (Domaine de l'Hyvernière) Marcel
Sautejeau produces Muscadet de Sèvre-et-Maine, which is bottled
sur lie at the estate. In its *négociant* form, it handles wines from
Anjou, Saumur and Vouvray. The domaine's history goes back to
medieval times when it was visited by the French King Henri IV
when he came to sign the Edict of Nantes in 1598.
Open: By appointment only.

Sauvion et Fils (Château du Cléray)
44330 Vallet. Vineyards owned: 30ha. 200,000 bottles. VP-R and N
The Château du Cléray estate is the heart of a *négociant* business
which produces a range of qualities of Muscadet. The *négociant*
side takes 80 percent of production and it makes Carte d'Or and
Lauréat brands as well as Château du Cléray, which is bottled *sur
lie*, and the *prestige cuvée* Cardinal Richard. Quality is high in all
these wines, the style generally being soft, with attractive earthy
overtones. The firm is careful to assess the quality of each
vineyard from which wine is bought. La Nobleraie is a brand
name for the wine produced from bought-in grapes.
Open: Mon–Fri 9am–noon, 2–5pm.

André Vinet
12 Rue du Progrès Uilbaud, 44330 Vallet.
Vineyards owned: None. 3 million bottles. N
A *négociant* specialising in the wines of the Pays Nantais. It makes
Muscadet de Sèvre-et-Maine and some Gros Plant, plus a
sparkling *blanc de blancs*. The range varies, with the wines from
some estates being bottled separately – one of them, Château la
Touché, is run on organic lines. *Open: By appointment only.*

COTEAUX D'ANCENIS VDQS

Jacques Guindon
La Couleuverdière, St-Géréon, 44150 Ancenis.
*Vineyards owned: Ancenis 6ha, Muscadet Coteaux de la Loire
12ha, Gros Plant 2ha. 92,500 bottles. VP-R*

Monsieur Guindon is one of the few strong producers of Muscadet Coteaux de la Loire whose wines reach further than the local restaurants. His principal wine is this Muscadet, but he also makes Gros Plant and smaller amounts of Coteaux d'Ancenis VDQS. His cellars are on the north side of the Loire, away from the Sèvre-et-Maine vineyards but close to Ancenis.

Open: Mon–Sat 9am–noon, 2–6pm.

Les Vignerons de la Noëlle

BP 102, 44150 Ancenis. Vineyards owned: 459ha.
2 million bottles. Coop (300 members).

One of the few cooperatives in the Muscadet area, this one produces large quantities of simple Muscadet from 220 hectares under a number of different brand names. Other wines include red Coteaux d'Ancenis from 50 hectares of Gamay, Gros Plant and red Vin de Pays du Jardin de la France. It also makes red and white wines under the Anjou AC, plus a small amount of Crémant de Loire from Chardonnay grapes. Standards are improving with the installation of new equipment. *Open: By appointment only.*

FIEFS VENDÉENS VDQS

Ph et X Coirier

La Petite Groie, Pisotte, 85200 Fontenay-le-Comte. Vineyards owned: Fiefs Vendéens Pisotte 16ha. 50,000 bottles. VP-R

Over half the production here is of red and rosé wines – a blend of Gamay, Pinot Noir and Cabernet Sauvignon. The red is a light-coloured wine, best drunk chilled and at its peak a year after the vintage. The white is a fragrant blend of Colombard with Chenin Blanc and Muscadet. *Open: Appointments preferred.*

Mercier Frères (Domaine de la Chaignée)

La Chaignée, 85770 Vix.
Vineyards owned: Fiefs Vendéens Vix 25ha. 9,000 bottles. VP-R

All the wines at this small estate are made in stainless steel. White comes from a blend of Chenin Blanc, Sauvignon and Chardonnay; rosé from Gamay, Pinot Noir and Cabernet Franc. Red wine from Gamay, Cabernet Franc and Cabernet Sauvignon is made by a semi-carbonic maceration method.

Arsene Rambaud

Follet, Bosnay, 85320 Mareuil-sur-Lay.
Vineyards owned: Fiefs Vendéens 4ha. 6,000 bottles. VP-R

Red and rosé Fiefs Vendéens are produced from a range of grapes: Gamay, Pinot Noir, Cabernets Franc and Sauvignon and Négrette. About 40 percent of production is sold to *négociants. Open: By appointment only.*

Alsace

Alsace wines are often said to be Germanic wines made in a French way. But that, I feel, is to play up the German element of the equation and to play down the French. Because there is no doubt that, despite differences in history and philosophy, Alsace produces wines that could only be French.

It is true that if you listened to an Alsace grower talking to a colleague from the next village, you could be forgiven for thinking you were on the east bank of the Rhine and not the west. Between themselves, Alsatians often speak a curious dialect which is much more German than French. As one grower put it "we think we're talking a dialect, but really we're talking German".

But that is hardly surprising. Alsace became part of modern France only in 1648 at the end of the 30 Years' War. Before that, it had either been part of the Holy Roman Empire or part of the Frankish kingdom of the Merovingians. Its history has certainly not been without troubles. Twice reoccupied by Germany (from 1870 to 1919 and from 1940 to 1945), it has been fought over for centuries. Now it is French but European as well; the European Parliament meets in Strasbourg, the capital of Alsace.

Alsace is well to the north in terms of French vineyards and to the south in terms of German vineyards – level with south Baden and the Kaiserstuhl. But geography is kinder to Alsace than history has been: the sheltering Vosges mountains run from north to south for virtually the whole length of Alsace, parallel to the River Rhine.

The vineyards lie in the eastern lee of the mountains, in a narrow strip that is never more than two miles wide. The Vosges protect the vines from rain – in Colmar in the central vineyards of Alsace the rainfall is the lowest in France, apart from Perpignan in the deep south. The result is that for weeks on end in the summer the skies of Alsace can be clear and blue, while a few miles away in the uplands of the Vosges it can be raining hard.

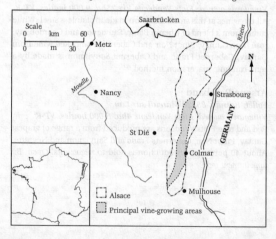

Alsace is picturesque wine country. The ribbon of vineyards is broken by small villages full of tall, overhanging half-timbered houses, decorated in the summer with brightly planted window boxes. Curious medieval signs indicate the cellars of wine producers, who often invite visitors to taste their wines. Everyone seems to be connected in some way with wine.

The most northerly Alsace vineyards virtually touch the German border near the southern end of the Pfalz wine region. The vineyards of Rott and Cleebourg have only recently been expanded and now there are 120 hectares of vines. Little of the wine, however, travels far beyond Strasbourg.

The main Alsace vineyard area begins 30 miles to the south, through the northern outcrops of the Vosges, where the village of Marlenheim marks the beginning of the Alsace wine road. From Marlenheim to Orschwiller, south of Sélestat, the vineyards are in the Bas-Rhin *département* (ie, lower down the course of the Rhine). While they have never achieved the fame of the vineyards further south, they give a definite character of their own to the wines. Some would describe this northern Alsace wine as lighter and drier than the wine of the south. The rainfall here is certainly higher, because the Vosges are lower, and the grapes tend not to ripen so quickly or so completely. Many of the grapes for the sparkling Crémant d'Alsace (*see* page 78) come from the Bas-Rhin vineyards. Famous wine villages in the Bas-Rhin include: Wangen, Barr, Goxwiller, Mittelbergheim, Itterswiller, Dambach-la-Ville, Kintzheim and Orschwiller.

At St-Hippolyte the Haut-Rhin *département* begins. The vineyards run the full length of this *département*, passing the famous villages of Bergheim, Ribeauvillé, Riquewihr, Kaysersberg, Ammerschwihr, Eguisheim, Husseren-les-Châteaux, Rouffach, Guebwiller and Soultz and ending with the small vineyard concentration around Thann, just west of Mulhouse. Here the Vosges are higher, the rainfall lower and the grapes ripen over a long growing period which runs into warm, dry autumns.

Négociants (merchants) used to dominate the Alsace wine trade, just as they did – until recently – in Burgundy. Many families have been in the business for centuries. The reason for this is the same as it was in Burgundy: the vineyards are owned by many growers with small holdings, who could not afford or did not wish to bottle and sell their own wine. Even now, there are 9,000 growers farming the 12,000 hectares of vineyard.

Today, the place of the *négociants* has been overtaken by the cooperatives which now take 39 percent of the region's production. Growers are also starting to bottle their own wine, as they realise they can obtain high prices to cover their costs: now nearly 25 percent – including some of the very best Alsace wine – is bottled by the growers.

Inevitably with such northerly vineyards, white wines dominate the viticulture. White and sparkling white wine make up 95 percent of production, and although Alsace growers like to show their red wines at a tasting, when it comes to the meal it is bottles of Bordeaux that will be drunk.

Although grape vines have grown in Alsace probably since Roman times and certainly since the Merovingians in the eighth and ninth centuries, the development of the Alsace vineyard as we know it today is relatively new – dating from after the First World War. The Appellation Contrôlée system reached Alsace in 1962.

When they were introduced, the new AC laws recognised a system of labelling unique to France – and not one inherited from Germany. Until recently (*see* page 76, Alsace Grand Cru) the whole Alsace vineyard – from the north by the border with Germany, down to the Swiss border near Basle – was covered by only one appellation. Everything was classified as AC Alsace.

On the labels, a system operates which will be familiar to Californian and Australian wine drinkers but which is still much less common in the rest of France: labelling wines with the name of the grape variety. The grape named must make up 100 percent of the contents of the bottle. This applies to wines exported from Alsace. At home, Alsatians drink blended wines quite happily – calling them Edelzwicker or using a brand name.

Another revolutionary system was adopted at the same time – revolutionary that is when compared with the system working the rest of France. The rules stipulate that all Alsace AC wines must be bottled in Alsace – not elsewhere in France, let alone abroad. This, above all else, has given Alsace its reputation for reliability. As a consequence, it is almost unknown to find a bad bottle of Alsace wine – bad, that is, in the sense of faulty.

Alsace Grape Varieties

The permitted grape varieties, with characteristics of the wine they produce, are as follows:

Chasselas This used to be a widely planted grape, but the area planted has now dropped to about 3.5 percent of the vineyard. It is also grown in Savoie and Switzerland. In Alsace it appears only as part of an Edelzwicker blend. When tasted by itself, it has a smoky, herby taste with soft, low-acid fruit flavour.

Gewürztraminer The grape that has brought more fame to the Alsace region than any other. It has a distinctive, spicy, full, oily taste; high alcohol, and sometimes a bitter finish and dryness in even the sweetest examples. It is the grape most frequently used in the late-picked *Vendange Tardive* and *Sélection des Grains Nobles* wines. Gewürztraminer wines are not wines to drink in vast quantities, but they are excellent with some of the rich Alsace cooking such as *choucroute* (pickled cabbage), spicy sausages and Münster cheese.

Muscat The grape that in the south of France produces the sweet sparkling Clairette de Die and the *vins doux naturels* such as Beaumes-de-Venise, in Alsace makes a wine that is a perfect combination of sweetness and lightness, dry yet with a honeyed tone, absolutely delicious as an aperitif wine. The trouble is that there is very little of it in Alsace: it is a difficult vine to grow so far north, and growers are reluctant to devote much of their vineyard space to a variety that yields well only in good years. As with the Pinot Blanc, there are two types of Muscat: the Muscat Blanc à Petits Grains (or Muscat d'Alsace) and the Muscat Ottonel. While the latter causes fewer growing problems, the former produces the finer wine.

Pinot Noir Rosé and red wines in Alsace come from this grape. Until the last decade most of the region's red wines were pale and uninteresting. With the arrival of modern techniques – such as the Vinimatic rotating fermenting tank – colour and tannin extraction has been made possible, and there are now many respectable reds from Pinot Noir – some are even aged in wood. As a consequence, plantings have increased and the wines are much in demand locally.

Pinot Blanc (Klevner) This produces some of the most readily drinkable wines in Alsace. It is no surprise that it has been such a success in London wine bars: it is very quaffable on its own as it is relatively low in alcohol, fresh tasting, soft with a pleasing touch of acidity and not too pronounced a character. There are two forms of the Pinot Blanc in Alsace – the Pinot Blanc itself and the Pinot Auxerrois. The latter is generally regarded as producing the better quality wine, but the two are normally blended and sold under the name Pinot Blanc – or further blended with other grapes and sold as Edelzwicker or a branded wine.

Riesling By general assent, the Riesling makes the finest wine in Alsace and epitomises the difference between Alsatian and German winemaking. In Alsace, the Riesling produces a wine that has medium alcohol, is bone dry with a flinty, steely taste, very fresh and often acidic when young, softening with maturity to give a superb wine with a petrolly taste. In very fine vintages it is allowed to make sweeter wines which still retain a dryness and firmness no German wine is ever intended to achieve.

Sylvaner A widely planted grape (it covers 20 percent of the Alsace vineyard) which produces a neutral, reliable wine, good for quaffing and often used as a component of Edelzwicker blends. It is especially popular in the northern Bas-Rhin vineyards where its early ripening and low acidity cope well with the cooler, wetter weather.

Tokay-Pinot Gris or Tokay d'Alsace This bears no relation to the Hungarian Tokay or Tokaji (which is made with a different grape variety, Furmint), but has links with eastern Austria and western Hungary as well as with parts of northern Italy. The name Tokay, while formally banned by the EC because of the confusion with the Hungarian wine, is still widely used – and most producers now refer to the wine as Tokay-Pinot Gris. Many Alsatians would call this their favourite style of wine: full, rich, soft, well-balanced with much acidity, a touch of pepper, quite high in alcohol and with the ability to age well. Tokay d'Alsace is often served with foie gras, which it certainly complements perfectly. If ever I am given the choice of Alsace wines, I am generally torn between a good Tokay and a good Riesling.

The Appellations

APPELLATIONS CONTRÔLÉES

Virtually all the wine made in Alsace has AC status. Alsace produces 20 percent of all white AC wine in France – around 143 million bottles a year.

Alsace This general Appellation Contrôlée covers all Alsace vineyards. Any of the permitted grape varieties (*see* pages 74–5) grown in any village in any AC vineyard can qualify.

Alsace Grand Cru First introduced with the '85 vintage. It covers specific vineyards for specific varieties. In other words, if *Grand Cru* vineyard X is designated as *Grand Cru* for Riesling, any Gewürztraminer in that vineyard will be simple AC Alsace. *Grand Cru* wines can be either 100 percent from one vineyard (which will be named on the label) or from a number of *Grand Cru* vineyards (when it will simply be called Alsace Grand Cru).

All Alsace Grand Cru wines must be 100 percent from one grape variety, and only the four top Alsace varieties – Riesling, Gewürztraminer, Tokay-Pinot Gris and Muscat – can produce *Grand Cru* wines. Permitted yields are also lower than for Alsace AC, at 65 hectolitres per hectare.

Like so many of the changes to AC laws all over France, local politics has played an important role in the designations. *Négociant* houses are not in favour of *Grand Cru* status as it implies that single-vineyard wines are better than wines blended from several top vineyards. The growers, however, are all for *Grand Cru* status (if they own *Grand Cru* land): it increases the price they can charge. There was much heated debate about the size of each designated *Grand Cru* and it took ten years for the first vineyards to be organised; the same was true for the second *tranche* of *Grands Crus* (*see* second list).

The first list of *Grand Cru* vineyards, which takes in ten percent of Alsace production and was delimited with the '83 vintage, is as follows. Commune, *département* and size are also listed.

Alsace Grands Crus: (first list)

Altenberg de Bergbieten (Bergbieten, Bas-Rhin)	29 hectares
Altenberg de Bergheim (Bergheim, Haut-Rhin)	35 hectares
Brand (Turckheim, Haut-Rhin)	57 hectares
Eichberg (Eguisheim, Haut-Rhin)	58 hectares
Geisberg (Ribeauvillé, Haut-Rhin)	8.5 hectares
Gloeckelberg (Rodern and St-Hippolyte, Haut-Rhin)	23 hectares
Goldert (Gueberschwihr, Haut-Rhin)	45 hectares
Hatschbourg (Hattstatt and Voegtlinshoffen, Haut-Rhin)	47 hectares
Hengst (Wintzenheim, Haut-Rhin)	76 hectares
Kanzlerberg (Bergheim, Haut-Rhin)	3 hectares
Kastelberg (Andlau, Bas-Rhin)	6 hectares

Kessler (Guebwiller, Haut-Rhin)	28 hectares
Kirchberg de Barr (Barr, Bas-Rhin)	40 hectares
Kirchberg de Ribeauvillé (Ribeauvillé, Haut-Rhin)	11 hectares
Kitterlé (Guebwiller, Haut-Rhin)	26 hectares
Moenchberg (Andlau and Eichhoffen, Bas-Rhin)	12 hectares
Ollwiller (Wuenheim, Bas-Rhin)	36 hectares
Rangen (Thann and Vieux-Thann, Haut-Rhin)	19 hectares
Rosacker (Hunawihr, Haut-Rhin)	26 hectares
Saering (Guebwiller, Haut-Rhin)	27 hectares
Schlossberg (Kaysersberg and Kientzheim, Haut-Rhin)	80 hectares
Sommerberg (Niedermorschwihr and Katzenthal, Haut-Rhin)	28 hectares
Sonnenglanz (Beblenheim, Haut-Rhin)	33 hectares
Spiegel (Bergholtz and Guebwiller, Haut-Rhin)	18 hectares
Wiebelsberg (Andlau, Bas-Rhin)	12 hectares

The second list covered another 25 vineyards. Producers were allowed to add the term *Grand Cru* to these vineyards' names from the '85 vintage even before the final decision was made in 1992. Alsace Grand Cru then rose to take in 15 percent of production.

Alsace Grands Crus: (second list)

Altenberg de Wolxheim (Wolxheim, Bas-Rhin)	28 hectares
Bruderthal (Molsheim, Bas-Rhin)	19 hectares
Engelberg (Dahlenheim, Bas-Rhin)	11 hectares
Florimont (Ingersheim, Haut-Rhin)	15 hectares
Frankstein (Dambach-la-Ville, Bas-Rhin)	53 hectares
Froehn (Zellenberg, Haut-Rhin)	13 hectares
Furstentum (Kientzheim and Sigolsheim, Haut-Rhin)	28 hectares
Kaefferkopf (Ammerschwihr, Haut-Rhin)	60 hectares
Mambourg (Sigolsheim, Haut-Rhin)	65 hectares
Mandelberg (Mittelwihr, Haut-Rhin)	12 hectares
Markrain (Bennwihr, Haut-Rhin)	45 hectares
Muenchberg (Nothalten, Bas-Rhin)	18 hectares
Osterberg (Ribeauvillé, Haut-Rhin)	24 hectares
Pfersigberg (Eguisheim, Haut-Rhin)	56 hectares
Pfingstberg (Orschwiller, Haut-Rhin)	28 hectares
Praelatenberg (Orschwiller, Bas-Rhin)	12 hectares
Schoenenbourg (Riquewihr, Haut-Rhin)	40 hectares
Sporen (Riquewihr, Haut-Rhin)	22 hectares
Steinert (Pfaffenheim, Haut-Rhin)	38 hectares
Steingrubler (Wettolsheim, Haut-Rhin)	19 hectares
Steinklotz (Marlenheim, Bas-Rhin)	24 hectares
Vorbourg (Rouffach and Westhalten, Haut-Rhin)	72 hectares
Wineck-Schlossberg (Katzenthal, Haut-Rhin)	24 hectares
Winzenberg (Blienschwiller, Bas-Rhin)	5 hectares
Zinnkoepflé (Westhalten and Soultzmatt, Haut-Rhin)	62 hectares
Zotzenberg (Mittelbergheim, Bas-Rhin)	34 hectares

Crémant d'Alsace A sparkling wine made by the classic method which can be produced from grapes grown anywhere in the Alsace AC area. The appellation was introduced with the '76 harvest. Permitted grape varieties for Crémant d'Alsace are: Pinot Blanc, Pinot Auxerrois, Pinot Noir, Pinot Gris, Riesling and Chardonnay. Most Crémant d'Alsace is made from Pinot Blanc and Pinot Auxerrois.

Vendange Tardive and Sélection des Grains Nobles Sweeter wines made either from bunches or selected berries that have particularly high sugar and potential alcohol levels. To that extent they correspond to the German wine categories of *Beerenauslese* and *Trockenbeerenauslese* with the vital difference that they never taste as sweet as the German equivalents. The taste of noble rot (*pourriture noble*) is often found in these wines, though not all the grapes used must necessarily be affected.

While the terms have been used for some time, it was only in 1984 (referring to the '83 vintage) that they were regulated.

LORRAINE VDQS

Côtes de Toul Red, rosé, *gris* and dry white wines from a small vineyard area around the city of Toul in the Meurthe-et-Moselle *département*. Most of the wine is *vin gris*, a pale rosé that is made from Gamay grapes. Pinot Noir and Pinot Meunier grapes are also planted.

Vin de Moselle Red and dry white wines from the *département* of Moselle. The red is made from Pinot Noir, Pinot Gris and Gamay, the white from Pinot Blanc and Sylvaner.

VINS DE PAYS

Departmental *vins de pays*

Vin de Pays de Bas-Rhin Wines from an area covering the whole of the Bas-Rhin *département*. A tiny amount of rosé and white wine is produced from the Alsace grapes as well as Chardonnay and Auxerrois.

Vin de Pays de Haut-Rhin A small quantity of wines, made from Alsace grapes as well as Chardonnay and Auxerrois. These wines may come from anywhere in the Haut-Rhin.

Vin de Pays de la Meuse An area covering the *département* of the Meuse in Lorraine. Production is mainly of white wines, coming from the Auxerrois, Chardonnay and a range of Alsatian grape varieties.

Bas-Rhin Producers

Domaine Bernhard-Reibel
20 Rue de Lorraine, 67730 Châtenois.
Vineyards owned: 12ha. VP-R
Domaine Weingarten wines are the ones to look out for from this small estate run by Cécile Bernhard-Reibel. The land runs from the Weingarten domaine in Châtenois to Haut-Koenigsbourg. The

main grape is Riesling, but there is a full range, including Pinot Noir. Organic viticultural techniques are used.

Open: By appointment only.

E Boeckel

67140 Mittelbergheim.
Vineyards owned: 20ha. 420,000 bottles. VP-R and N

Riesling wines are the speciality of this *négociant*, the biggest wine producer in Mittelbergheim. The vineyard holdings include two in *Grand Cru* vineyards – the Zotzenberg and the Wiebelsberg – as well as holdings in the Brandluft vineyard.

Curiously, despite Zotzenberg's previous reputation for producing high-class Sylvaner, E Boeckel has always concentrated on Riesling and Gewürztraminer from this vineyard. The wines, on the whole, should be drunk relatively young.

Open: By appointment only.

Lucien Brand

71 Rue de Wolxheim, 67120 Ergersheim.
Vineyards owned: Grand Cru Kaefferkopf 0.2ha, Alsace AC 7ha, Crémant d'Alsace 1ha. 60,000 bottles. VP-R

Charles Brand is the *oenelogue* at this small estate, where he practises ecological techniques in the vineyard. Gewürztraminer seems to be his most successful grape variety, although he also makes a *Grand Cru* Riesling from the Engelberg vineyard. Small quantities of Crémant d'Alsace are also made.

Open: Mon–Fri 9am–noon, 2–7pm; Sat 9am–noon, 2–6pm.

Cave Vinicole de Cléebourg

Route du Vin, 67160 Cléebourg. Vineyards owned: Alsace AC 162ha. 1.7 million bottles. Coop (189 members).

The members of this cooperative own some of the most northerly vineyards in Alsace, some of which lie against the German border. The cooperative was founded in 1946 when 300 hectares of former vineyard were replanted. The most interesting wines to come from this area are made with the Auxerrois (Pinot Blanc) including the cooperative's Crémant d'Alsace. One curiosity is its Pinot Noir which, it is claimed, is the most northerly red wine made in France.

Open: Mon–Sat 8am–noon, 2–6pm; Sun 10am–noon, 2–6pm.

Vignobles Raymond Engel et Fils

1 Route du Vin, 67600 Orschwiller. Vineyards owned: Grand Cru Praelatenberg 6ha, Alsace AC 9ha. 150,000 bottles. VP-R

The *Grand Cru* Praelatenberg vineyard supplies all four permitted grape varieties – Gewürztraminer, Riesling, Tokay-Pinot Gris and Muscat – which are labelled under the name Domaine des Prélats, while Monsieur Engel's other vineyards also produce the complete range of Alsace wines. He makes a small quantity of Crémant d'Alsace and a Rouge d'Alsace. The wines are normally aged briefly in wood before being bottled.

Open: Mon–Fri 8am–noon, 3–7pm.

Louis Gisselbrecht

67650 Dambach-la-Ville.
Vineyards owned: Alsace AC 12ha. 900,000 bottles. VP-R and N
This firm produces a full range of modern-style wines, vinified in stainless steel, attractively fresh and drinkable, but without great depth. It is proudest of its Riesling produced from its own vineyards in Dambach-la-Ville. *Open: Appointments preferred.*

Willy Gisselbrecht et Fils

5 Route du Vin, 67650 Dambach-la-Ville.
Vineyards owned: Alsace AC 145ha, Crémant d'Alsace 15ha.
1.2 million bottles. VP-R and N
A large *négociant* business producing a range of good-quality wines. A mixture of wood, glass-lined tanks and stainless steel is used and traditional vinification methods followed. The philosophy is to bottle the wines quickly to cut the use of sulphur to a minimum. The range covers all the varietal styles, plus Edelzwicker and Crémant d'Alsace. A small amount of *Grand Cru* Frankstein is also made. Brand names used are Willy Gisselbrecht and Antoine Heinrich.
Open: Mon–Fri 9am–noon, 2–6pm; Sat 9am–noon, 2–5pm.

Domaine André et Rémy Gresser

2 Rue de l'École, 67140 Andlau. Vineyards owned: Grand Cru Wiebelsberg 1ha, Grand Cru *Moenchberg 0.4ha,* Grand Cru Kastelberg 0.2ha, Alsace AC 8.5ha. 60,000 bottles. VP-R
This small family vineyard was established in 1667 but it has moved with the times. It now uses stainless steel for vinification, but still ages in wood. The largest production is of Sylvaner and Riesling and the finest wines, including the best *Grand Cru*, are all Riesling. Some of the Wiebelsberg wine is from 60-year-old vines. Also known as Domaine André-Rémy Gresser.
Open: Mon–Sun 9am–noon, 2–7pm.

Jean Hauller et Fils

92 Rue du Maréchal Foch, 67650 Dambach-la-Ville. VP-R and N
A large *négociant* firm that also owns some vineyards around Dambach-la-Ville, with Riesling from Schwerwiller and Gewürztraminer from Hahnenberg. However, the firm does not vinify its own grapes separately from fruit which it buys in. It makes *Vendange Tardive* from Gewürztraminer under the name Cuvée St-Sebastian. The quality is enjoyable rather than exciting. *Open: Mon–Sat 9–11.30am, 1.30–6pm.*

Domaine Pierre Hering

6 Rue du Docteur Sultzer, 67140 Barr. Vineyards owned: Kirchberg Grand Cru *and Alsace AC 10ha. 80,000 bottles. VP-R*
Apart from a holding in the Kirchberg *Grand Cru*, Pierre Hering has vines in two other vineyards: Clos de la Folie Marco (for Sylvaner) and Gaensbroennel (for Gewürztraminer). His best wine is the Riesling from the Kirchberg vineyard, but he makes a full range of wines. *Open: Mon–Sat 9am–6pm; Sun by appointment.*

Jean Heywang
7 Rue Principale, 67140 Heiligenstein. Vineyards owned: Grand
Cru *Kirchberg 0.5ha, Alsace AC 4.95ha. 35,000 bottles. VP-R*
The speciality of this house is Klevener de Heiligenstein, a variety
which has been planted in the village since 1700. This makes a
light, fresh, vivacious wine which is good with white meats,
according to Jean Heywang. The Gewürztraminer *Grand Cru*
Kirchberg is, however, the finest.
Open: Mon–Sat and Sun morning; closed 12.15–1.15pm.

Domaine Klipfel
6 Avenue de la Gare, 67140 Barr. Vineyards owned: Grands
Crus *7.2ha, Alsace AC 28ha. 1.2 million bottles. VP-R and N*
The largest merchant house in Barr. It operates under two names:
Louis Klipfel for estate wines and Eugène Klipfel for *négociant*
wines. Unsurprisingly, the estate wines are the better ones, and
examples such as the Gewürztraminer *Grand Cru* Clos Zisser are
well able to age. On the Freiberg estate, the firm makes some
deliciously spicy Tokay-Pinot Gris. *Open: 10am–noon, 2–6pm.*

Marc Kreydenweiss
12 Rue Deharbe, Andlau, 67140 Barr.
Vineyards owned: Grands Crus *Kastelberg, Wiebelsberg and*
Moenchberg 3ha, Alsace AC 8ha. 60,000 bottles. VP-R
Biodynamie, a belief in and respect for the properties of the soil, is
the foundation of the vineyard work of this talented wine
producer. His range of wines is considerable, but the finest
include the wines of Kritt vineyard (a Pinot Blanc, a late-picked
'Klevner' and a Gewürztraminer), the Riesling from the
Wiebelsberg *Grand Cru* and Tokay-Pinot Gris from *Grand Cru*
Moenchberg. He also innovates with wood-matured Sylvaner, a
blend of Riesling and Tokay-Pinot Gris and a *barrique*-aged
Chardonnay. *Open: By appointment only.*

Michel Laugel
102 Rue Général de Gaulle, 67520 Marlenheim. Vineyards
owned: Alsace AC 6ha. 4.5 million bottles. VP-R and N
A large *négociant* firm, now owned by Rémy Pannier of Saumur in
the Loire, which dominates the northern end of the Alsace region.
It produces a wide range, of which the most interesting is the
selection of village wines. These are varietals made from vineyards in villages which are particularly famous for specific grape
varieties: Riesling de Wolxheim, Gewürztraminer de Wangen,
Pinot Noir de Marlenheim (a rosé) and Pinot Rouge de
Marlenheim. It also produces Crémant d'Alsace.
Open: Mon–Fri 9am–noon, 2–5pm, by appointment.

Frédéric Mochel
56 Rue Principale, 67310 Traenheim.
Vineyards owned: Grand Cru *Altenberg de Bergbieten 5ha,*
Alsace AC 3ha, Crémant d'Alsace 0.8ha. 76,000 bottles. VP-R
Monsieur Mochel produces Sylvaner, Pinot Blanc (locally called

Klevner), Riesling, Muscat, Tokay-Pinot Gris, Gewürztraminer and Pinot Noir from his vineyards in and around Traenheim. His vineyard and winemaking methods are traditional. Riesling *Grand Cru* Altenberg de Bergbieten is his finest wine, and some of it forms a Cuvée Henriette, made from 30-year-old vines.
Open: Mon–Sat 9am–noon, 1.30–6pm.

François Muhlberger
1 Rue de Strasbourg, 67120 Wolxheim.
Vineyards owned: **Grand Cru Altenberg de Wolxheim 3ha,** *Alsace AC 7.5ha, Crémant d'Alsace 1.5ha. 70,000 bottles. VP-R*
Specialities from this small producer include *Grand Cru* Altenberg de Wolxheim Riesling and Gewürztraminer, Riesling Rothstein from the exclusivity of Clos Philippe Gras and a range of three wines under the Horn de Wolxheim name made from Klevner, Tokay-Pinot Gris and Pinot Noir. The family has had vineyards here since 1777. *Open: Mon–Sun 9am–7pm.*

Cave Vinicole d'Obernai Divinal
30 Rue du Général Leclerc, 67210 Obernai.
Vineyards owned: Alsace AC 800ha. 6 million bottles. Coop.
A modern cooperative founded in 1962, using stainless steel and making a full range of Alsace wines. Brand names include Clos Ste-Odile and Divinal. It also makes a Crémant d'Alsace called Fritz Kobus. *Open: By appointment only.*

Cave Vinicole d'Orschwiller
67600 Orschwiller.
Vineyards owned: **Grand Cru,** *Alsace AC and Crémant d'Alsace 110ha. 1.5 million bottles. Coop (141 members).*
This cooperative produces the full range of varietal wines from vineyards around Sélestat and Ribeauvillé. It has two labels, Moenchenbornes and the rather better Les Faîtières. Quality is good generally, and the wines are fresh, fruity and light in style.
Open: Mon–Sun 8am–noon, 1–6pm, by appointment.

Domaine Ostertag
87 Rue Finkwiller, 67680 Epfig.
Vineyards owned: **Grand Cru Muenchberg and Alsace AC** *10ha. 70,000 bottles. VP-R*
A small firm producing high-quality wine, making a play on its name (which means Easter Day) by incorporating a paschal lamb on the label. It makes the full range of varietals but the finest wine is the Riesling Muenchberg which is well balanced, green, steely and full. A small amount of Gewürztraminer is made in good years and a Crémant d'Alsace is also produced.
Open: By appointment only.

Schmitt
35 Rue des Vosges, 67310 Bergbieten.
Vineyards owned: **Grand Cru Altenberg de Bergbieten 2.2ha,** *Alsace AC 5.3ha. 70,000 bottles. VP-R*

A small vineyard with some very fine Rieslings: *Grand Cru* Altenberg de Bergbieten, Glintzberg Riesling and Riesling from old vines. *Open: By appointment only.*

Albert Seltz
21 Rue Principale, 67140 Mittelbergheim. Vineyards owned: Grand Cru *and Alsace AC 10ha. 100,000 bottles. VP-R*

This firm's Zotzenberg vineyard produces one of the best Alsace Sylvaners I have tasted. It has a small planting of Riesling in the Brandluft vineyard, but the *Grand Cru* wine is all Gewürztraminer. Brand names are Alsace Seltz and Pierre Seltz.
Open: Mon–Fri; weekends by appointment.

Domaine Siffert
16 Route du Vin, 67600 Orschwiller.
Vineyards owned: Grand Cru Praelatenberg *1.2ha, Alsace AC 6ha. 82,000 bottles. VP-R*

An old-established (1792) family holding which specialises in Riesling and Gewürztraminer. All the wine is matured in old wood for three months. The firm makes Gewürztraminer *Vendange Tardive* in good years. *Open: By appointment only.*

Charles Wantz
36 Rue St-Marc, 67140 Barr. Vineyards owned: Alsace AC 20ha. 1.5 million bottles. VP-R and N

A large-scale producer making quantities of well-priced wines and one or two gems: *Grand Cru* Riesling Wiebelsberg, Klevener de Heiligenstein and a range which has been given the Sigillé award. It makes a non-AC sparkling wine under the Goldlinger label.
Open: Mon–Fri 8am–noon, 1.30–6pm; and Sat morning.

Alsace Willm
BP 13, 32 Rue du Docteur Sultzer, 67140 Barr.
Vineyards owned: Grand Cru Kirchberg *3ha, Alsace AC 17ha. 900,000 bottles. VP-R and N*

The top wines from this medium-sized *négociant* firm are vinified in wood, while the standard range goes through stainless steel and early bottling. Apart from the usual range, labelled Alsace Willm, it makes a Riesling Kirchberg and a Gewürztraminer from Clos Gaensbroennel. The *réserve* wines are called Cuvée Émile Willm. It also produces a range of Crémant d'Alsace including Crémant Prestige from *réserve* wines. The cooperative of Eguisheim has bought an interest in the firm.
Open: Mon–Thurs 8am–noon, 2–6pm; Fri until 5pm.

A Zimmermann et Fils
3 Grand Rue, 67600 Orschwiller.
Vineyards owned: Alsace AC 14ha. 126,000 bottles. VP-R

The vineyard, on the slopes of the Haut Koenigsbourg château, has been in the Zimmermann family since 1693. Emphasis is on Riesling, Gewürztraminer and Tokay-Pinot Gris, and methods used are traditional. *Open: By appointment only.*

Haut-Rhin Producers

Les Caves Jean-Baptiste Adam

5 Rue de l'Aigle, 68770 Ammerschwihr. Vineyards owned:
Grand Cru *and Alsace AC 14ha. 800,000 bottles. VP-R and N*
This large merchant house has been in existence since 1614 and is
now the largest producer in Ammerschwihr. Its small vineyard
holding includes some land in the Kaefferkopf vineyard (the
most famous in the village), from which it makes Riesling and
Gewürztraminer Cuvée Jean Baptiste, which is a speciality of the
house. The *Grand Cru* holding is in the Sommerberg vineyard.
The firm mixes modern and traditional techniques to produce a
range of rich, particularly fruity wines.
Open: Mon–Sat 8am–noon, 2–6pm.

Lucien Albrecht

68500 Orschwihr.
The biggest domaine in Orschwihr, in existence since 1770. The
wines, especially Riesling and Gewürztraminer, are often of
high quality. *Grand Cru* wines such as the *Grand Cru* Riesling
Pfingstberg can age gracefully for many years. Of the less
expensive wines, the Riesling Himmelreich has excellent zest.
Gewürztraminers include the Cuvée Martine, named after one of
the daughters of the family.

Domaine Barmès-Buecher

30 Rue Ste-Gertrude, 68920 Wettolsheim.
Vineyards owned: Grand Cru Hengst *and* Steingrubler 1.9ha,
Alsace AC *12.5ha. 75,000 bottles. VP-R*
A small-scale producer whose best wines come from Riesling
vines growing in *Grand Cru* Hengst and Gewürztraminer from
Steingrubler. He also makes a Tokay-Pinot Gris from Herrenweg,
as well as a Crémant d'Alsace. The style is traditional, although
vinification is now in stainless steel.
Open: Mon–Sat 9am–noon, 2–7pm (appointments preferred).

Caves Vinicole de Beblenheim et Environs

Rue de Hoen, 68980 Beblenheim.
Vineyards owned: Grand Cru *and Alsace AC 400ha. 4 million*
bottles. Coop (200 members).
Newly installed modern equipment at this large cooperative
produces the usual range of varietal wines, which are sold under
the Baron de Hoen brand, including some *Grands Crus* from the
Sonnenglanz vineyard. The standard is average, and the wines
are drunk with pleasure but without too much seriousness.
Open: Mon–Sat 8am–noon, 2–6pm; Sun 10am–noon, 2.30–7pm.

J Becker

4 Route d'Ostheim, Zellenberg, 68340 Riquewihr.
Vineyards owned: Grand Cru *and Alsace AC 30ha.*
280,000 bottles. VP-R and N
One-third of the production at this firm is from its own vineyards,

two-thirds is from bought-in grapes and wine. Wines tend to a dry style and the firm is keen to produce wines that age well. In recent years, particularly since the '88 vintage, its wines have reached a new level of quality. It vinifies grapes from its own vineyards separately and makes quite a range of single-vineyard wines as well as the generic varietals. The brand names are J Becker and Gaston Beck. *Open: (Summer) Mon–Sun 8am–noon, 2–6pm. (winter) Mon–Fri 8am–noon, 1.15–5.15pm and Sat morning.*

Les Caves de Bennwihr

3 Avenue de Général de Gaulle, 68630 Bennwihr. Vineyards owned: Alsace AC 350ha. 3 million bottles. Coop (220 members).
Bennwihr's vineyards were devastated in World War II; the cooperative took over the replanting and now nearly every grower in the village is a member. It has modern equipment that allows them to make clean, simple wines which can be very pleasant to drink. They are sold under the Bennwihr name.
Open: Mon–Fri 8am–noon, 2–6pm; July and August Mon–Fri 8am–7pm; Sat/Sun 9am–noon, 2–6pm.

Léon Beyer

2 Rue de la Première Armée, 68420 Eguisheim. Vineyards owned: Alsace AC 20ha. 840,000 bottles. VP-R and N
A most respected firm which dates back to 1580, making it one of the oldest in Alsace. The usual range of Alsace varietals is made with the top wines being Riesling Cuvée des Écaillers and Cuvée Particulière and Gewürztraminer Cuvée des Comtes d'Eguisheim, for which Eguisheim is noted. This is one of the few large producers that remains opposed to the concept of *Grand Cru*. *Open: July and Aug Mon–Sun 10am–noon, 2–7pm; or by appointment.*

Paul Blanck et Fils

32 Grand-Rue, Kientzheim, 68240 Kayserberg. Vineyards owned: 25ha. 183,000 bottles. VP-R and N
This firm operates both as *négociant* and as *viticulteur* for its own domaine. It owns a portion of the *Grand Cru* Schlossberg from which it produces a Riesling; other parts of the production include Gewürztraminer from Furstentum and Riesling from Patergarten. It specialises in Tokay-Pinot Gris (a Comte de Lupfen is reputed to have brought the vine from Hungary, and his is a brand name they use). The *négociant* side of their business goes under the name of Blanck Frères. *Open: Mon–Sat 9am–noon, 1.30–6.30pm.*

Albert Boxler et Fils

78 Rue des Trois-Épuis, 68230 Niedermorschwihr. Vineyards owned: Grand Cru and Alsace AC 9.5ha. 70,000 bottles. VP-R
One of the more exciting producers in Alsace, capable of making great wines from his vineyard holdings in *Grand Cru* Brand (Riesling and Tokay-Pinot Gris) and from the *Grand Cru* Sommerberg (Riesling). His style is strong on rich fruit, which seems to lend itself to ageing.
Open: By appointment only.

Paul Buecher et Fils

15 Rue Ste-Gertrude, Wettolsheim, 68000 Colmar.
Vineyards owned: Grand Cru, Alsace AC and Crémant
d'Alsace 25ha. 185,000 bottles. VP-R
This firm owns vineyards in eight communes which allows it
the possibility of producing blends which are very typical of
Alsace. The *Grand Cru* wine comes from the Hengst vineyard in
Wintzenheim. All the wines are vinified in wood and then go into
stainless steel. *Open: Mon–Sun 8am–noon, 2-6pm.*

Domaine Joseph Cattin et ses Fils

12 Rue Roger-Frémeaux, 68420 Voegtlinshoffen. Vineyards
owned: Grand Cru *and Alsace AC 27ha. 240,000 bottles. VP-R*
Joseph, or Jacques, Cattin makes a serious but elegant range
of wines from a good-sized vineyard holding which includes
Gewürztraminer in the *Grand Cru* Hatschbourg. A new ageing
cellar was constructed recently, but techniques continue to make
the best of the traditional, half the wine being matured in wood
and half in stainless steel. *Open: Mon–Sun 8am–noon, 2-6pm.*

Théo Cattin

68420 Voegtlinshoffen. Vineyards owned: Grand Cru *and*
Alsace AC 16.7ha. 180,000 bottles. VP-R and N
A cousin of Jacques Cattin, Théo Cattin makes wine in the classic
style with rich Riesling from *Grand Cru* Hatschbourg and ripe
Gewürztraminer from *lieu dit* Bollenberg. Pinot Noir is made as
well as Pinot Blanc which is produced slightly off dry. The Cattin
family has been in Voegtlinshoffen since the 17th century.
Open: By appointment only.

Marcel Deiss

15 Route du Vin, 68750 Bergheim. Vineyards owned: Grand
Cru Altenberg de Bergheim 2.5ha, *Grand Cru* Schoenenbourg
0.7ha, Alsace AC 16.8ha. 150,000 bottles. VP-R
One of the stars of the Alsace wine scene, Jean-Michel Deiss
continues to make wonderful wine. His vineyards help – two plots
from *Grand Cru* land and fine sites elsewhere, particularly in
Bergheim – and *terroir* is very important to his view of winemaking. Perhaps his finest wines are from his Riesling vines, of
which he has seven hectares. *Open: By appointment only.*

Dopff 'Au Moulin'

2 Avenue J-Preiss, 68340 Riquewihr. Vineyards owned: Grand
Cru 12.3ha, Alsace AC 50ha. 2.4 million bottles. *VP-R and N*
Seventy-five percent of the firm's grapes are bought in from 600
growers. Production is on a large scale, covering the complete
varietal range plus some *Grand Cru* wines from Brand in
Turckheim and Sporen and Schoenenbourg in Riquewihr. The firm
pioneered Crémant d'Alsace, and for many years was the only
major producer. Today its Cuvée Bartholdi and Brut Sauvage are
among the very best sparkling wines made in Alsace. Most Alsace
wine drinkers will have enjoyed bottles from this firm. The 'Au

Moulin' was added to their name to avoid confusion with Dopff et Irion (*see below*). The families are related but there are no business connections. *Open: Mon–Sun 9am–noon, 2–6pm.*

Dopff et Irion (Château de Riquewihr)

68340 Riquewihr. Vineyards owned: **Grand Cru** *and Alsace AC 31ha. 200,000 bottles. VP-R and N*

The largest producer in Riquewihr, whose old premises occupy one side of the courtyard behind the Hôtel de Ville with an immense warehouse and bottling facilities on the edge of the village. Most of the production is in stainless steel, and pressing is effected with modern pneumatic presses rather than the more common Vaslin press. The wines are highly enjoyable considering the scale of the operations, and I particularly like the wines from the firm's own estates – Riesling Les Murailles, Gewürztraminer Les Sorcières, Muscat Les Amandiers and Tokay-Pinot Gris Les Maquisards. The style is light and fresh, but some *Vendange Tardive* and *Sélection des Grains Nobles* wines are also made. *Open: April 1–Nov 15; by appointment in winter.*

Cave Vinicole d'Eguisheim

6 Grand Rue, 68420 Eguisheim. Vineyards owned: **Grand Cru** *and Alsace AC 1,200ha. 14 million bottles. Coop (850 members).*

The largest cooperative in Alsace, drawing its grapes from nine communes surrounding Eguisheim. In addition it bottles wine for the cooperatives at Dambach-la-Ville and Cave Vinicole du Vieil Armand. Under the brand name Wolfberger it makes a full range of wines, from standard quality to special *cuvées*. *Grand Cru* wines come from Hengst, Eichberg, Steingrubler, Hatschbourg, Ollwiller, Spiegel and Pfersigberg vineyards.

Open: Mon–Sat 8am–noon, 2–6pm; Sun 10am–noon.

Henri Ehrhart

2 Rue du Romarin, 68770 Ammerschwihr.
Vineyards owned: Alsace AC 6ha. 360,000 bottles. VP-R and N

A producer whose strength lies in his good-quality generic Alsace wines, made with consistency of style and ripe fruit. Riesling and Tokay-Pinot Gris are his best styles, and his Riesling *Grand Cru* Kaefferkopf is probably his finest wine. Some of his wines are sold under the Domaine Ehrhart label.

Open: By appointment only.

Paul Ginglinger

8 Place Charles de Gaulle, 68420 Eguisheim. Vineyards owned: **Grand Cru** *and Alsace AC 9ha. 80,000 bottles. VP-R*

This small firm, which dates back to 1636, is best known for its light, dry wines. It uses wood for much of the vinification and for maturing. The largest production is of Riesling, but it also makes the usual range of varietal wines. Also produced are a Crémant d'Alsace and *Vendange Tardive* wines. *Grand Cru* wines come from the Eichberg and Pfersigberg vineyards in Eguisheim.

Open: Mon–Sat, morning and afternoon.

Hugel et Fils

3 Rue de la Première Armée, 68340 Riquewihr. Vineyards owned: Grand Cru *Sporen 8ha,* Grand Cru *Schoenenbourg 3.8ha, Alsace AC 13.2ha. 1.2 million bottles. VP-R and N*

The most famous name in Alsace wine, the Hugel firm, founded in 1639, lives up to its reputation. The style is for full, rich wines, but the standard range of high-quality varietals is appealingly fresh and clean. The finest wines are matured in wood, but Hugel also uses stainless steel and as few chemicals as possible. The firm pioneered the idea of late-harvest wines – the *Vendange Tardive* and *Sélection des Grains Nobles* – and its superb examples are never cloyingly sweet. Recently it has been producing quite the best red Pinot Noir wine in Alsace. The range consists of three levels: standard varietals, Cuvée Tradition and Réserve Personnelle, topped up by the late-harvest wines. A new wine, Gentil Hugel, a blend of Sylvaner with a little Riesling, Gewürztraminer and Muscat, revives a tradition of superior blended wines. *Open: Visits by appointment only, Mon–Fri 9am–noon, 2–6pm. Shop open April–Nov 9am–noon, 1.30–6.30pm.*

Cave Coopérative d'Ingersheim

45 Rue de la République, 68040 Ingersheim.
Vineyards owned: Grand Cru *and Alsace AC 270ha. 3 million bottles. Coop (210 members).*

A full range of varietals in a simple, attractive, drinkable style. More serious wines include Gewürztraminer from Letzenberg and Florimont vineyards, Riesling from Steinweg vineyard and Riesling *Grand Cru* Sommerberg. The brand name is Jean Geiler.
Open: April–Dec Mon–Sun 8am–noon, 2–7pm; Jan–March 8am–noon, 1.30–5pm and Sat morning.

Jos Meyer

75 Rue Clémenceau, 68920 Wintzenheim. Vineyards owned: Grand Cru *and Alsace AC 31ha. 300,000 bottles. VP-R and N*

Vineyards in Turckheim and Wintzenheim (including some in *Grand Cru* Hengst) form the core of this grower-*négociant* business. One of the specialities is Pinot Blanc, but the Rieslings are good, especially Les Pierrets, as is the Gewürztraminer Les Archenets. The Hengst vineyard produces fine Riesling and Gewürztraminer including some *Vendange Tardive*. The wines are often dry and elegant although some of the top examples have a fuller style. *Open: Mon–Fri 8am–noon, 2–6pm; Sat 8am–noon.*

Cave Vinicole de Kientzheim-Kaysersberg

10 Rue des Vieux Moulins, 68240 Kientzheim.
Vineyards owned: Grand Cru *16ha, Alsace AC 148ha, Crémant d'Alsace 5ha. 1.7 million bottles. Coop (150 members).*

All the Alsace varietals are used, including some from the Schlossberg, Kaefferkopf and Altenberg de Bergheim *Grands Crus*. Crémant d'Alsace is also produced.
Open: Mon–Thurs 8am–noon, 2–6pm; Fri 8am–noon, 2–5pm; in summer also open Sat and Sun 10am–noon, 2–6pm.

André Kientzler

50 Route de Bergheim, 68150 Ribeauvillé.
Vineyards owned: **Grands Crus** *Geisberg, Kirchberg and Osterberg 3.7ha, Alsace AC 6.3ha. 70,000 bottles. VP-R*
Riesling and Gewürztraminer from his *Grand Cru* sites in Geisberg and Osterberg are André Keintzler's finest wines, but equally impressive in their way are his Chasselas and Auxerrois. He is also proud of his Tokay-Pinot Gris Réserve Particulière and *Sélection des Grains Nobles* from Gewürztraminer, Riesling and Tokay-Pinot Gris. He vinifies in wood which gives his wines an extra richness and character. *Open: Appointments preferred.*

Kuentz-Bas

14 Route du Vin, Husseren-les-Châteaux, 68420 Herrlisheim.
Vineyards owned: **Grand Cru** *2.5ha, Alsace AC 10ha, Crémant d'Alsace 1ha. 350,000 bottles. VP-R and N*
A medium-sized firm producing excellent wines. There are two ranges: Cuvée Tradition from bought-in grapes, and Réserve Personnelle from its own vineyards. *Vendange Tardive* wines are called Cuvée Caroline. In recent years the firm has increased the number of wines so as to make smaller quantities of each *cuvée*. I have particularly enjoyed the Muscat and the Tokay-Pinot Gris Réserve Personnelle, but all the wines are of high quality and are elegantly restrained.
Open: Mon–Sat 9am–noon, 1–6pm; winter (on Sat) by appointment.

Seppi Landmann

20 Rue de la Vallée, 68570 Soultzmatt.
Vineyards owned: **Grand Cru** *Zinnkoepflé 2ha, Alsace AC 4ha, Crémant d'Alsace 1ha. 60,000 bottles. VP-R*
A range whose quality is best expressed in the drier styles such as Riesling and Gewürztraminer from *Grand Cru* Zinnkoepflé as well as the generic range of Vallée Noble wines which includes a very dry Muscat. The Crémant d'Alsace is particularly good. Monsieur Landmann's cellars date back to 1574. He recently withdrew from the local cooperative and set up on his own.
Open: Mon–Sun 9am–8pm, by appointment.

Gustave Lorentz

35 Grand Rue, 68750 Bergheim. Vineyards owned: **Grand Cru** *Altenberg de Bergheim and* **Grand Cru** *Kanzlerberg 13.5ha, Alsace AC 17ha. 1.8 million bottles. VP-R and N*
A large-scale firm which manages to retain high quality in a wide range of wines including *Vendange Tardive* and *Sélection des Grains Nobles*. It uses some modern equipment in the cellars, with temperature-controlled fermentation, and uses only the natural yeast from the grapes because it "gives a natural quality to the wine". The vineyards are mainly in Bergheim, but the firm also buys from growers in Ribeauvillé and Bergheim. Better wines are matured in wood, lesser ones in glass-lined tanks. *Grand Cru* wines come from the Altenberg de Bergheim and Kanzlerberg vineyards. *Open: Mon–Fri 8am–noon, 2–5pm; Sat 9am–noon.*

Domaine Albert Mann

13 Rue du Château, 68920 Wettolsheim. Vineyards owned:
Grands Crus Hengst, Schlossberg, Steingrubler, Furstentum,
Pfersigberg 4ha, Alsace AC 11ha. 110,000 bottles. VP-R

A family firm, now run by the Barthèlme brothers who are related
by marriage to the Mann family. The firm uses temperature-
controlled stainless steel and believes in minimum intervention
in the winemaking to produce wines that are both rich and full of
character. The Pinot Blanc is particularly good of its type, as is a
fruity Pinot Noir. Best, however, are the Gewürztraminers, both
the generic and that from *Grand Cru* Hengst. *Open: Mon–Sat
8am–noon, 1.30–6.30pm; Sun by appointment.*

Muré (Clos St-Landelin)

68250 Rouffach. Vineyards owned: Grand Cru *Vorbourg Clos
St-Landelin 16ha, Alsace AC 25ha, Crémant d'Alsace 10ha.
400,000 bottles. VP-R and N*

The land in the Clos St-Landelin *Grand Cru* Vorbourg vineyard is
treated without chemicals, and the wine vinified traditionally in
wood. This vineyard produces about 140,000 bottles a year.
Grand Cru varietals are Riesling, Tokay-Pinot Gris, Muscat and
Gewürztraminer. Standard Alsace AC wines include the full range
of varietals. Since 1982 it has also made a Crémant d'Alsace. All the
wines tend to be full and soft and the *Grand Cru* wines often age
particularly well. *Open: Mon–Sat 8am–7pm.*

Cave Vinicole de Pfaffenheim

5 Rue du Chai, 68250 Pfaffenheim.
Vineyards owned: Grands Crus Steinert 39ha, Goldert 35ha,
and Hatschbourg 6ha, Alsace AC 110ha. 2.5 million bottles.
Coop (220 members).

A well-run modern cooperative, using stainless steel and making
wines that are attractive when young. It makes a full range,
but the largest production is of Sylvaner, Pinot Blanc and
Gewürztraminer. The *Grand Cru* Goldert wine is Gewürztraminer.
Company names used are Hartenberger, J Hornstein and Ernest
Wein, plus a range of *cuvée* names including Cuvée Rabelais for a
Tokay-Pinot Gris, Cuvée des Dominicans for a particularly good
Pinot Noir and Cuvée Lafayette for a Chasselas.
*Open: Beginning of May to end Oct: Mon–Fri 8am–7pm; Sat 8am–
noon, 2–6pm; Sun 10am–noon, 2–6pm. Beginning of Nov to end April:
Mon–Sat 8am–noon, 2–6pm; Sun 10am–noon, 2–6pm.*

Preiss-Zimmer

42 Rue du Général de Gaulle, 68340 Riquewihr.
Vineyards owned: Alsace AC 9ha. 120,000 bottles. VP-R

Now owned by the Cave Coopérative of Turckheim, the firm of
Preiss-Zimmer continues to make wine from vineyards still
owned by the Zimmer family. Gewürztraminer and Riesling are
both good. The Zimmers also own the shop where their wines are
sold, as well as a restaurant in Riquewihr.
Open: (shop only) Mon–Sat 9am–noon, 2–6pm.

Cave Coopérative de Ribeauvillé et Environs
2 Route de Colmar, 68150 Ribeauvillé. Vineyards owned:
Alsace AC 175ha. 2 million bottles. Coop (90 members).
Pinot Blanc, Riesling and Sylvaner are the main wines from what
is probably the oldest cooperative in France, founded in 1895. The
modern equipment produces some good, if middle-of-the-road,
wines. The small Clos de Zahnacker (planted with Riesling,
Gewürztraminer and Tokay-Pinot Gris) produces the best. Brand
names used include Martin Zahn, Traber, Medaillon and
Armoires. The Crémant d'Alsace is called Giersberger. *Open:*
Mon-Sat 9am-noon, 2-5.30pm; Oct-March by appointment only.

Rolly Gassmann
1-2 Rue de l'Église, Rorschwihr, 68590 St-Hippolyte.
Vineyards owned: Alsace AC 17ha. 150,000 bottles. VP-R
Louis Gassmann and his wife Marie-Thérèse (née Rolly) have built
up an enviable reputation for high-quality wines, including the
Gewürztraminer Kappelweg, Riesling Silberberg, the Tokay-Pinot
Gris Réserve and a ripely aromatic Pinot Blanc. Louis Gassmann
likes to vinify the grapes from his different vineyards separately in
order to produce wines with strong individual characteristics.
Open: by appointment only.

Edgard Schaller et Fils
1 Rue du Château, 68630 Mittelwihr.
Vineyards owned: Grand Cru Mandelberg 0.4ha, Alsace AC
3.1ha, Crémant d'Alsace 3ha. 85,000 bottles. VP-R
One of the many ancient family firms, founded in 1609. Much of
the production is of Crémant, but it also makes a full range of
varietals. The house style is for very dry, almost austere wines
which benefit from ageing. *Open: 9am-7pm.*

André Scherer
12 Route du Vin, Husseren-les-Châteaux, 68420 Herrlisheim.
Vineyards owned: Grands Crus Eichberg and Pfersigberg,
Alsace AC 8ha. 120,000 bottles. VP-R and N
A wide range is produced by this firm. Half the wines come from
its own vineyards, half from grapes which are bought locally. It
makes the usual range of varietals and *Grand Cru* wine from the
Eichberg vineyard of Eguisheim. Brand names include Cuvée
Jean-Baptiste and Cuvée Blanche. One of the best varietals is the
Tokay-Pinot Gris, and André Scherer is one of the rare Alsace
producers whose red Pinot Noir is full-bodied and has good colour.
Open: Mon-Sun 9am-7pm, by appointment only.

Charles Schléret
1-3 Route d'Ingersheim, 68230 Turckheim.
Having established a modern cellar in Turckheim this grower
produces a range of true-to-type varietal wines. He is best known
for his Tokay-Pinot Gris, Gewürztraminer and Pinot Noir, from
which he gets more colour than usual by means of heated fermentation vats. *Open: 8am-noon, 1.30-7pm, by appointment only.*

Domaines Schlumberger

100 Rue Théodore Deck, 68500 Guebwiller. Vineyards owned:
Grand Cru 60ha, Alsace AC 80ha. 1 million bottles. *VP-R*
Schlumberger dominates the village of Guebwiller, controlling
much of the vineyard area. Being the largest private vineyard
owner in Alsace, the firm is able to develop new techniques of
large-scale planting in horizontal rows on the steep slopes above
Guebwiller, which contrasts with the normal Alsace method of
vines growing up single stakes. It makes *Grand Cru* wines from
the Kitterlé, Kessler, Spiegel and Saering vineyards. The wines
can be variable but the Riesling Kitterlé and Gewürztraminer
Cuvée Christine Schlumberger are both good.
Open: By appointment only.

Domaine Schoffit

27 Rue des Aubépines, 68000 Colmar. VP-R
One of the rising stars of Alsace, Bernard Schoffit makes Riesling,
Gewürztraminer and Tokay-Pinot Gris from holdings in *Grand
Cru* Rangen Clos St-Théobald and Chasselas from the Harth
vineyard in Colmar. His style is characterised by intense flavours,
enhanced by very low yields. *Open: By appointment only.*

Domaine Sick-Dreyer

*17 Route de Kientzheim, 68770 Ammerschwihr. Vineyards
owned:* **Grand Cru *and* Alsace AC 13ha. 80,000 bottles.** *VP-R*
The finest wine from this small estate is the Gewürztraminer
from its holding on the famous Kaefferkopf vineyard. It makes
the full range of varietals to a good quality level, using a mix of
traditional and modern techniques and vinifying 90 percent of
the wine in wood. Most of the vineyards are in Ammerschwihr
but it also owns land in Eguisheim, Katzenthal and Sigolsheim.
Open: Mon-Fri 8.30–11.30am, 2–6pm; Sat 8.30–11.30am, 2–5pm.

Société Coopérative Vinicole de Sigolsheim et Environs

12 Rue St-Jacques, Sigolsheim, 68240 Kaysersberg.
Vineyards owned: **Grand Cru 31.5ha, Alsace AC 248ha.**
3 million bottles. *Coop (230 members).*
One of the largest cooperatives in Alsace, with modern equip-
ment and a wide range of quality wines. It produces wines from
the *Grand Cru* Mambourg and the Vogelgarten vineyards, plus
Vendange Tardive and *Sélection des Grains Nobles* – all from
Gewürztraminer. The brand names used include Comte de Sigold
for Crémant d'Alsace. *Open: Mon-Fri 8–10.30am, 2–4.30pm; on
Sun during summer; appointments preferred for groups.*

Louis Sipp

5 Grand'Rue, 68150 Ribeauvillé. Vineyards owned: **Grand Cru**
Kirchberg de Ribeauvillé 2.2ha, Osterberg 1.8ha, Alsace AC
27ha. 1.2 million bottles. *VP-R and N*
A firm that has concentrated on producing commercial wines,
both from its vineyard holdings and from bought-in grapes. The
best wines, which can sometimes age well, are from Riesling and

Gewürztraminer. The firm vinifies grapes from its holding in the *Grand Cru* Kirchberg de Ribeauvillé separately, but otherwise does not identify the estate wines. *Open: By appointment only.*

Pierre Sparr et ses Fils

2 Rue de la Première Armée Française, 68240 Sigolsheim.
Vineyards owned: **Grand Cru** *and Alsace AC 77ha.*
855,000 bottles. VP-R and N

This firm of *négociants* buys in three-quarters of its requirements from other growers in the Sigolsheim and Kaysersberg area. The firm's own vineyards are in Sigolsheim (including *Grand Cru* Mambourg), Kientzheim and Turckheim (including *Grand Cru* Brand). Brand names used include Cuvée K, for a blend of Gewürztraminer and Tokay-Pinot Gris from the Kaefferkopf vineyard, Symphonie for a blend of Riesling, Tokay-Pinot Gris, Pinot Blanc and Gewürztraminer, and Diamant d'Alsace (for Pinot Blanc). It makes *Vendange Tardive* from Tokay-Pinot Gris and *Sélection des Grains Nobles* from Gewürztraminer. *Open: Mon–Thurs 8am–noon, 2–6pm; Fri 8am–noon, 2–5pm; Sat 8am–noon.*

F E Trimbach

68150 Ribeauvillé.
Vineyards owned: Alsace Grand Cru and Alsace AC 28ha.
750,000 bottles. VP-R and N

One of the oldest firms in Alsace (founded in 1626), with a long tradition of making fine wines both as a merchant house and vineyard owner. Its Riesling from the Clos Ste-Hune vineyard is often considered the greatest Riesling in Alsace. The firm makes three quality levels: standard, Réserve and Réserve Personnelle. Its own vineyards include land in Ribeauvillé, Hunawihr, Bergheim, Riquewihr and Mittelwihr. Top *cuvées* are of Clos Ste-Hune, Frédéric Émil and Seigneurs de Ribeaupierre.
Open: By appointment only.

Cave Coopérative de Turckheim

68230 Turckheim.
Vineyards owned: **Grand Cru** *20ha, Alsace AC 275ha, Crémant d'Alsace 15ha. 3 million bottles. Coop (230 members).*

One of the most go-ahead cooperatives in Alsace, it has had great success with its well-priced wines which are widely available in the export markets. Wines such as the Pinot Blanc and Gewürztraminer regularly win awards. The cellars of the cooperative are highly modern with rows of stainless-steel tanks and rely on the latest computer technology.
Open: Mon–Sat 8am–noon, 2–6pm; Sun 10am–noon, 3–6pm.

Domaine Weinbach

68240 Kaysersberg.
Vineyards owned: Alsace AC 25ha. 180,000 bottles. VP-R

Madame Théo Faller and her children, who run the Domaine Weinbach estate (also known as the Clos des Capucins), have established an enviable reputation for top-quality Alsace wines.

The firm has stayed faithful to traditional methods, vinifying in wood and avoiding the centrifuging which so many Alsace producers seem to favour. The resulting wines are full-bodied yet perfectly characteristic. The grapes are harvested late to give the wines considerable ageing potential. Cuvée Théo is the best Riesling from this estate.
Open: By appointment only.

Cave Coopérative Vinicole de Westhalten

52 Rue de Soultzmatt, 68250 Westhalten.
Vineyards owned: Grand Cru *and Alsace AC 270ha. 3 million bottles. Coop (220 members).*

This cooperative now controls the *négociant* firm of Alfred Heim, also based in Westhalten. It makes a wide range of wines at different levels of quality, including *Grand Cru* wine from the Vorbourg and Zinnkoepflé vineyards. The quality of some of the more basic wines is disappointing, but some in the top ranges are good, especially Muscat d'Alsace (Westhalten is in a sheltered side valley which is advantageous for the ripening of Muscat) and Gewürztraminer. The Heim wines are still sold under separate labels. *Open: Mon–Sat 8am–noon, 2–6pm.*

Maison Wiederhirn

7 Rue du Cheval, 68340 Riquewihr. Vineyards owned: Grands Crus *Schoenenbourg 0.8ha, Sporen 0.3ha and Mandelberg 0.25ha, Alsace AC 4.1ha. 47,500 bottles. VP-R*

High-quality but small-scale producer who has a small holding in the Schoenenbourg and Sporen vineyards. His methods are traditional, with much wood in evidence in his small cellar. Monsieur Wiederhirn's wines age well – especially his Riesling and Tokay-Pinot Gris – perhaps because of their richness and slight sweetness. He makes small quantities of Gewürztraminer *Vendange Tardive. Open: Mon–Sat, by appointment only.*

Domaine Zind-Humbrecht

Route de Colmar, 68230 Turckheim.
Vineyards owned: Grands Crus *Rangen 5.3ha, Goldert 0.8ha, Brand 1.6ha and Hengst 1.4ha, Alsace AC 32.8ha. 250,000 bottles. VP-R*

For Alsace, this is a large vineyard holding, now producing some of the region's best wines thanks to the inspired partnership between father Leonard and son Olivier Humbrecht. Production includes 30 percent Riesling and 34 percent Gewürztraminer, but as well as the full range of varietals. From brand new cellars just outside Turckheim, which would look more at home in California than Alsace, the firm bottles its wines *sur lie*, without filtration, which gives them extra body and considerable depth of flavour. The *Grand Cru* wines come from Brand in Turckheim, Goldert in Gueberschwihr, Hengst in Wintzenheim and Rangen in Thann – the southernmost vineyard in Alsace, which Zind-Humbrecht has effectively resurrected in recent years.
Open: Mon–Fri 9am–noon, 2–6pm

Jura

The Jura vineyard is a mere shadow of its former self. As is the case with so many out-of-the-way areas, the phylloxera epidemic of the last century is to blame for the decline. But traditions have survived in this remote corner of France and at least two remarkable wines are still made here. Today new ideas are reviving old fortunes. The vineyard area of 1,450 hectares is on the eastern slopes of the Saône Valley, facing the Burgundian Côte d'Or. The vines grow at heights of between 250 and 500 metres above sea level in wooded valleys and between half-timbered towns. The Burgundian influence is here in some of the grape varieties – Chardonnay and Pinot Noir – but there is also a flourishing set of local grapes which are still commonly planted.

Red, white, rosé and sparkling wines are all made in the Jura. Some of the rosé is known as *vin gris*, on account of the pale pink colour achieved before fermentation. Little Jura wine – apart from *vin jaune* (*see below*) – is seen outside the area. Methods tend to be old-fashioned, although the main producer of the region (Henri Maire) has an ultra-modern plant. Traditionally, the wines are aged for considerable periods, which can make them too oxidised for modern tastes. Sparkling wine is increasing in popularity.

Red grapes include Poulsard (or Plousard), a light-coloured grape used to make rosé. Because of its paleness it can be left in contact with the must for several days, so Jura rosés tend to have great weight and are akin to the southern Rhône's Tavel. The Trousseau is used to give bite in red wines and to make a sparkling *blanc de noirs*.

Chardonnay is used to make many of the white Jura wines but the local grape, Savagnin (a type of Traminer), is used in the most unusual wines of the region. *Vin jaune* – yellow wine – is a sherry-type wine, made by ageing Savagnin in small barrels for a minimum of six years. A type of yeast – like the *flor* of Jerez – grows on the surface of the wine, producing a characteristic dry,

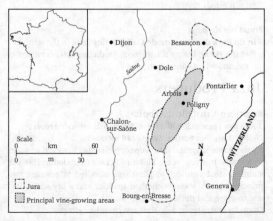

oxidised taste. The barrels are not topped up, thus allowing the *flor* to develop in the air. The wine is bottled in the traditional *clavelin* of Jura, which has a capacity of 64 centilitres (the amount left from a litre after evaporation), a long neck and sloping shoulders.

The other rare wine of the region – rarer now than *vin jaune* – is called *vin de paille*. This is a sweet wine made from grapes dried on straw (*paille*) mats until they are like raisins. The nearest equivalent is the Italian Vin Santo. Vintages: reds '82, '85, '87, '88, '89, '90, '93, '95; *vin jaune* '89, '90, '95. Whites and rosés should be drunk within two years.

The Appellations

APPELLATIONS CONTRÔLÉES

Arbois Red, dry white, rosé, *gris* and *vin jaune*.

Arbois Mousseux Sparkling wines fermented in the same bottle.

Arbois Pupillin Red, dry white and rosé from the commune of Pupillin. Slightly richer than straight Arbois.

Château-Chalon Tiny appellation making only 70,000 bottles a year but producing the best *vin jaune*.

Côtes du Jura Catch-all for red, dry white, rosé, *gris* and *vin jaune*.

Côtes du Jura Mousseux Sparkling wines.

L'Étoile White wines made from Chardonnay, Savagnin and Poulsard (vinified as white). Also *vin jaune* and *vin de paille*. Small production but good quality.

L'Étoile Mousseux Sparkling version of above, using a blend of Chardonnay and Savagnin.

VINS DE PAYS

Regional *vin de pays*

Vin de Pays de la Franche-Comté A *vin de pays* covering the Jura and Haute-Saône *départements*, using Chardonnay and Auxerrois for its whites and Pinot Noir, Pinot Gris and Gamay for the reds.

Zonal *vin de pays*

Vin de Pays des Coteaux de Coiffy A tiny zone in the southeast of the Haute-Marne *département*, producing 500 hectolitres of red and white wines each year.

Jura Producers

Fruitière Vinicole d'Arbois

2 Rue des Fossés, 39600 Arbois. Vineyards owned: Arbois 200ha. 1 million bottles. Coop (140 members).

As the name suggests, this cooperative is also involved in other fruit crops. It is one of the oldest in France (founded in 1906). A stainless-steel vinification plant was installed to produce two principal wines: a classic-method sparkler and a dry white. Red and rosé are also made.

Open: By appointment only; there is a charge for groups.

Château d'Arlay
Arlay, 39140 Bletterans. Vineyards owned: Côtes du Jura 27ha.
95,000 bottles. VP-R and N

The English King William III was, among other things, Baron d'Arlay, a title still held by the Dutch Royal family. The estate has a history stretching back to the Middle Ages and vines cover the slopes beneath its medieval castle. A 19th-century château is home to the present owner, Comte de Laguiche. Quality is important at the estate and only the free-run juice is used for the top Château d'Arlay range of red, rosé and white. Modern vinification is followed by wood-ageing (seven years for *vin jaune*). The new equipment has allowed the firm to make a fresh, lively Savagnin-based white, bottled straight after second fermentation called Fleur de Savagnin. A small quantity of top-quality *vin jaune* is made, and in '85 for the first time, some *vin de paille*. *Négociant marques* include Comte de Guichebourg, Baron de Proby and Cuvée de l'Épinette.
Open: Mon–Sat 8am–noon, 2–7pm; Sun 2–7pm.

Caves Jean Bourdy
Arlay, 39140 Bletterans. Vineyards owned: Côtes du Jura
4.5ha, Château-Chalon 0.5ha. 20,000 bottles. VP-R and N

Vin jaune and Château-Chalon are the star wines from this old-established (1781) firm. It buys in finished wine as well as making Côtes du Jura white and red from its own vineyards. A Marc de Franche-Comté is also made. A highly reliable producer. *Open: Mon–Fri 9am–noon, 2–7pm; appointments necessary for groups.*

Cave Coopérative de Château-Chalon et Côtes du Jura
39120 Voiteur. Vineyards owned: 66ha. 240,000 bottles.
Coop (69 members).

The importance of this small cooperative is that it is one of the few sources for the *vin jaune* of Château-Chalon AC. But it also makes Côtes du Jura AC white, rosé and *vin jaune*.
Open: By appointment only.

Hubert Clavelin et Fils
Le Vernois, 39120 Voiteur.
Vineyards owned: Côtes du Jura 24ha. 100,000 bottles. VP-R

The bulk of production here is of a good classic-method sparkling wine made from Chardonnay, but Monsieur Clavelin also makes Côtes du Jura white and red and *vin jaune* (from Savagnin). Methods are traditional and vinification takes place in wood.
Open: By appointment only.

Château de l'Étoile
39570 L'Étoile. Vineyards owned: 26ha. 100,000 bottles. VP-R

An ancient vineyard, records of which go back to the 13th century and which has been in the possession of the Vandelle family since 1883. The firm makes white L'Étoile from Chardonnay and a *vin jaune* from Savagnin as well as a sparkling wine and a red and rosé Côtes du Jura. *Open: Mon–Sun 8am–noon, 2–7pm.*

Grand Frères
Route de Frontenay, 39230 Passenans.
Vineyards owned: 20ha. 100,000 bottles. VP-R
A full range of Jura wines is made by this firm, from sparkling *crémant* made from Chardonnay, to the *vin de paille* and *vin jaune*. All the wines are aged in wood. The firm has a promotional arrangement with a local restaurant, Le Domaine du Revermont, which offers the perfect opportunity of tasting the wines at leisure and with food.
Open: Mon–Sun, in working hours; closed weekends in Jan and Feb.

Château Gréa
Rotalier, 39190 Beaufort. Vineyards owned: Le Clos (Rotalier) 3.3ha, Sur Laroche (Rotalier) 0.7ha, Le Chanet (Rotalier) 1.5ha, En Cury (Rotalier) 1ha. 30,000 bottles. VP-R
A small domaine which has been in the same family since 1679. The existing château dates from the 1770s. The vineyards are all in the Côtes du Jura general AC. Modern methods are used to make a clean rosé and a classic-method sparkling *brut* from Chardonnay and Pinot Noir. A fine, richer white, Le Chanet, is made from a blend of Chardonnay and Savagnin which is given three years in wood. Around 2,000 bottles of *vin jaune*, called En Cury, are made in good years. Fine *eau-de-vie* wines are also produced here.
Open: Mon–Fri 10am–12.30pm, 2–7pm; appointments preferred.

Henri Maire (Château Montfort)
39600 Arbois.
Vineyards owned: 321ha. 4.8 million bottles. VP-R and N
Henri Maire dominates Jura in a way that few producers can ever dominate larger wine producing areas. The firm has revitalised the region, and its base houses a fine collection of glasses as well as the largest stocks of *vin jaune* anywhere. The estate is located mainly around Montfort, Grange Grillard, Sorbief and La Croix d'Argis. All the Jura AC wines are made, including one of the very best *vins jaunes*, plus a number of brands (sparkling Vin Fou is the best known). *Open: By appointment only.*

Domaine Désiré Petit
Pupillin, 39600 Arbois. Vineyards owned: Pupillin 12.6ha, Arbois 1.1ha, Côtes du Jura 3.3ha. 114,000 bottles. VP-R
Modern vinification in stainless steel produces white, rosé and red wines that need little ageing. A *vin jaune* is also produced and this is aged in wood. The firm is one of the important landowners in the Arbois Pupillin AC.
Open: Mon–Sun 9am–noon, 1.30–7pm.

Fruitière Vinicole de Pupillin
Pupillin, 39600 Arbois. Vineyards owned: Arbois Pupillin 56ha. 340,000 bottles. Coop (35 members).
The cooperative keeps this tiny village alive. The bulk of production is rosé from the Poulsard grape. Red is made from Pinot

Noir, white from Chardonnay. Classic-method sparkling and rosé are made under the brand name Papillette. There are also small quantities of *vin jaune* produced.
Open: Mon–Sun 8am–noon, 2–6.30pm.

Rolet Père et Fils
Montigny-lès-Arsures, 39600 Arbois. Vineyards owned: Arbois 35ha, Côtes du Jura 20ha. 350,000 bottles. VP-R.
The second biggest producer in the Jura, this family business is run by father, two sons and a daughter. As befits the firm's size it has modern production facilities specialising in making single-variety wines which are unusual in the area. Reds include a Trousseau and a Pinot Noir, while there is a rosé from Poulsard and a white from Chardonnay which matures in new wood.
Open: Mon–Sat at shop in Arbois, opposite the town hall.

André et Mireille Tissot
Quartier Bernard, Montigny-les-Arsures, 39600 Arbois.
Vineyards owned: Montigny-les-Arsures (Arbois) 12.8ha.
140,000 bottles. VP-R.
Founded in 1962, when André Tissot cultivated a mere 0.27 hectares. Red and rosé are made from a blend of Trousseau, Poulsard and Pinot Noir, giving the red considerable depth of colour for the region. The white is 100 percent Chardonnay. All wines are aged in wood for at least 18 months and treatments are minimal. *Vin jaune* and *vin de paille* are also made. *Open: Mon–Sun.*

Domaine Jacques Tissot
39 Rue de Courcelles, 39600 Arbois. 150,000 bottles. VP-R.
The old cellars of Jacques Tissot are where Louis Pasteur made his studies of vine diseases. They have been supplemented by a brand new *chai* where Arbois red, rosé and white are made. Monsieur Tissot also makes *vin de paille* and *vin jaune*.
Open: Mon–Sat 9.15am–noon, 2–7pm.

Savoie

The Alpine vineyards of Savoie lie south of Lake Geneva. Most are set along the upper valley of the Rhône as it flows towards Lyon, in its tributary valley with the Lac du Bourget, and along the valley of the Isère southwest to Grenoble. Slopes lying at an altitude of around 300 metres above the lakes or the Rhône are the most favoured sites.

Important towns in the area include Annecy and Aix-les-Bains as well as Chambéry, which is the home of France's best vermouths. It is almost as if the wines of Savoie were designed for the après-ski parties during which they are consumed in quantity.

Both the reds and the whites are best drunk within a year of the harvest and are refreshing if undemanding wines. The sparkling wines are the only examples that leave the region in any quantity. As the vineyards of Savoie are so scattered, microclimates play an important role. The two lakes, Geneva and Bourget near Aix-les-Bains, moderate the Alpine conditions, as do the fast-moving rivers.

There is a hint of Switzerland in the wines made from the Chasselas grape on the southern shores of Lake Geneva at Crépy, and an influence from Beaujolais in the Gamay which is used to make light red wines. But there are also local grape varieties in the 1,500 hectares of vineyard. The Mondeuse makes a simple full-bodied red; the Jacquère is a widely planted white grape which makes crisp wines to be drunk young; the Altesse (or Roussette) makes soft wines, while the Bergeron (akin to the Roussanne of the southern Rhône) makes finer whites around Chambéry. The sparkling wines, made in the region of Seyssel, are a blend of Chasselas with Altesse and Molette.

Most Savoie wines need to be drunk young. Wines made from the Mondeuse grape occasionally repay keeping for a couple of years, otherwise '93, '95 and '96 were good recent vintages.

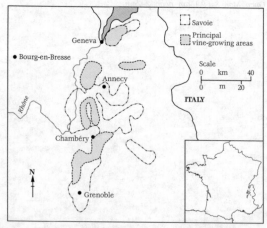

The Appellations

APPELLATIONS CONTRÔLÉES

The AC system is probably more complex than the styles of wine warrant: this is because the vineyards are so widely scattered.

Crépy Dry, slightly sparkling whites from the southern shore of Lake Geneva. The grape is the Chasselas (Swiss Fendant). Some claim they age, but the chance to prove this is rare since most are drunk young and locally.

Roussette de Savoie Dry white wines made mainly around Frangy, north of Lac du Bourget, and around Cruet in the Isère Valley. The wine is normally a blend of Roussette (or Altesse) and Chardonnay (called Petite Ste-Marie locally) with Mondeuse.

Roussette de Savoie Crus Four communes have the right to add their name to the generic Roussette de Savoie AC – Frangy, Marestel, Monterminod and Monthoux.

Seyssel Dry white wines from the commune of Seyssel on the Rhône. Only the Roussette (or Altesse) grape is permitted.

Seyssel Mousseux Classic-method sparkling wines made from the Altesse and Chasselas grapes.

Vin de Savoie Widespread AC taking in reds, dry whites and rosés. Reds and rosés are more from Mondeuse, Gamay and Pinot Noir; whites from Jacquère and Altesse with smaller amounts of Chardonnay, Aligoté and Chasselas.

Vin de Savoie Crus The 17 communes allowed to add their name to generic Vin de Savoie are: Marignan, Maurin and Ripaille (on Lake Geneva); Ayse, Charpignat, Chautagne and Jongieux (on Lac du Bourget); les Abimes, Apremont, Arbin, Chignin, Chignin-Bergeron, Cruet, Montmélian, St-Jean-de-la-Porte and Ste-Jeoire-Prieuré (south of Chambéry) and Ste-Marie d'Alloix (towards Grenoble).

Vin de Savoie Ayse Mousseux Classic-method sparkling wine made in the commune of Ayse.

Vin de Savoie Mousseux Mainly white (but also a little rosé) classic-method sparkling wine produced from other Vin de Savoie *Cru* villages.

Vin de Savoie Pétillant Lightly sparkling, sometimes sweet wines are made in the Roussette de Savoie *Cru* villages of Frangy, Marestel and Monthoux.

VINS DE PAYS

Regional *vin de pays*

The regional *vin de pays* of Comtes Rhodaniens (*see also* the Rhône) covers the whole Savoie area. The wines come from a wide range of grape varieties: Cabernet Sauvignon, Cinsaut, Syrah, Grenache and Merlot for reds; Chardonnay, Marsanne, Roussanne, Sauvignon Blanc, Viognier, Ugni Blanc, Clairette and Grenache Blanc for the whites. Of the total production, 70 percent is of red wines. There are two subzones in Savoie: Vin de Pays des Coteaux du Grésivaudan and Vin de Pays des Balmes Dauphinoises.

Zonal *vin de pays*

Vin de Pays de l'Allobrogie Mainly white wines made from
Jacquère, Chardonnay or Chasselas grapes, in a region to the
west and south of Annecy. Some reds are also made from
Gamay, Pinot Noir and Mondeuse grapes.

Savoie Producers

Canelli-Suchet
Château de la Tour de Marignan, 74140 Sciez.
Vineyards owned: Vin de Savoie 5ha. 30,000 bottles. VP-R
This family has been in Savoie for more than three centuries and
the name recalls that the area was once part of Italy. Wines are
made traditionally and organically from Chasselas grapes. The
range includes still wine aged in cask under the Marignan name
and a small amount of classic-method dry and medium-dry
sparkling wine called La Perle. *Open: Appointments preferred.*

Cave Coopérative de Chautagne
73310 Ruffieux.
Vineyards owned: Chautagne 133ha, Vin de Savoie 10ha,
Roussette de Savoie 10ha. 900,000 bottles. Coop (190 members).
The grapes for this cooperative come from the area north of Lac
du Bourget. Unusually for Savoie, over half the production here is
of red and rosé wine, mainly from the Gamay, with some Pinot
Noir and Mondeuse. Some reds are aged in wood after stainless-
steel vinification. The Pinot Noir wines age well for a couple of
years. *Open: Summer Tues–Sun 9am–noon, 2–7pm; closed Sun Sept
15 to Easter.*

Cave Coopérative des Vins Fins de Cruet
73800 Cruet. Vineyards owned: 275ha. 3.1 million bottles.
Coop (340 members).
This is by far the largest producer in the Savoie region, making an
enormous range of wines from tiny quantities of Chardonnay to
huge amounts of Gamay and Jacquère. The most highly esteemed
wines are red Arbin and white Chignin and Cruet.
Open: Mon–Sun 8am–noon, 2–6pm.

Domaine Dupasquier
Aimavigne, 73170 Jongieux.
Vineyards owned: 9ha. 77,000 bottles. VP-R
A traditional family domaine, making six different wines
including Jacquère Vin de Savoie and Altesse Roussette de Savoie,
along with smaller quantities of reds. The cellars are situated in a
pretty village, and most of the wines spend some time in old
wood. *Open: Mon–Sat, by appointment.*

Caveau du Lac St-André (J-C Perret)
*St-André-les-Marches, 73800 Montmélian. Vineyards owned: 10ha
(including some in the Cru of Apremont). 100,000 bottles. VP-R*
The main production in this modern winery is of an attractively

perfumed white Vin de Savoie Apremont, made in stainless steel with a long cool fermentation to bring out the fruit. Red and rosé are made from Gamay using carbonic maceration.
Open: By appointment only.

L Mercier et Fils
Grande Cave de Crépy, 74140 Douvaine. Vineyards owned: Crépy (Vin de Savoie AC) 30ha. 350,000 bottles. VP-R and N
The principal wine made by this large firm is a white slightly sparkling Chasselas Vin de Savoie Goutte d'Or, which is vinified traditionally in wood. Mercier also acts as *négociant*.
Open: Mon–Fri 5–6pm; by appointment only.

Michel Million Rousseau
Monthoux, 73170 St-Jean de Chevelu.
Vineyards owned: Vin de Savoie 4ha, Roussette de Savoie Monthoux 1ha. 40,000 bottles. VP-R
The range of Vin de Savoie AC from this small family firm includes Gamay, Mondeuse, Pinot Noir and Jacquère wines, all of which are vinified and sold separately. Monsieur Million Rousseau also makes small quantities of an attractive fresh Roussette de Monthoux. The reds need around three to seven years, but the whites need to be drunk young.
Open: Mon–Sat 8am–noon, 2–7pm.

Michel et Jean-Paul Neyroud
Les Aricoques, Designy, 74270 Frangy.
Vineyards owned: Les Aricoques (Frangy) 3ha, Planaz (Designy) 3.5ha. 35,000 bottles. VP-R
While most of this firm's production is a nutty white Roussette de Savoie from Frangy, made in a modern style using stainless steel, there is also some more traditional red Vin de Savoie made from the Mondeuse grape which can age well for two or three years. The other wine made is a Gamay, Vin de Savoie Rouge.
Open: During working hours; appointments necessary for groups.

J Perrier et Fils
St-André-les-Marches, 73800 Montmélian. Vineyards owned: Apremont 9ha, Les Abîmes 6ha. 217,000 bottles. VP-R and N
Apart from its own vineyards at Apremont and Les Abîmes which produce 100 percent Jacquère Vin de Savoie AC, the firm also makes a range of wines including a white Chignin and Roussette de Savoie, Gamay de Savoie and Gamay de Chautagne. Pinot Noir is also bought in to make a Pinot de Savoie, while Mondeuse is bought from Arbin. Recent launches include a classic-method sparkling and a *pétillant* wine. The quality from this, one of the largest firms in the area, is generally good if not particularly exciting. *Open: Mon–Fri 8am–noon, 2–6pm; by appointment only.*

André et Michel Quénard
Torméry, 73800 Chignin. Vineyards owned: Chignin and Chignin-Bergeron 17ha. 150,000 bottles. VP-R

All the wines made in this modern winery are 100 percent varietals. Chignin Blanc is from Jacquère; Chignin-Bergeron is Roussanne; Vin de Savoie rouge is Mondeuse and has some ageing potential; Vin de Savoie rosé is Gamay. The brand name is Coteaux de Torméry. The top wine made is a rich, intense Chignin-Bergeron. *Open: By appointment only.*

Les Fils René Quénard

Les Tours, 73800 Chignin. Vineyards owned: Vin de Savoie Chignin 13.5ha, Vin de Savoie 1.5ha. 128,000 bottles. VP-R
Another branch of the Quénard family. This firm makes Chignin and Chignin-Bergeron. The Chignin Coteaux de la Maréchale is dry while the Chignin-Bergeron Coteaux de Mont-Ronjoux is medium-sweet and made from Roussanne grapes.
Open: Mon–Sat 9am–7pm, by appointment only.

Le Vigneron Savoyard

73190 Apremont.
Vineyards owned: Apremont AC 25ha, Les Abîmes AC 8ha, Vin de Savoie AC 3ha. 40,000 bottles. Coop (10 members).
White Vin de Savoie from the two *Cru* villages of Apremont and Les Abîmes is the main production of this cooperative. Small quantities of red Vin de Savoie are also made. Modern equipment produces straightforward, attractive clean wines. The cellars are in the farm of the château at Apremont.

Marcel Tardy et Fils

La Plantée, Apremont, 73190 Challes-les-Eaux.
Vineyards owned: 5ha. 40,000 bottles. VP-R
Small producer making a very attractive white Vin de Savoie Apremont, adding a touch of Sauvignon to give it extra crispness and freshness. *Open: By appointment only.*

Varichon et Clerc

Les Sechallets, 01420 Seyssel. Vineyards owned: Seyssel 20ha, Mousseux de Bugey Cerdon 18ha, Crémant de Bourgogne 20ha. 1.8 million bottles. VP-R and N
Good-quality sparkling wines are the speciality of this firm now owned by Boisset, the Burgundy firm. Some, such as the Royal Seyssel, are made from local grapes, but the Seyssel Mousseux is made from grapes bought in from other areas. Varichon et Clerc also produces a Pétillant de Savoie from the Jacquère grape, as well as making wines in Bugey and a Crémant de Bourgogne from land owned in Burgundy. *Open: Appointments preferred.*

Bugey

Bugey lies immediately to the west of the Savoie vineyards. This small VDQS area has recently returned to life after a long period when it was almost moribund. In style the white wines are directly related to Savoie, while the reds (made principally from the Gamay) are closer to the Jura. The various appellation names are extraordinarily complex for such a minor area.

BUGEY VDQS

Mousseux de Bugey/Pétillant de Bugey A classic-method sparkling wine and naturally semi-sparkling white made with the white grapes used in Vin de Bugey. The commune of Cerdon can attach its name to this wine.

Roussette de Bugey A white made from Roussette (Altesse) and Chardonnay.

Roussette de Bugey *Cru* A 100 percent Roussette wine from six communes: Anglefort, Arbignieu, Chanay, Lagnieu, Montagnieu and Vineu-le-Grand.

Vin de Bugey Red, dry white and rosé from Gamay, Pinot Noir, Poulsard, Mondeuse (red and rosé) and Altesse, Jacquère, Mondeuse Blanche, Chardonnay, Aligoté and Pinot Gris (white).

Vin de Bugey *Crus* As above. Five communes may use their names: Cerdon, Machuraz, Manicle, Montagnieu, Vineu-le-Grand.

Bugey Producers

Le Caveau Bugiste
01350 Vognes. Coop.
The main cooperative of the area producing a full range of wines to an acceptable standard, and a mouth-watering Gamay that reminds you that these vineyards are not too far from Beaujolais.

Eugène Monin
Vongnes, 01350 Culoz.
Vineyards owned: 20ha. 150,000 bottles. VP-R
The largest private producer in Bugey. Monsieur Monin makes a number of wines: a Chardonnay, which he regards as his best wine; a Roussette de Bugey, which has 75 percent Chardonnay and 25 percent Roussette (Altesse); a sparkling wine with Jacquère, Chardonnay, Aligoté and Molette; and, for reds, Pinot Noir and Gamay. Stainless steel is now used to make the white.
Open: 8am–noon, 2–7pm, appointments preferred.

The Rhône

The red wines of the Rhône were traditionally regarded as among the finest in France. Hermitage had pride of place long before Bordeaux achieved its present eminence. Today, the area's best wines can achieve the same quality as Bordeaux and provide much greater reliability than burgundy.

The Rhône vineyards are now the most exciting source of red wine in France. Exciting because the greatness of Hermitage, Côte Rôtie and Cornas has been rediscovered, and because the vast sprawl of the Côtes du Rhône has come to life with wines of both quality and value. Even the whites – not normally considered an important part of the area's product – have improved with the arrival of new equipment. The wines of the two small areas of Condrieu and Château-Grillet command extravagantly high prices.

Conventionally, the Rhône vineyards are divided into two areas: Northern Rhône and Southern Rhône. Northern Rhône starts south of Lyon at the ancient Roman city of Vienne, which faces the first vineyards of northern Côtes du Rhône and Côte Rôtie. In this first stretch, the valley is narrow – the eastern edge of the Massif Central cut in two by the fast-flowing river. Vineyards are steeply terraced, expensive to work and spectacular to look at. The red wine vineyards of Côte Rôtie, facing east and southeast, run into the small AC white areas of Condrieu and the tiny plot of Château-Grillet. Immediately after this white interlude, the northern end of the St-Joseph AC is reached, and before long – on the opposite bank – the vineyards of Crozes-Hermitage begin.

The Crozes-Hermitage vineyards skirt the edge of the dome-shaped hill of Hermitage which marks the end of the steep slopes on the eastern bank. On the western bank, the town of Tournon faces Tain l'Hermitage. The terraced vineyards behind Tournon produce the best St-Joseph and only a short gap divides them from Cornas and then St-Péray. Here the Northern Rhône ends.

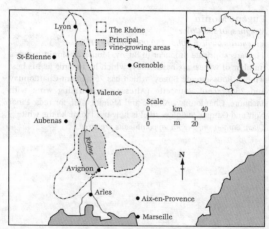

There are no vineyards around the nougat town of Montélimar, except a small area of Côtes du Rhône vineyards around Brezème. Perhaps the smell of all that sweet sticky stuff does not agree with the vines. South of Montélimar the valley opens out in both directions – east towards the foothills of the Alps and west to the Cévennes. Coteaux du Tricastin is on the east bank of the Rhône. Next, the vast Mistral-swept plain of the Côtes du Rhône begins, the boundary of the ancient Roman Provincia (Provence) is passed – and you arrive in a mediterranean landscape.

On the eastern edge of the Côtes du Rhône, where the Alps begin, are the prime hillside vineyard sites of many of the Côtes du Rhône Villages, Vacqueyras and Gigondas. The new AC of Côtes du Ventoux runs along the southern edge of Mont Ventoux. Facing Mont Ventoux and hard on the eastern bank of the Rhône is the outcrop of rolling hills which marks Châteauneuf-du-Pape, facing, on the western bank, Tavel and Lirac. By the time the city of Avignon has been reached, the Côtes du Rhône has run its course. The only vineyards left are the outlying Côtes du Lubéron and the Coteaux de Pierrevert away to the east. The latter are hardly separated from Aix-en-Provence and are grouped with the wines of Provence, which they resemble more closely.

In the past the division between north and south has been a question not only of convenience, but one of styles of wine. The Northern Rhône vineyards were dominated by the Syrah grape; the Southern by a mélange of grape varieties, of which Grenache and Cinsaut were perhaps the most important.

Today the differences are becoming a little more blurred. One change has come from the movement of grape varieties – in particular the Syrah grape. Syrah fulfils the same role in the Rhône as the Cabernet Sauvignon does elsewhere. It has become what the French call a *cépage améliorateur* – a noble grape variety which is used to lift the quality of local wine. The increasing use of the Syrah in Southern Rhône vineyards – along with Mourvèdre which has travelled north from the mediterranean vineyards of Bandol – is one of the chief reasons for the improvement in quality of Côtes du Rhône.

Another has been the development of new techniques of winemaking. Some producers are now blending together wine made from free-run juice with wine that is the result of a long maceration of the grapes, stalks and all. The maceration brings out the colour and fruit (with the stalks adding some tannin) while the free-run juice gives elegance and freshness.

There has also been considerable investment in new equipment, the cellars tend to be cleaner than they used to be, and many of the younger generation of wine producers have been to colleges and universities to study their craft. The Rhône Valley has also been given its very own Université du Vin. Housed in a spectacular château in the village of Suze-la-Rousse, in the middle of the Côtes du Rhône vineyards, this runs courses particularly for local producers but also for producers from other parts of France. It has a fine library and tasting rooms. For any visitors to the area, a tour round the château is a must (tel [0475] 04 86 09).

While the Côtes du Rhône is the heart of the Southern Rhône vineyards, there has also been a development of vineyards in the surrounding areas. New ACs and VDQSs have been created – Ventoux, Tricastin, Lubéron, Vivarais – which have brought recognition and an improvement in quality to areas that were previously comparatively unknown.

The Southern Rhône has the potential for a range of quality wines at affordable prices. A very different situation applies in the north, where demand regularly outstrips supply. Here the vineyard area is long established and in some areas the best-quality hillside vineyards have already been planted, leaving little room for expansion without a diminution of quality. Prices for the Northern Rhône wines, especially Hermitage and Côte Rôtie, represented superb value a few years ago, but have recently rocketed. Much of the running has been made by a few of the *négociant* firms who dominate this area, and who argue that they are simply charging the prices the wines are worth. They have forced the individual growers along in their wake. But from the less popular ACs – St-Joseph, Crozes-Hermitage and, to a lesser extent, Cornas – the wines are still affordable.

The Appellations

CÔTES DU RHÔNE AC

The huge area of the Côtes du Rhône AC stretches from vineyards behind the slope of the Côte Rôtie in the north to Avignon in the south. In all, there are 41,000 hectares of vines in six *départements*: Rhône, Loire, Ardèche, Drôme, Vaucluse and Gard. Most of the vineyards are on the wide plain east of Orange and north of Avignon, but areas of good quality are also found on the edges of the Crozes-Hermitage AC area in the north and around the edges of Tavel and Lirac in the south.

Red, rosé and white wines are made under this general AC. The reds and rosés must have at least 70 percent of the noble grape varieties: Cinsaut, Grenache, Mourvèdre and Syrah, with Carignan allowed at up to 30 percent and Camarèse, Counoise, Muscardin, Vaccarèse and Terret Noir also permitted. Whites are made from Bourboulenc, Clairette, Grenache Blanc, Marsanne, Roussanne and Ugni Blanc. The reds are best drunk comparatively young – probably within three years of the vintage – although in great years some wines will age very well. Vintages: '89, '90, '91, '93, '94, '95. For producers *see* Southern Rhône.

NORTHERN RHÔNE AC

Château-Grillet The smallest AC in France, and one of only two that are entirely owned by one producer (the other is Coulée de Serrant in the Loire). Here white wine is produced from the Viognier grape from a 2.6-hectare vineyard arranged in a semi-circle high above the Rhône, south of the town of Condrieu. Some years (such as '78) may produce only about 4,000 bottles; others (such as '80) may yield as many as 16,500. The taste of the wine is like an intense version of Condrieu –

apricots, honey and ripe fruits are often cited, but the wine is dry. It is bottled in brown flute bottles – the only wine on the Rhône to use this shape and colour. It can live for up to ten years in good vintages, sometimes even longer. Vintages: '86, '88, '89, '90, '91, '93, '95.

Condrieu A slightly larger area than Château-Grillet with 200 hectares available for planting, but a little over 100 hectares actually in use. The vineyard has declined not least because of the attraction of local industry and the notoriously low yield and unreliability of the Viognier grape. But with its increasing popularity, as well as better clones, the star of Condrieu has begun to wax again. Unlike Château-Grillet, there are two styles of Condrieu – a sweet and a dry. The dry, although somewhat more obvious than Château-Grillet, has similar attractions, with its intense spicy fruit and apricots and honey bouquet. The wine does not keep for as long as Château-Grillet: it reaches maturity after three to four years and rarely goes beyond ten. Vintages: '89, '90, '91, '93, '95.

Cornas 100 percent Syrah wine from the steep hillside on the western bank of the Rhône, south of Tournon and Tain l'Hermitage. The vineyard area was once 25 percent larger, but now has only 60 hectares planted on the slope above the village of Cornas. New housing, low prices and the sheer physical difficulty of working the land were the main reasons for the decline. A rise in price after the '83 and '85 vintages put this situation into reverse. The wine is fuller than a Côte Rôtie, very closed and tannic when young, but in good years the fruit of the Syrah breaks through with intense earthy, spicy, violet flavours; often the equal of Hermitage. Lighter wines are made lower down on sandy soil. Top wines are not ready for drinking for ten years; lighter wines are maturing after four to five. Vintages: '85, '86, '88, '89, '90, '91, '94, '95.

Côte Rôtie The vineyards start just south of Vienne on the west bank on steep hillsides, facing south and southeast, and have ideal exposure – hence the name 'roasted slope'. The core of the vineyard, level with the village of Ampuis, is divided into the Côte Brune (on clay soil) and the lighter soil (and hence lighter wine) of the Côte Blonde. Some wines are labelled as a blend of the two vineyards, but most Côte Rôtie is a blend of more than just these two. A small amount of white Viognier is normally blended with the Syrah to lighten its tannic intensity and about five percent of the vineyard has the white vine. Recent plantings on the plateau above the hill have brought the total area under vine to 130 hectares. Most tasters, however, agree that the plateau does not produce the right style of wine and the best growers have nothing to do with these new plantings. The wine is rich, very smooth when mature, with the characteristic spicy fruit of the Syrah toned down by the Viognier. Vintages: '85, '86, '88, '89, '90, '91, '94, '95.

Coteaux du Lyonnais Not strictly in the Northern Rhône orbit – it comes from the Gamay rather than the Syrah – the Coteaux du Lyonnais is more an outlying district of the Beaujolais. The vineyards cover an area south of Villefranche-sur-Saône and around Lyon. Reds are from the Gamay; whites from Chardonnay, Aligoté and Melon de Bourgogne. Cheap, cheerful and mainly consumed in Lyon.

Crozes-Hermitage Long regarded as the poor relation of Hermitage, this large vineyard area is now coming into its own following the price rise in Hermitage and an improvement of quality in Crozes. The village of Crozes-Hermitage itself lies behind the Hermitage hill, but the vineyards stretch along the Rhône's eastern bank, around the base of the hill and out into the plain as far as Roch-de-Glun and Pont d'Isère to the south. The total area is now over 800 hectares. Red is from Syrah while the small proportion of white comes from Marsanne and Roussanne grapes. Some producers are now bottling single-estate wines, although in the past most Crozes-Hermitage has been bought in by *négociants*. Quality of the top estates is very good, approaching that of Hermitage, but there is still some indifferent wine under anonymous labels. Good wines have a spicy aroma, with the presence of blackcurrant fruit when young. They develop quite fast – within three to four years – and age up to six and eight years for better wines. Vintages: '88, '89, '90, '91, '93, '94, '95.

Hermitage The superb position of the vineyards on the hill of the Hermitage, which receives the sun virtually the whole day, guarantees the high quality of this AC. The Hermitage is a small chapel at the top of the hill once occupied by a crusading knight and now a magnificent viewing point. The band of Hermitage vineyards stretches around the hill from the top almost into the town of Tain l'Hermitage. They are divided into a number of smaller sections, whose names sometimes appear on the labels: Chante-Alouette, la Chapelle, les Bessards, les Greffieux and le Méal are among the best known. The total AC Hermitage area is small – 125 hectares – and almost completely planted. While nearly all the granitic soil of the vineyard is covered with Syrah, a small amount of Marsanne and Roussanne are grown which can be added to the red (up to 15 percent) or used to make a white Hermitage. All attention, however, is focussed on the reds with their superb keeping powers, their intense blackcurrant fruit when young and their chocolatey richness when mature. Along with fine Côte Rôtie and the occasional Cornas, Hermitage is the finest wine on the Rhône. Wines from good years seem capable of surviving almost for ever and should not be touched before ten years. Vintages: '76, '78, '80, '83, '85, '86, '88, '90, '91, '94, '95.

St-Joseph This vineyard runs parallel to Crozes-Hermitage on the opposite (western) bank of the river, stretching much further north to the southern edge of Condrieu and a little further south almost to Cornas – a distance in total of nearly 70 kilometres. The original area was the southern end, around the town of Tournon and into the side valleys a little to the south. But changes in the AC legislation in 1972 extended the area from the previous 240 hectares to around 600 hectares. Sadly, as with Côte Rôtie, the new plantings do not produce such good wine as the original, and the best wines still come from the southern communes of Tournon, Mauves and St-Jean de Muzols. The style of St-Joseph – even the best – is much lighter than Crozes-Hermitage, deriving its character from the sand and gravel which are mixed with the granite base of the vineyard soil. It brings out the fruit of the Syrah rather than the intense flavours, and makes it a wine to enjoy younger than some other wines from the area. After three years it is certainly mature, and very few St-Joseph wines last beyond ten or 11 years. Vintages: '88, '89, '90, '91, '94, '95.

St-Péray At the Northern Rhône vineyards a 60-hectare white wine AC appears. The white is made in both a still and sparkling style (*see below*). The still wine from Marsanne and Roussanne is dry, has high natural acidity, a pale gold colour and a relatively short life-span (two to three years).

St-Péray Mousseux The more interesting version of St-Péray. This sparkling wine comes from the sandy clay soil around the small town of St-Péray and the surrounding villages which stretch into the side valley towards Lamastre. It is made by the classic method and is generally a blended non-vintage wine, although a few growers do make vintage wines. Full and fruity, it is popular in France but rarely seen abroad.

SOUTHERN RHÔNE AC

Châteauneuf-du-Pape From the road north leaving Avignon, the truncated tower of the papal palace can be seen standing over the small town of Châteauneuf-du-Pape and its surrounding vineyards. The flat Rhône Valley floor and the rolling slopes rise towards this symbol of medieval papacy: the vineyards with their characteristic gnarled vines and huge stones which reflect the heat. Châteauneuf-du-Pape mainly produces red wine although a small amount of white is also made. The vineyards are large, covering 3,000 hectares in five communes. There are 13 grape varieties permitted for the red (in order of importance): Grenache (Noir and Blanc), Syrah, Mourvèdre, Cinsaut, Clairette (white), Bourboulenc (white), Roussanne (white), Picpoul (white), Counoise, Terret Noir, Vaccarèse, Muscardin and Picardan (white). Very few growers actually use more than five, although two of the best – Château de Mont-Redon and Château de Beaucastel – use all 13. Châteauneuf-du-Pape is a highly alcoholic wine, but the richness and smoothness of the fruit should compensate for this. White Châteauneuf comes from Grenache Blanc, Clairette, Bourboulenc and Roussanne. It tends to be flowery but on the full side. Domaine-bottled wines come in bottles bearing the papal coat of arms; *négociant*-bottled wines are unmarked. Vintages (reds): '86, '88, '89, '90, '91, '93, '94, '95.

Coteaux Diois East of the main Rhône Valley vineyards are two small appellations in the heart of Alpine scenery, of which this is one, centred on the little town of Châtillon-en-Diois in the valley of the Bez. Red, white and rosé wines are made. The red comes from Gamay, Syrah and Pinot Noir; the whites from Chardonnay and Aligoté. The occasional Chardonnay can be attractive, but on the whole they are not exciting.

Clairette de Die Still wines from the same area as the Mousseux (*see below*). Not often seen outside Die – and really best as a base for the sparkling wines.

Clairette de Die Mousseux Another small area only a few miles from Châtillon, back in the valley of the Drôme, but still in spectacular mountain scenery. Medium sweet sparkling wines are made from Clairette and Muscat à Petits Grains. The dry is sometimes made by the classic method, while the medium-sweet adopts the local *méthode dioise*, using sugar left over from an arrested first fermentation to start the second fermentation. The medium-sweet Clairette de Die is similar to, if a little drier than, sparkling Asti and quite as delicious.

Crémant de Die A dry sparkling wine from the same area as Clairette de Die; made by the classic method using Clairette grapes.

Coteaux du Tricastin Red, rosé and dry white wines from a large (2,000-hectare) area south of Montélimar and at the northern end of the big Côtes du Rhône plain around Orange. The soil is clay with large stones. Reds and rosés come from Grenache and Syrah, with smaller amounts of the Carignan, Cinsaut and Mourvèdre grape varieties. Whites come from Marsanne and Bourboulenc. Little distinguishes these wines from their Côtes du Rhône neighbours, especially with the increasing use of Syrah, and their quality, like those of the Côtes du Rhône, is getting better all the time. Best drunk within two to three years of the vintage, when their full fruit and peppery flavour are at their best. Vintages: '90, '91, '93, '94, '95.

Côtes du Lubéron Red, rosé and dry white wines from the southern slopes of the Montagne de Lubéron in the Durance Valley, east of Avignon. The reds and rosés come from Grenache, Syrah, Mourvèdre, Cinsaut and some Gamay. The whites are from Grenache Blanc, Clairette, Bourboulenc, Marsanne and some Ugni Blanc, and some Chardonnay and Sauvignon Blanc is being planted. The quality from the better producers is good and improving.

Côtes du Rhône-Villages Superior (in alcohol and, generally, quality) Côtes du Rhône which can either be simply AC Côtes du Rhône-Villages (if it is a blend from a number of different, specified, communes) or can come from a specific one of 16 communes – in which case the name of the commune will appear on the label. Red, rosé and dry white wines are made. Reds and rosés come from Grenache (maximum 65 percent), Carignan (maximum ten percent) and at least 25 percent in total of Syrah, Mourvèdre and Cinsaut. Whites are made from Bourboulenc, Clairette and Roussanne. The 16 Villages communes are mainly on the eastern edges of the Côtes du Rhône plain: Rousset-les-Vignes, St-Pantaléon-les-Vignes, Valréas, Visan, Vinsobres, St-Maurice-sur-Eygues, Roaix,

Cairanne, Rochegude, Rasteau, Séguret, Sablet and Beaumes-de-Venise. On the west side of the Rhône, opposite Orange, are the three communes of St-Gervais, Chusclan and Laudun. Until its promotion to separate AC, Vacqueyras was also a Côte du Rhône-Villages. The red wines last a little longer than ordinary Côtes du Rhône – up to eight or nine years for good vintages. Vintages (red): '88, '89, '90, '91, '93, '94, '95.

Côtes du Ventoux Along the southern slopes of Mont Ventoux are the 6,400 hectares of Côtes du Ventoux. Red, rosé and dry white are produced on sedimentary soil. The red and rosé are made from Grenache, Syrah, Mourvèdre and Cinsaut, with smaller amounts of Camarèse, Counoise, Muscardin, Terret Noir and Vaccarèse. Whites come from Bourboulenc, Clairette, Grenache Blanc, Marsanne and Roussanne. The reds are lighter in style than Côtes du Rhône and are best drunk two or three years after the vintage. The whites can be very fresh if made with modern equipment. Vintages (reds): '91, '93.

Gigondas Lies between the Côtes du Rhône village of Sablet and Vacqueyras and shares many of the characteristics of each (it was a Villages wine until 1971). Only red and rosé wines are made on the 1,200 hectares. Grapes are: Grenache (maximum 80 percent), Syrah, Mourvèdre and Cinsaut. Clay soil produces very rich reds, with spicy fruit and often a vegetal farmyard smell. The wines can last seemingly for ever and are not really drinkable for four to five years after the vintage. Vintages: '86, '88, '89, '93, '94, '95.

Lirac Mainly red and rosé wines (and a tiny amount of white) from a small area (650 hectares) northwest of Avignon on the west side of the Rhône, adjacent to Tavel (*see below*). The red and rosé come from Grenache (minimum 40 percent), Syrah, Mourvèdre and Cinsaut; the whites come from Bourboulenc, Clairette, Picpoul, Calitor and Macabeo. The reds are a sort of lighter version of Châteauneuf-du-Pape, more long-lasting than Côtes du Rhône, and worth keeping for five years. At the moment they are some of the best-value red Rhônes around. The rosés are a little heavy. The whites are also very good, fresher and more acidic than many Rhône whites. All in all, an AC producing wines that are worth looking out for. Vintages (reds): '88, '89, '90, '93, '94, '95.

Tavel The most famous rosé AC in France, with vines planted on nearly 750 hectares of clay soil west of Avignon. The wines are made from Grenache, Cinsaut, Syrah and Mourvèdre with the permitted addition of the white grapes of Bourboulenc, Picpoul and Clairette. The wine is invariably very dry, with only a little fruit and rather more tannin, a characteristic onion-skin colour from wood, and comparatively low acidity. More modern techniques are enhancing the fruit and acidity and decreasing the use of wood. The wines age for around four years but are at their best after two to three years.

Vacqueyras Promoted from Côtes du Rhône-Village status in 1990, the appellation of around 1,500 hectares lies between Gigondas and Beaumes-de-Venise. The grapes are the same as those used in Villages wines: Grenache, Carignan, Cinsaut, Syrah and Mourvèdre for reds and rosés – but with a greater emphasis on Syrah and Mourvèdre and less on Carignan and Cinsaut. The style is powerful, emphasising vigour rather than elegance. Little white is made, but the grapes used are Bourboulenc and Roussanne. Reds can age up to ten years or more. Vintages (reds): '86, '88, '89, '90, '93, '94, '95.

SOUTHERN RHÔNE VDQS

Côtes du Vivarais Red, rosé and dry white wines from the west bank of the Rhône between Pont St-Esprit and Montélimar. Red and rosé come from the standard Côtes du Rhône grapes with the addition of Gamay. Whites (of which the production is very small) also come from Côtes du Rhône varieties. Three communes are allowed to add their name to the basic appellation: Orgnac, St-Montan and St-Remèze. Reds are lighter than Côtes du Rhône and delicious slightly chilled.

VINS DOUX NATURELS

Two communes in the Côtes du Rhône-Villages AC also produce fortified sweet *vins doux naturels*, which have separate appellations:

Muscat de Beaumes-de-Venise A Muscat-based sweet white VDN, made from the Muscat de Frontignan, which has achieved greater worldwide popularity than any other VDN from the south of France. It has the grapey, honeyed, smooth taste characteristic of all these wines.

Rasteau A VDN made from the Grenache, which can be either red or pale tawny (made by removing the skins early in the fermentation). There is also a version called Rasteau Rancio which results from leaving the wine in cask.

VINS DE PAYS

Regional *vins de pays*

Vin de Pays des Comtes Rhodaniens A large region covering eight *départements* (the Ain, Ardèche, Drôme, Isère, Loire, Rhône, Savoie and the Haute-Savoie). Most of the *vin de pays* wines produced within its boundaries are actually entitled to the zonal *vin de pays* classification, and therefore in practice this wine is rarely seen.

Vin de Pays de la Drôme Wine production mainly from the south of the *département* of Drôme, east of Montélimar. Most of that made – 92 percent – is red wine from the normal varieties of Carignan, Cinsaut and Syrah, supplemented by Gamay, Cabernet Sauvignon and Merlot.

Other regional *vins de pays*:

Vin de Pays de l'Ardèche

Vin de Pays du Puy-de-Dôme

Zonal *vins de pays*

Vin de Pays des Collines Rhodaniennes Situated in the heart of the Rhône Valley, among the Côtes du Rhône vineyards, this *vin de pays* takes in mainly outlying non-AC areas.

Production is mainly of red wines, from Gamay and Syrah grapes, and a little Merlot.

Vin de Pays du Comté de Grignan East of Montélimar, this area, producing almost entirely red wines, includes peripheral Côtes du Rhône vineyards, using the same mix of grapes.

Vin de Pays des Coteaux de l'Ardèche In the southern half of the Ardèche *département*, to the west of the Côtes du Rhône AC area, this zone has built a reputation for the production of 100 percent varietal *vins de pays*, most notably Chardonnay and Gamay, but also including a selection of grapes from Burgundy, Bordeaux and the south of France. The arrival of Burgundian *négociants* in the area has given impetus to the development of these wines.

Vin de Pays des Coteaux des Baronnies In the southeast of the Drôme *département*, to the east of Nyons, this zone brings together Rhône grapes plus Merlot and Cabernet Sauvignon. For the small production of whites, Chardonnay is also used in the blend.

Vin de Pays de la Principauté d'Orange Around Orange, just east of the Châteauneuf-du-Pape vineyards, this is an area of predominantly red wines from local grape varieties. There is a tiny production of rosé, and an even smaller amount of white.

One other zonal *vin de pay*:

Vin de Pays des Balmes Dauphinoises

Northern Rhône Producers

CHÂTEAU-GRILLET AC

Neyret-Gachet (Château-Grillet)
42410 Vérin. Vineyards owned: 3.4ha. 12,000 bottles. VP-R
The one and only producer of Château-Grillet from the smallest AC in France, M Neyret-Gachet actually lives in Lyon, where he is a businessman during the week. At weekends, however, he is down on his farm, where *maître de chai* A Canet is in charge. The wines, although considered by some to be overpriced because of their rarity value, are never to be forgotten. Almost luscious, yet dry, they taste of ripe peaches or apricots with a hint of sweet spice. The figure of 12,000 bottles per year is at the top end of the scale – in '78 only 3,800 bottles were made.
Open: By appointment only.

CONDRIEU AC

Domaine du Chêne
Le Pêcher, 42410 Chavanay. Vineyards owned: Condrieu 2.5ha, St-Joseph 5.1ha, vin de pays 2.5ha. 58,000 bottles. VP-R
Marc Rouvière makes both Condrieu and St-Joseph from his vineyards. His whites are made in stainless steel and are designed for early drinking. His red St-Joseph, including top *cuvée* Anaïs, is matured in *barriques*. He also makes red *vin de pays*.
Open: Mon–Sun, by appointment only.

Pierre Dumazet
Limony, 07340 Serrières.
Vineyards owned: 1.6ha. 7,800 bottles. VP-R
Monsieur Dumazet produces tiny quantities of Condrieu from a vineyard on the terraces above the river. Much of the wine goes to top restaurants in France, but a little does get exported. He uses a mix of wood and stainless steel and blends together wine made by both methods. All the apricot flavours of ripe Condrieu are the result. Small quantities of St-Joseph and Côtes du Rhône are also made. *Open: 7am–noon, 2–7pm (including Sun), by appointment.*

Philippe Faury
La Ribaudy, 42410 Chavanay. Vineyards owned: Condrieu 2ha,
St-Joseph 4.5ha, vin de pays 0.9ha. 81,000 bottles. VP-R
A producer whose cellars have recently been expanding into new premises, allowing him to use stainless steel for white wines while keeping wood for reds. He makes Condrieu for early consumption, and white as well as red St-Joseph. He also makes small amounts of Vin de Pays des Collines Rhodaniennes, white and red. *Open: Appointments preferred.*

Domaine Niero-Pinchon
20 Rue Cuvillière, 69420 Condrieu.
Vineyards owned: Condrieu 2.6ha, Côte Rôtie 0.6ha, Côtes du
Rhône 0.25ha. 10,000 bottles. VP-R
While he makes small amounts of red wine, the Condrieu is Robert Niero's main claim to fame. Formerly he worked at a bank in Lyons, but seems to have adjusted to viticulture well, making what is often seen as one of the finest Condrieus. It has some wood-ageing, and is not normally released until a year after the vintage. *Open: Weekday afternoons and all day Sat.*

André Perret
42410 Chavanay. Vineyards owned: Condrieu 4ha,
St-Joseph 3.8ha. 31,000 bottles. VP-R
The Perrets' vineyard on the steepest slopes of Condrieu may be difficult to work, but it does produce concentrated wines which repay some ageing. André Perret also makes red St-Joseph and some white from old vines. His St-Joseph *cuvée* is called Les Grisières. *Open: Sat, and by appointment during the week.*

Domaine du Château du Rozay
Le Rozay, 69420 Condrieu. Vineyards owned: Condrieu 2.3ha,
Côtes du Rhône 1ha. 10,000 bottles. VP-R
The Multier family make two styles of Condrieu. One, from old vines, is called Château du Rozay; the second is a straight Condrieu from younger vines. The wine is fermented in a mixture of stainless steel and wood. Those who admire the style of the Condrieu will be delighted to know that more land has just been planted. The family also owns a small plot of Syrah vines from which it produces Côtes du Rhône.
Open: By appointment only.

Georges Vernay

1 Rue Nationale, 69420 Condrieu. Vineyards owned: Condrieu 6ha, Côte Rôtie 2ha, St-Joseph 1ha. 52,000 bottles. VP-R

Traditional methods and modern equipment are sensibly combined to give wines of considerable style. Monsieur Vernay makes about 30,000 bottles of Condrieu a year. He uses ten percent new wood each vintage for both red and white wines. *Open: By appointment only.*

CORNAS AC

Guy de Barjac

07130 Cornas.

Very traditional winemaking is the order of the day here. There is a long fermentation, no fining or filtration, which means the wines throw a sediment in the bottle. Old vines – the average age is 50 years – help the concentration of the wines, giving a deep, dark colour. They mature over a ten-year period, and continue to hold their quality.

Auguste Clape

07130 Cornas. Vineyards owned: Cornas 4ha, Côtes du Rhône 1ha. 17,000 bottles. VP-R

Superb wines are made by M Clape, who has now been joined by his son in his small cellar on the main road of Cornas. His vineyards are high on the hill above. Although impenetrable when young, there is plenty of fruit lurking in the inky black wine. With age – at least ten years – they are rich, earthy, spicy, perfumed and surprisingly elegant. *Open: By appointment only.*

Jean-Luc Colombo

07130 Cornas. Vineyards owned: Cornas 4ha, Côtes du Rhône 0.5ha, vin de pays 0.5ha. 16,000 bottles. VP-R

Monsieur Colombo's influence is much greater than the size of his vineyard would suggest, since he acts as consultant to many growers, advocating the use of new wood and the de-stalking of the grapes, thereby lessening tannins. His own Cornas, les Ruchets, stays in wood for 18 months. His Côtes du Rhône is entirely Syrah. *Open: By appointment only.*

Juge

Place de la Salle des Fêtes, 07130 Cornas. Vineyards owned: Cornas 3ha, St-Péray 0.35ha. 18,000 bottles. VP-R

"My style never changes", writes Monsieur Juge. And he is right. Heavy and tannic when young, his Cornas develops into rich, soupy wine full of herby fruit and with immense ageing ability. *Open: By appointment only.*

Robert Michel

Grande Rue, 07130 Cornas. Vineyards owned: Cornas 7ha, vin de table 0.5ha. 26,000 bottles. VP-R

M Michel makes three styles of Cornas. The lightest comes from vineyards at the foot of the hill. The second in quality and depth comes from the hillside itself, while the third comes from old vines on the hill: this *cuvée* is called La Geynale. The wine is bottled unfined, giving a very rich, earthy taste. Old fashioned style. *Open: Mon–Sat; appointments preferred.*

Noel Verset
07130 Cornas.

Monsieur Verset produces what is certainly one of the longest lived Cornas' – and one of the best. It comes from vineyards which have an ideal exposure on the steep slopes of Cornas, and his yields are the lowest in the appellation. The results are aged in a bewildering variety of barrels, fined with egg white and then bottled unfiltered.

Alain Voge
Rue de l'Équerre, 07130 Cornas. Vineyards owned: Cornas 7ha, St-Péray 3.5ha. 57,000 bottles. VP-R

Monsieur Voge must be one of the few producers of Cornas who uses cement tanks in his cellar. This softens the tannin that can sometimes cover the fruit, and his wines mature comparatively quickly. His St-Péray is made with Marsanne (98 percent) and Roussanne.
Open: Mon–Fri 8am–noon, 2–7pm; by appointment at weekends.

CÔTE RÔTIE AC

Gilles Barge
Route de Baucharcy, 69420 Ampuis. Vineyards owned: Côte Rôtie 5ha, Condrieu 0.5ha, St-Joseph 1ha. 32,000 bottles. VP-R

Gilles Barge has taken over from his father Pierre, and concentrates mainly on Côte Rôtie. He uses traditional wood-ageing for up to 24 months, although the cellar also has stainless steel for vinification. *Open: Appointments preferred.*

Bernard Burgaud
69420 Ampuis.

A relatively young vineyard, mainly at the top of the Côte Rôtie slopes, with a portion on the flat plateau above. The wine is fermented at a high temperature to extract colour and concentration, and then aged in small barrels, some of which are new. Bernard Burgaud is seen as a rising star in the appellation. *Open: Appointments preferred.*

Émile Champet
69420 Ampuis.

The main part of Monsieur Champet's vineyard is on the Côte Brune, and he owns a portion of the La Viaillère vineyard. Wines contain five percent Viognier and are matured in a wide range of old barrels, from small to large. The style is slightly rustic and the wines are not the weightiest Côte Rôties, but they have plenty of fragrant fruit flavours. *Open: Appointments preferred.*

Domaine Clusel-Roch
Route du Lacat, Verenay, 69420 Ampuis. Vineyards owned: Côte Rôtie 3ha, Condrieu 0.5ha. 13,000 bottles. VP-R

Gilbert and Brigitte Clusel-Roch own land on the Grandes Places vineyard which has vines up to 60 years old. The top wine, which takes the vineyard's name, is vinified traditionally and aged in Burgundian casks. The top *cuvée* is les Grands Places. The Domaine also produces a Cuvée Classique and a Condrieu Coteau de Chery. The style of the wines is elegant rather than overwhelming.
Open: By appointment only.

Marius Gentaz-Dervieux
69420 Ampuis. VP-R

A producer of small quantities of very fine Côte Rôtie from Côte Brune vineyards. Monsieur Gentaz-Dervieux' cellar has only old barrels, and the wines stay in wood for up to 22 months. Despite very traditional methods, the wines veer more to elegance, even with huge colour, than to overwhelming power.
Open: By appointment only.

E Guigal
Ampuis, 69420 Condrieu. Vineyards owned: Côte Rôtie 75ha, Condrieu 25ha. 480,000 bottles. VP-R and N

The major force in Côte Rôtie, now that the company owns Vidal-Fleury (*see page 120*). Happily, its size does not adversely affect quality, which has a justifiably high reputation. Vinification is in stainless steel, but more recently the wines have undergone a considerable amount of new-wood ageing. Three styles of Côte Rôtie are made: a traditional blended Côte Brune and Côte Blonde; a lighter Côte Blonde, La Mouline, which is 12 percent white Viognier; and La Landonne, which is 100 percent Syrah: deep, well structured and seemingly able to live for ever. Guigal makes many other Rhône wines, including a very superior Côtes du Rhône and Gigondas. *Open: 8am–noon, 2–6pm (by appointment).*

Joseph Jamet
69420 Ampuis.

Very big, very concentrated wines, sometimes almost black in colour, coming from vineyards scattered about the hillside of Côte Rôtie. The wines mature after 15 to 20 years. The estate is now run by Joseph's sons, Jean-Paul and Jean-Luc.

Robert Jasmin
Ampuis, 69420 Condrieu.
Vineyards owned: 3.5ha. 12,000 bottles. VP-R

One of the top producers in Côte Rôtie, Monsieur Jasmin's tiny cellars in the centre of Ampuis are a delight to visit. He blends wines from the Côte Brune and Côte Blonde for his Chevalière d'Ampuis, pressing and then leaving the must to macerate for around ten days – all in wood. The results are surprisingly soft in character, full of fruit even when young. He expects them to reach maturity after ten years. *Open: By appointment only.*

René Rostaing

'Le Port', 69420 Ampuis. Vineyards owned: Côte Rôtie 6.5ha, Condrieu 1.5ha. 30,000 bottles. VP-R

Monsieur Rostaing has taken over the vineyards of his father-in-law Albert Dervieux, giving him fine holdings and the ability to produce four *cuvées* of Côte Rôtie: a straight *cuvée*, a Côte Blonde, La Landonne and La Viaillère. While there is stainless steel for fermentation, Monsieur Rostaing also ages his wines for between one to three years in wood. *Open: By appointment only.*

Domaine de Vallouit

Château de Châteaubourg, 07130 St-Péray.
Vineyards owned: Côte Rôtie 10ha, Hermitage 1.5ha, St-Joseph 2ha, Condrieu 0.5ha, Crozes-Hermitage 6ha, Cornas 0.5ha, vin de pays 5ha. 140,000 bottles. VP-R

The estate has dropped its *négociant* function in order to concentrate on its vineyards. It has also moved into the 11th-century castle of Châteaubourg. The wines cover almost the full gamut of Northern Rhône appellations, but the firm's main concentration is in Côte Rôtie, where its top *cuvée* is Les Roziers. Other wines of importance include St-Joseph les Anges and Cornas.
Open: Tasting room in Ampuis open Mon, Tues, Thurs–Sun.

Vidal-Fleury

BP 12, Ampuis, 69420 Condrieu.
Vineyards owned: 8ha. 32,000 bottles. VP-R and N

Now owned by Guigal (*see* page 119), Vidal-Fleury makes Côte Rôtie from the Côte Brune and Côte Blonde, both separately and together, using vineyard names such as La Chatillonne, Le Clos, La Turque, La Pommière and Pavillon-Rouge. The firm is the oldest in the area, having been founded in 1781, and its reputation has been high for much of that time. It remains firmly committed to traditional ways. *Open: By appointment only.*

CROZES-HERMITAGE AC

Belle Père et Fils

Quartier Les Marsuriaux, 26600 Larnage. Vineyards owned: Crozes-Hermitage 17.5ha, Hermitage 1.5ha. 17,500 bottles. VP-R

Albert Belle, one of the producers who is setting high standards in Crozes, moved his grapes in 1990 from the local cooperative and is now making much of his own wine. He ages his reds in *barriques*, of which 30 percent are new. The small quantities of white are produced in stainless steel. *Open: By appointment only.*

Cave des Clairmonts

Beaumont-Monteux, 26600 Tain l'Hermitage.
Vineyards owned: 98ha. 132,000 bottles. Coop.

Red and a small amount of white Crozes-Hermitage are made in this modern grouping of four growers, headed by Jean-Michel Borja. Cave des Clairmonts makes full use of autovinification and temperature control. These techniques produce a modern, fresh

white and a soft, young-maturing red with plenty of colour and simple fruit. The red is more attractive than the white.
Open: Mon–Sat (appointments for groups).

Domaine Collonge
26600 Mercurol. Vineyards owned: Crozes-Hermitage 34ha, St-Joseph 6.20ha. VP-R
A relatively large-scale producer of both Crozes-Hermitage and St-Joseph, with reds being made traditionally and whites in a more modern style. Red St-Joseph is partially aged in large wooden barrels. *Open: Mon–Sun 9am–noon, 2–6.30pm.*

Desmeure Père et Fils
Domaine des Remizières, Route de Romans, 26600 Mercurol. Vineyards owned: Crozes-Hermitage 14.5ha, Hermitage 2.5ha, vin de pays 2.7ha. VP-R
Red and white Crozes-Hermitage and Hermitage are made by Philippe Desmeure. His style is modern, with softer tannins in the reds than many, and plenty of new-wood tastes – they are aged for up to 18 months in wood. Whites are also wood-aged.
Open: Mon–Sun 9am–noon, 2–6pm.

Domaine des Entrefaux
GAEC de la Syrah, Chanos-Curson, 26600 Tain l'Hermitage. Vineyards owned: Crozes-Hermitage 30ha. 85,000 bottles. VP-R
Red and white Crozes-Hermitage are made by Charles Tardy and Bernard Ange, using traditional methods and ageing the wine in wood, with a proportion of new oak. The quality of the wines is very high indeed: an '83 Domaine des Entrefaux tasted in 1986 was quite the best Crozes-Hermitage I have ever drunk. Other names used include Domaine des Pierrelles and Domaine de la Beaume, after portions of the estate. *Open: Mon–Sat 9am–noon, 3–7pm.*

Alain Graillot
26600 Tain l'Hermitage. Vineyards owned: Crozes-Hermitage 18ha, Hermitage 0.12ha, St-Joseph 0.5ha. VP-R
One of the real rising stars who is making Crozes-Hermitage more than just an appendage of Hermitage. His top *cuvée* of Crozes, La Guiraude, is a wood-matured wine that emphasises fruit as much as tannins and other characteristics. He also makes small quantities of Hermitage: big, rich wines by any standards.
Open: By appointment only.

Domaines Pochon
Château de Curson, 26600 Chanos-Curson. Vineyards owned: 13ha. 67,000 bottles.
Étienne Pochon makes four wines. His top wines are called Château Curson, his second Domaine Pochon. Both top wines are aged in wood – the white for three months, the red for up to ten months. Monsieur Pochon's cellars are in a 16th-century building which once belonged to Diane de Poitiers.
Open: Sat 2–6pm; July–Sept every afternoon 2–7pm.

Domaine Pradelle
26600 Chanos-Curson.
Vineyards owned: 23.5ha. 70,000 bottles. VP-R
Both a red and a white are produced on this estate on the east side of the Hermitage hill. The red is better than the white, ageing in wood for one year, with a full, if slightly rustic, character.
Open: Mon–Sat 8am–noon, 2–6pm.

Raymond Roure
26600 Gervans.
Very low yields from vineyards on the hilly slopes by the Rhône in the north of the AC produce highly concentrated wines that spend up to two years in wood. They are sold under the name of Les Picaudières. *Open: Appointments preferred.*

HERMITAGE AC

M Chapoutier
18 Rue du Dr Paul Durand, 26600 Tain l'Hermitage.
Vineyards owned: Hermitage 30ha, Crozes-Hermitage 5ha,
St-Joseph 6ha, Côte Rôtie 3ha, Châteauneuf-du-Pape 27ha.
1 million bottles. VP-R and N
One of Hermitage's largest *négociant* and vineyard-owning firms, Chapoutier remains firmly under family control but has changed dramatically since the youngest generation – Marc and Michel – took over in 1990. The firm makes the full range of Northern Rhône wines, and has a major holding on the hill of Hermitage itself – which boldly displays its name. In some respects, the whites are more remarkable than the reds – especially Hermitage Chante-Alouette which ages for a considerable time. As a *négociant* firm, it also makes Côtes du Ventoux, Châteauneuf-du-Pape, Coteaux du Tricastin, Tavel, Cornas and Gigondas. *Open: By appointment only.*

Domaine Jean-Louis Chave
39 Avenue du St-Joseph, Mauves, 07300 Tournon.
Vineyards owned: 15ha. 45,000 bottles. VP-R
One of the great names in Hermitage, Gérard Chave, now joined by his son Jean-Louis, produces thoroughly traditional reds and whites which seem to live forever. The Hermitage is made from 100 percent Syrah – unlike that of some other Hermitage producers – and all the winemaking takes place in wood. The family has recently celebrated 500 years of winemaking from the same vineyard on the hill of Hermitage. *Open: By appointment only.*

Delas Frères
07300 Tournon. Vineyards owned: Hermitage 25ha,
Cornas 12ha, Côte Rôtie 6ha, Condrieu 5ha. VP-R and N
An old-established firm of *négociants* which owns vineyards in the main Northern Rhône ACs and buys in wine from the Southern Rhône. It has maintained traditional standards while expanding the business. Now owned by the champagne firm of Deutz.
Open: By appointment only.

Bernard Faurie
07300 Touron. Vineyards owned: Hermitage 1.7ha, St-Joseph 2ha, Crozes-Hermitage 0.7ha. VP-R

Small scale does not mean small wines at M Faurie's cellar. He makes some of the most intense wines in the Hermitage appellation from vines on Les Greffieux and Le Méal.

Open: By appointment only.

Caves Fayolle
Les Gamets, 26600 Gervans.
Vineyards owned: 11ha. 40,000 bottles. VP-R

Fermentation of reds is in wood at this traditional family firm. It vinifies the crops from each parcel of land separately: Le Dionnières for Hermitage, Le Pontaix and Les Voussères for red Crozes-Hermitage (Les Blancs for white). Of the Crozes-Hermitage wines, Le Pontaix is probably the best. Vinification takes place in a mixture of wood and cement tanks and the whole process is very traditional. *Open: By appointment only.*

Paul Jaboulet Aîné
BP 46, 76600 Tain l'Hermitage. Vineyards owned: Hermitage 28ha, Crozes-Hermitage 47ha. 2 million bottles. VP-R and N

The most successful and most go-ahead firm in the Northern Rhône, pioneering new, lighter styles of wine and making the running for the increasing reputation of this area's wines. The Hermitage La Chapelle is the firm's most famous wine, but a full range is also produced from other areas of the Rhône. Their Crozes-Hermitage Domaine de Thalabert is generally considered one of the best wines of that AC. *Négociant* wines take in Châteauneuf-du-Pape, Côtes du Rhône (including the well-known Parallèle 45), Côtes du Ventoux, St-Joseph and Côte Rôtie. A modern plant outside Tain l'Hermitage is the outward symbol of their success.

Open: Mon–Fri 8–11.30am, 1.30–5.30pm, by appointment.

Marc Sorrel
Avenue Jean-Jaurès, 26600 Tain l'Hermitage.
Vineyards owned: Hermitage 3ha. 16,000 bottles. VP-R

Old vines are behind the quality from this small vineyard, where traditional methods reign. Monsieur Sorrel has vineyards exclusively in Hermitage: Le Méal, Les Bessards, Les Greffieux and Les Rocoules. He makes a red Hermitage, Le Gréal, and a white (100 percent Marsanne), Les Rocoules.

Open: By appointment only.

Cave Coopérative de Tain l'Hermitage
22 Route de Larnage, 26600 Tain l'Hermitage.
Vineyards owned: Hermitage 31ha, Crozes-Hermitage 696ha, St-Joseph 79ha, Cornas 13ha, St-Péray 28ha, vin de pays 107ha. 2 million bottles. Coop (500 members).

Besides having members with vineyards in Crozes-Hermitage, St-Péray, St-Joseph and Cornas, this cooperative controls two-thirds of the Hermitage AC. Standards are good, if old fashioned, and quality is on the whole sustained. The wines tend not to have the infinite ageing ability achieved by some of the private producers, but are attractive after nine or ten years. Whites, made in a modern style, are fresh and crisp. *Open: Mon–Sun (during working hours).*

ST-JOSEPH AC

Domaine de Boisseyt-Chol
RN 86, 42410 Chavanay.
Vineyards owned: St-Joseph 5.8ha, Côte Rôtie 0.8ha, Côte du Rhône 2ha, classic-method Pétillant 1ha. 36,000 bottles. VP-R
Didier Chol owns this estate based at Boisseyt. He has land above Chavanay where he makes his St-Joseph. These wines are ready to drink after about five years. Other wines include small amounts of Côte Rôtie and Côtes du Rhône, and a sparkling wine made from Clairette grapes. *Open: Mon–Sat 9am–noon, 2–6pm.*

Pierre Coursodon
Place du Marché, Mauves, 07300 Tournon.
Vineyards owned: 11.5ha. 54,000 bottles. VP-R
Le Paradis, St-Pierre and l'Olivaie are names that Monsieur Coursodon uses for his red and white produced from vineyards in the southern part of the St-Joseph AC. The red is from 100 percent Syrah grapes – fermentation takes place in open wood vats. The white is from 100 percent Marsanne and made in lined tanks. *Open: Mon–Fri 8am–noon, 2–7pm.*

Émile Florentin
Route Nationale, Mauves, 07300 Tournon.
Vineyards owned: St-Joseph 4ha. 16,000 bottles. VP-R
Monsieur Florentin produces red and white St-Joseph called Clos de l'Arbalestrier on his small estate. His vines are old and yields are low, resulting in complex wines. The red is perhaps a little too tannic for the fruit, but the white, from Roussanne, is very good indeed. *Open: By appointment only.*

Bernard Gripa
Mauves, 07300 Tournon. Vineyards owned: St-Joseph 4ha, St-Péray 1ha. 25,000 bottles. VP-R
Wood fermentation is still the only way wine made *chez* Gripa, and the resultant quality makes him probably the best producer of St-Joseph. His vineyards are actually in the heart of the appellation in the area known as St-Joseph. The red has the soft richness typical of the AC; the white, from Marsanne, is made from 50-year-old vines. Monsieur Gripa's still St-Péray (he does not make a sparkling wine) is from a blend of 90 percent Marsanne and ten percent Roussanne. *Open: By appointment only.*

Jean-Louis Grippat
La Sauva, 07300 Tournon. Vineyards owned: St-Joseph 4.4ha, Hermitage 1.5ha. 31,000 bottles. VP-R
A small yield from the terraces of St-Joseph gives Monsieur

Grippat an intense wine but one whose fruit and life bring it round comparatively quickly – after five years. Part of his holding is in the St-Joseph AC. His white Hermitage (which, like the red Hermitage, is from the Les Murets vineyard) is very highly regarded and can age well for five or six years. Monsieur Grippat and Monsieur Gripa (*see previous entry*) are cousins.
Open: Appointments preferred.

J Marsanne et Fils

25 Avenue Ozier, 07300 Mauves. Vineyard owned: St-Joseph 1.3ha, Crozes-Hermitage 0.8ha. 8,000 bottles. VP-R
This is a traditional small-scale operation, producing rich, long-lived powerful wines which live on their tannins as much as their fruit. The wine is fermented and aged in wood for up to 12 months. *Open: By appointment only.*

Cave de St-Désirat

07340 St-Désirat.
Vineyards owned: St-Joseph 140ha, Côtes du Rhône 150ha, Condrieu 3ha. 700,000 bottles. Coop (82 members).
The main cooperative in St-Joseph producing a good standard of wine from its vineyards, including a special *cuvée*, Medaille d'Or, from steep terraces above the river. Visitors can see the coop's Maison des Vins by this vineyard.
Open: Mon–Sun 8am–7pm, by appointment.

Raymond Trollat

St-Jean-de-Muzols.
Monsieur Trollat's vineyard in St-Jean-de-Muzols is in the southern part of the appellation, with the hillside sites. His reds are firmly fruity and can age for anything up to ten years; his whites are similarly fruity, with a lovely peachy flavour.

ST-PÉRAY AC

Jean-François Chaboud

21 Rue F Malet, 07130 St-Péray.
Vineyards owned: 16ha. 50,000 bottles.
Monsieur Chaboud makes mainly sparkling St-Péray, with a smaller proportion of still wines as well. The sparkling wine, which is better, is made from 100 percent Marsanne, while the still wine has 20 percent Roussanne. *Open: By appointment only.*

Southern Rhône Producers

CHÂTEAUNEUF-DU-PAPE AC

Château de Beaucastel

Société Fermière des Vignobles Pierre Perrin, 84350 Courthézon. Vineyards owned: Châteauneuf 70ha, Côtes du Rhône 30ha. 350,000 bottles. VP-R
This large family estate has pioneered organic methods, cutting

out artificial fertilisers in the vineyard and adopting heat treatment of the grapes in the cellar before fermentation to give greater extract and avoid the need for sulphur. The vineyard has many old vines and yields are low, but the extra efforts are well rewarded by one of the top two or three Châteauneufs available. It ages superbly and is full of rich, vegetal fruit. In addition to the Château de Beaucastel which is Châteauneuf AC (and uses all 13 permitted grape varieties), a white Châteauneuf and an equally fine Côtes du Rhône Cru du Coudoulet (*see* page 135) are produced on part of the estate which is outside the Châteauneuf area.
Open: 9–11.30am, 2–5.30pm.

Domaine de Beaurenard

84230 Châteauneuf-du-Pape. Vineyards owned: Châteauneuf 30ha, Côtes du Rhône Rasteau 25ha. 200,000 bottles. VP-R
Domaine de Beaurenard is the name for both the Châteauneuf and the Côtes du Rhône wine produced here. The Domaine is one of the oldest concerns in the area, started in 1695, and Paul Coulon is the seventh generation. He uses a mixture of carbonic maceration and juice from pressed grapes to give a rich, fruity wine, low in tannin. The Côtes du Rhône Rasteau is a good, quick-maturing wine, which again is full of fruit.
Open: By appointment only.

Domaine Berthet-Rayne

Route de Roquemaure, 84350 Courthézon.
Vineyards owned: 6.7ha. 15,000 bottles. VP-R
This small estate produces Châteauneuf and Côtes du Rhône, using thermovinification at controlled temperatures. It also makes a small amount of Châteauneuf white.
Open: By appointment only.

Le Bosquet des Papes

Route d'Orange, 84230 Châteauneuf-du-Pape.
Vineyards owned: 26ha. 104,000 bottles.
Going up the lane to the ruins of the papal castle you pass the medium-sized vineyard of Les Bosquets des Papes, run by the Boiron family. Both white and red Châteauneuf are made. The red is a blend of 70 percent Grenache plus Syrah, Mourvèdre and Cinsaut. The wines are concentrated and age well.

Maison Brotte

BP 1, 84230 Châteauneuf-du-Pape. Vineyards owned: Côtes du Rhône 42ha, vin de pays 11ha. 2 million bottles. VP-R and N
Owned by J-P Brotte, president of the local Syndicat, this is one of the biggest firms in the area. It acts as *négociant* for wine from all over the Rhône, especially Côtes du Rhône, Côtes du Rhône-Villages, Coteaux du Tricastin, Côtes du Ventoux and Gigondas, as well as Châteauneuf where it sells the wine from estates such as Domaine de la Petite Bastide and Clos Bimard and makes a Cuvée Prestige. A fascinating museum at its cellars in Châteauneuf is well worth a visit. *Open: Mon–Sun 9am–noon, 2–6pm.*

Domaine de Cabrières-les-Silex
Route d'Orange, CD 68, 84230 Châteauneuf-du-Pape.
Vineyards owned: 65ha. 208,000 bottles. VP-R
One of the top estates of Châteauneuf, both because it is at the
highest point of the AC area and because of the quality of the
wine. The 'soil' here consists almost completely of the large round
stones (*galets roulées*) so often seen in pictures of the Châteauneuf
vineyards. Traditional methods are used, fermenting and ageing
in wood for the herby, meaty, spicy red. The white is also full and
traditional in style. *Open: By appointment only.*

Les Cailloux (Domaine André Brunel)
84230 Châteauneuf-du-Pape.
Vineyards owned: 31.5ha. 120,000 bottles.
Two separate vineyards make up this estate: one, Les Cailloux, for
Châteauneuf and one, called Domaine de la Bécassanne, for Côtes
du Rhône. There is as much as 70 percent Grenache in the wine,
but this is being reduced in favour of Syrah and Mourvèdre.
Vinification is a mixture of traditional long maceration after
crushing, and the newer method of vinifying using whole berries.
There is some new-wood ageing. A quick-maturing white is also
made. *Open: Tasting cellar at Cave Reflets, 3 Chemin du Bois de la
Ville in Châteauneuf: Mon–Fri 8am–noon, 2–6pm.*

Domaine Chante-Cigale
Avenue Louis Pasteur, 84230 Châteauneuf-du-Pape.
Vineyards owned: 42ha. 100,000 bottles. VP-R
Everything is in wood here, and the intense colour of the wine
achieved by macerating the grapes for nearly three weeks. Only
Grenache, Cinsaut, Mourvèdre and Syrah are used and the wine
is kept for 18 months in wood. A white is now also made.
Open: Mon–Fri 8am–noon, 2–6pm; by appointment Sat and Sun.

Domaine Chante Perdrix
84230 Châteauneuf-du-Pape.
Vineyards owned: 20ha. 60,000 bottles. VP-R
Big, old-style wines are made on this estate on the western edge
of the Châteauneuf AC area which makes only a red wine.
Open: By appointment only.

Domaine les Clefs d'Or
84230 Châteauneuf-du-Pape.
Very traditional wines, with great power and richness, from an
estate divided into two parts. The cellars are on the edge of the
town of Châteauneuf. Both a red and a white wine are made.
Vinification for the red wine is carried out with a mixture of
traditional and whole-berry maceration.
Open: Appointments preferred.

Domaine Durieu
84230 Châteauneuf-du-Pape.
The underground cellars of Paul Durieu are in the middle of the

town of Châteauneuf. Here he keeps wines that are in an elegant, not too heavy style and that mature well for up to ten years. The proportion of Grenache grapes planted in his vineyards is being increased. *Open: Appointments preferred.*

Château des Fines Roches
84230 Châteauneuf-du-Pape.
Vineyards owned: 24ha. 110,000 bottles. VP-R and N
The Mousset family owns a large *négociant* firm which produces wines from all over the Rhône Valley. In addition it owns the mock-Gothic Château des Fines Roches (part of which has now been converted into an up-market restaurant). The Châteauneuf estates are owned by different members of the family; besides Château des Fines Roches, there are also Château du Bois de la Garde, Domaine Fabrice Mousset, Domaine de la Font du Roi, Domaine de Clos du Roi and Clos St-Michel.
Open: By appointment only.

Château de la Font du Loup
Route du Châteauneuf-du-Pape, 84350 Courthézon.
Vineyards owned: Châteauneuf 21ha. 60,000 bottles. VP-R
While the fermentation process has in recent years been moved into stainless steel, ageing remains in wood. The red is elegant, less tannic than some Châteauneuf. The white is produced in small quantities, using a microvinification technique which gives considerable fruit and freshness and cuts down the tannin.
Open: By appointment only.

Château Fortia
84230 Châteauneuf-du-Pape.
Vineyards owned: 27ha. 93,000 bottles. VP-R
A traditional red and a modern-style white Châteauneuf are made at Château Fortia, which is generally regarded as one of the top Châteauneuf estates. The owning family, Le Roy de Boisaumarié is proud of the fact that it was one of its forebears, Châteauneuf's most famous grower the late Baron Le Roy, who in 1923 mapped out the best land in Châteauneuf and instigated what became the first Appellation Contrôlée area in France.
Open: Mon–Sat 9am–noon, 2–6pm.

Château de la Gardine
84230 Châteauneuf-du-Pape.
Vineyards owned: Châteauneuf 54ha, Côtes du Rhône-Villages 48ha. 400,000 bottles. VP-R
Members of the Brunel family have been *vignerons* since 1670, working on land to the west of Châteauneuf. Vinification here is modern and innovative, with investment in the cellar, the use of *pigeage* to extract colour, and the use of new wood. The Brunels produce a Cuvée Génération which is entirely aged in new wood – as are portions of the white wine. The Côtes du Rhône-Villages comes from the villages of Rasteau and Roaix.
Open: Mon–Fri 8.30am– 5.30pm.

Domaine du Grand Tinel
84230 Châteauneuf-du-Pape. Vineyards owned: 72ha
Very powerful wines are made here by Elie Jeune. The vineyards are in the eastern part of the appellation, around Courthézon, with some more centrally placed near the village of Châteauneuf. There is also a second label, Les Caves St-Paul.

Domaine de la Janasse
84350 Courthézon. Vineyards owned: 45ha. VP-R
Both Courthézon and Côtes du Rhône are made here, from a widely scattered vineyard of 50 different parcels. Christophe Sabon is a keen experimenter and makes many different *cuvées*, trying to reflect differences in the soil. His best Châteauneuf is called Chaupin (the name of a parcel of vines) and is 100 percent Grenache. Cuvée Vieilles Vignes is a particularly powerful wine. *Open: By appointment only.*

Domaine de Monpertuis
7 Avenue St-Joseph, 84230 Châteauneuf-du-Pape.
Vineyards owned: 17.2ha. 60,000 bottles. VP-R
The Jeune family makes old fashioned wines with a high proportion of Grenache, also with Syrah and Mourvèdre and year-long wood-ageing. A special *cuvée*, Cuvée Tradition, is made almost entirely from selected Grenache. White Châteauneuf is also made, as well as a little red Vin de Pays de la Principauté d'Orange. *Open: Mon–Sun July to October (by appointment only).*

Clos du Mont-Olivet
15 Avenue St-Joseph, 84230 Châteauneuf-du-Pape.
Vineyards owned: Châteauneuf 25ha, Côtes du Rhône 10ha,
vin de table 2ha. 155,000 bottles. VP-R
Traditional Châteauneuf style: big, robust reds with plenty of herby, spicy flavour and which need good ageing. A small amount of white wine is also made, plus Côtes du Rhône red from vineyards to the east of Châteauneuf at Bollène.
Open: Mon–Fri 8am–noon, 2–6pm; Sat by appointment.

Château de Mont-Redon
84230 Châteauneuf-du-Pape.
Vineyards owned: Châteauneuf 94ha, Côtes du Rhône 18ha.
530,000 bottles. VP-R
Château de Mont-Redon is one of the largest Châteauneuf estates – and also one of the best. The Châteauneuf vineyard is on the high plateau to the west of the AC area, facing north towards Orange. All 13 varieties of vines permitted under the Appellation Contrôlée rules are grown and there are small plantings of some varieties which have otherwise virtually disappeared. Each variety is vinified separately before being blended. The Abeille and Fabre families are seriously committed to producing aromatic, very fruity wines, using some carbonic maceration. The firm also own a Côtes du Rhône vineyard at Roquemaure to the southwest. *Open: Mon–Sun 8am–7pm, by appointment only.*

Domaine de Nalys
Route de Courthézon, 84230 Châteauneuf-du-Pape.
Vineyards owned: 52ha. 240,000 bottles. VP-R
All 13 permitted varieties are planted at this large estate, which was founded in 1778 and is set to the east side of the AC area. Aged for 12 months in wood the wines are quick-maturing with a floral, perfumed bouquet and a soft texture. Smaller quan-tities of white are also made. *Open: Mon–Fri 9am–noon, 2–6pm.*

Château la Nerthe
Route de Sorgues, 84230 Châteauneuf-du-Pape.
Vineyards owned: 90ha. 336,000 bottles. VP-R
Now part of Burgundy *négociants* Richard and David Foillard, this estate has a great Châteauneuf tradition. A state-of-the-art winery has recently been constructed. The wine is matured in wood, some of which is new each year. It makes a white wine, Clos de Beauvenir, and also two reds, Château la Nerthe and the top Cuvée des Cadettes. The estate was formerly known as de la Nerte. *Open: Mon–Fri 8.30am–12.30pm, 2.30–6.30pm.*

Clos de l'Oratoire des Papes
Rue St-Joseph, 84230 Châteauneuf-du-Pape.
Vineyards owned: 40ha. 140,000 bottles. VP-R
Red and white Châteauneuf are produced from a vineyard that boasts its own 18th-century altar. The owner, Madame Amouroux, runs the estate traditionally, making comparatively lightweight wines. *Open: Mon–Fri 8am–noon, 2–6pm.*

Clos des Papes
84230 Châteauneuf-du-Pape.
Vineyards owned: 37ha. 110,000 bottles. VP-R
Paul Avril, whose family has been making wine in the area for 300 years, produces traditional Châteauneuf with a high percentage of Grenache, using a long maceration and wood-ageing for up to 18 months. His wines are well structured, if tannic, and need a long time in bottle before they are ready to drink. Red makes up 90 percent of production; the remainder white. *Open: By appointment only.*

Domaine de Pegaü
Avenue Impériale, 84230 Châteauneuf-du-Pape.
Vineyards owned: 13ha. 60,000 bottles. VP-R
This is a strongly traditional estate, owned by the Féraud family who have been making wine here since 1670. The wines are big, concentrated, with a high proportion of Grenache, and need plenty of ageing time. *Open: By appointment only.*

Domaine Pierre Quiot
Château Maucoil, 84100 Orange.
Vineyards owned: Châteauneuf 30ha, Gigondas 14ha, Côtes du Rhône 14ha. 150,000 bottles. VP-R
Four brand names are used at this estate: Château Maucoil and

Quiot St-Pierre for Châteauneuf, Pradets for Gigondas and
Patriciens for Côtes du Rhône. The Châteauneuf vineyard is
probably the oldest named land in the area and records date back
to the 16th century. The style is traditional throughout the range.
Open: Appointments preferred.

Château Rayas
*84230 Châteauneuf-du-Pape. Vineyards owned: Châteauneuf
13ha, Côtes du Rhône 12ha. VP-R*
A small estate in Châteauneuf terms, but one which is highly
regarded for the quality of its traditionally-made red Châteauneuf.
Unusually, this is made from 100 percent Grenache, with low
yields even for Châteauneuf, and aged in wood for up to three
years. Côte du Rhône red and white are also produced from the
estate of Château de Fonsalette. *Open: By appointment only.*

Domaine de la Solitude
*84230 Châteauneuf-du-Pape. Vineyards owned: Châteauneuf
41ha, Côtes du Rhône 47ha. 490,000 bottles. VP-R*
A combination of traditional and modern techniques including
carbonic maceration for the red wines, with an increasing return
to tradition. The Châteauneuf has a high proportion (20 percent)
of Mourvèdre, which gives some power as well as an attractive
perfume. Monsieur Lançon makes white wines in both AC areas.
The estate has been in the family since the 16th century.
Open: Mon–Sun 8am–noon, 1–6pm.

Cuvée du Vatican
*Route de Courthézon, BP 33, 84230 Châteauneuf-du-Pape.
Vineyards owned: Châteauneuf 17ha, Côtes du Rhône 5ha, vin
de pays 30ha. 140,000 bottles. VP-R*
The sure-fire name Cuvée du Vatican is used both for the
Châteauneuf and the Côtes du Rhône produced by this firm. The
Châteauneuf has a long fermentation on the skins, giving it a very
deep colour. Monsieur Diffonty also makes Vin de Pays du Gard
in red, rosé and white, which are sold under the name Mas de
Brès. *Open: Mon–Sat 8am–noon, 2–6pm.*

Domaine de la Vieille Julienne
84100 Orange. Vineyards owned: 34ha. VP-R
While Côtes du Rhône occupies the bulk of the land of this
domaine, Châteauneuf is obviously the prime love of the Daumen
family. The style, from vines in the north of Châteauneuf, is
perfumed and there is some new-wood ageing. A white wine is
modern in style and has some wood-ageing.
Open: By appointment only.

Domaine du Vieux Télégraphe
*84370 Bedarrides.
Vineyards owned: Châteauneuf 50ha. 70,000 bottles. VP-R*
A very traditional estate producing concentrated, firm wines
which need many years to reach maturity. The Brunier family

vineyard is planted with 80 percent Grenache and also Cinsaut, Mourvèdre and Syrah. The yields are low and the reds have two years' ageing in large wood barrels, giving wines that are rich, supple and never too tannic. *Open: During working hours, and at 2 Avenue Louis Pasteur in Châteauneuf.*

CLAIRETTE DE DIE AC

Albert Andrieux
26340 Saillans.
Vineyards owned: Clairette de Die 11ha. 50,000 bottles. VP-R
This estate produces a range of Clairette wines – from still, dry Domaine du Plot to the dry classic-method and semi-dry *méthode dioise* sparkling wines. *Open: Mon–Fri 8am–noon, 2–6pm.*

Buffardel Frères
Boulevard de Cagnard, 26150 Die.
Vineyards owned: None. 300,000 bottles. N
Sweet and dry Clairette de Die are the only wines produced by this firm of *négociants*. Both are made by the classic method and sold under a number of different brand names: Buffardel Frères, Albert Reymond, Leblanc Père et Fils, J & R Leblanc and Jacques Leblanc. The dry wine is probably the best.
Open: By appointment only.

Union Producteurs du Diois
Cave Coopérative de la Clairette, Avenue de la Clairette, 26150 Die. Vineyards owned: 800ha. 3.2 million bottles.
Coop (530 members).
This cooperative controls 80 percent of Clairette de Die production: these are attractive Muscat wines made by the *méthode dioise*. A dry classic-method sparkling, Voconces Brut, is also made, as is still Clairette de Die and Châtillon-en-Diois.
Open: During working hours.

Domaine de Magord
Barsac, 26150 Die. Vineyards owned: 9ha. 60,000 bottles. VP-R
A small firm producing sweet Clairette de Die by *méthode dioise*, and a classic-method *brut* version. *Open: Appointments preferred.*

COTEAUX DU TRICASTIN AC

Domaine du Château des Estubiers
26290 Les Granges-Gontardes.
Vineyards owned: 146ha. 600,000 bottles. VP-R
A large vineyard producing red and rosé wines using stainless steel. The red is bottled 18 months after the harvest.
Open: Mon–Fri 8am–6pm; Sat by appointment.

Domaine de Grangeneuve
26230 Roussas. Vineyards owned: 95ha. 500,000 bottles. VP-R
This estate, along with the Domaine des Lones, is owned by

Madame Odette Bour whose main product is an excellent red wine made with a large proportion of Syrah. A little rosé and white are also made. The labels are particularly floral.
Open: Mon–Sun 9am–noon, 2–7pm.

Domaine de la Tour d'Elyssas
26290 Les Granges-Gontardes
By far the most interesting estate in this appellation. A number of wines are made including two single-vineyard wines, called Le Devoy and Les Échirousses; and a 100 percent Syrah *cuvée*. The quality is high and prices are low.

CÔTES DU LUBÉRON AC

Château de Canorgue
Route de Roussillon, 84480 Bonnieux.
Vineyards owned: 30ha. 120,000 bottles. VP-R
Red, rosé and white are made, the white and rosé wines in a fresh style and the red with some ageing in wood. Both styles are attractive and easy to drink. Biodynamic methods are followed in the vineyard. *Open: Mon–Fri 9am–noon, 3–7pm.*

Cellier de Marrenon
Quartier Notre-Dame, 84240 La Tour d'Aigues. Vineyards owned: Côtes du Lubéron 11,000ha, Côtes du Ventoux 3,000ha. 15 million bottles. Coop (combining 16 cooperative cellars).
This huge cooperative dominates the Côtes du Lubéron and has done much to bring the quality of the wines from the area up to an acceptable level. Red, rosé and white Côtes du Lubéron and Côtes du Ventoux are made: the red made by carbonic maceration for drinking young. The firm also produces Vin de Pays de Vaucluse, a little Côtes du Rhône and Châteauneuf-du-Pape, and *vin de table. Open: Mon–Sat 8am–noon, 2–6pm; Sun 8am–noon.*

Château de Mille
84400 Apt. Vineyards owned: 55ha. 290,000 bottles. VP-R
Highly praised Côtes du Lubéron is produced by Conrad Pinatel. Red, rosé and white wines are made and, unusually for most Côtes du Lubéron, the reds have ageing ability.
Open: Mon–Sun 8am–noon, 2–6pm.

Château Val-Joanis
84120 Pertuis. Vineyards owned: 170ha. 1.2 million bottles. VP-R
This model estate produced its first wine in '82, and has set new standards for the whole of the Côtes du Lubéron. The Chancel family have invested a fortune in top-class equipment for the vineyard and winery. The wines themselves are improving year by year. Chardonnay and Sauvignon Blanc have been planted as well as Ugni Blanc for whites; reds are made from Cinsaut, Grenache and up to 60 percent Syrah. Gamay is used for rosés. Vin de Pays de Vaucluse is also made.
Open: At the château 9am–5pm; in Pertuis a shop is open 10am–7pm.

CÔTES DU RHÔNE AC

For producers making Côtes du Rhône-Villages from a specific village, *see* next section.

Vignerons Ardèchois
Route de Vallon, Quartier Chaussy, 07120 Ruoms.
Vineyards owned: 6,363ha. 6 million bottles. Coop (a grouping
of 21 cooperatives with 4,228 members).
The largest single wine production unit in the Rhône Valley, this Union des Coopératives brings together smaller cooperatives in the Côtes du Rhône, Coteaux du Tricastin and Côtes du Vivarais. While the vast production of 4.2 million bottles of Vin de Pays des Coteaux de l'Ardèche (much of it as single varietal wines such as Syrah, Merlot, Gamay, Chardonnay – some of which goes to Louis Latour in Burgundy) dominates the operation, a good deal of Appellation Contrôlée wines are also made. The Côtes du Rhône is basic, sound wine, and there is a smaller amount of Côtes du Rhône-Villages made from 80 percent Grenache and 20 percent Syrah. Côtes du Vivarais is also made. *Open: Mon–Sat 8am–1pm, 2–7pm (shops at Ruoms and St-Didier-sous-Aubenas).*

Domaine de la Berthete
Route de Jonquières, 84850 Camaret sur Aigues.
Vineyards owned: 28ha. 200,000 bottles. VP-R
Traditional and modern techniques mix in these cellars and a combination of stainless steel and lined cement tanks is used for vinification. The wine's quality is good, especially the fresh white Côtes du Rhône, made from Grenache, Bourboulenc and Clairette. White Vin de Pays de la Principauté d'Orange and red Vin de Pays de Vaucluse are also produced. *Open: Mon–Sat 9am–noon, 2–6pm.*

Domaine du Cabanon
5 Place de la Fontaine, Saze, 30650 Rochefort-du-Gard.
Vineyards owned: 18ha. 120,000 bottles. VP-R
M Payan uses some carbonic maceration for his red Côtes du Rhône, which is the only wine he makes. The blend includes ten percent Syrah which gives a deep, long-lasting colour to the wine. It is not designed for ageing. *Open: Mon–Sun 10am–noon, 2–6pm.*

Domaine de Cabasse
84000 Séguret. Vineyards owned: 24ha. 96,000 bottles. VP-R
Côtes du Rhône and Côtes du Rhône-Villages Séguret are the wines produced on this estate. The Côtes du Rhône is an easy-to-drink wine, while the Côtes du Rhône-Villages is more serious and takes some bottle-age. *Open: By appointment only.*

Coopérative Vinicole Le Cellier des Templiers
84600 Richerenches. Vineyards owned: 870ha. 9 million
bottles. Coop (160 members).
While much of the wine here goes for bottling elsewhere, a small amount of Côtes du Rhône-Villages, Côtes du Rhône and Coteaux

du Tricastin is bottled on site. The wine generally tends to be on the light side and should be drunk young.

Open: Mon–Sat 8am–noon, 2.30–6.30pm; Sun April 15–Sept 15.

Chambovet Père et Fils
Rue St-Jean Prolongée, 84100 Orange.

Vineyards owned: 82ha. 300,000 bottles. VP-R

The vineyards belonging to this company are near the village of Suze-la-Rousse. They are from three estates: Château d'Estagnol, La Serre du Prieur and Domaine Ste-Marie. All three estates produce excellent wines – although my preference is for La Serre du Prieur, which is dominated by Syrah. In addition to reds, the firm also makes white Côtes du Rhône, including an unusual 100 percent Bourboulenc with apricot flavours and good fresh acidity.

Open: By appointment only.

Domaine de la Chartreuse de Valbonne
St-Paulet de Caisson, 30130 Pont St-Esprit.

Vineyards owned: 6ha. 30,000 bottles. VP-R

This beautiful Carthusian monastery founded in 1203 is now a medical centre which owns the surrounding vineyard. The red Côtes du Rhône is of good quality though production is limited. It is 60 percent Grenache and 30 percent Syrah yet the flavours of the Syrah dominate.

Open: Mon–Fri 9–11.30am, 2–6pm; Mon–Sun in summer.

Cru du Coudoulet
Château de Beaucastel, 84350 Courthézon.

This Côtes du Rhône vineyard is next door to the Châteauneuf-du-Pape vineyard of Château de Beaucastel (*see* page 125). Both are owned by the Perrin family, and the 'soil' of the Coudoulet vineyard is virtually identical to the huge stony pebbles of Châteauneuf. The quality is high, among the best of any Côtes du Rhône, and the wines are made using the same organic methods as Château de Beaucastel. Syrah, Cinsaut, Mourvèdre and Grenache are used in the blend. *Open: Appointments preferred.*

Château de Domazan
30390 Domazan. Vineyards owned: 30ha. VP-R

Modern vinification techniques produce a richly fruity Côtes du Rhône based on Grenache, Syrah and Cinsaut. The wines are not for keeping, but are immensely enjoyable when drunk young. The Chaudéracs, who have been at Domazan for several hundred years, have joined forces with a group of other producers (Domaine des Roches d'Arnaud, Domaine de Sarrazin, Mas d'École and Domaine Reynaud) to market their wines in bottle under the name of Caveau du Château de Domazan.

Open: Appointments preferred.

Domaine de l'Espigouette
84150 Violès. Vineyards owned: 20ha. 60,000 bottles. VP-R

Two vineyards make up this estate. The first, the Domaine de l'Espigouette, produces a Côtes du Rhône, predominantly of Grenache with ten percent Syrah and other varieties. The second, Plan de Dieu, makes Côtes du Rhône-Villages, with 80 percent Grenache and 20 percent Syrah, Cinsaut and Mourvèdre. Fermentation at controlled temperatures gives good colour and depth to both wines. Small amounts of white and rosé are also made. *Open: Mon–Sat 8am–noon, 1–7pm.*

Château de Fonsalette
84290 Lagarde-Paréol.

Owned by Jacques Reynaud of the Châteauneuf estate of Château Rayas (*see* page 131),this is a highly regarded Côtes du Rhône estate. Two *cuvées* of Côtes du Rhône are made, with 50 percent Grenache, 30 percent Cinsaut and 20 percent Syrah, a traditional blending but one which, through low yields and careful selection, produces rich, concentrated, powerful wines. There is also a 100 percent Syrah wine which has been compared to the wines of Hermitage. Wine that is not considered good enough for Château Rayas has also been used in the blend, increasing its quality still further. A white Côtes du Rhône is also made.
Open: Appointments preferred.

Château du Grand Moulas
Mornas, 84420 Piolenc.
Vineyards owned: 29ha. 96,000 bottles. VP-R

Monsieur Ryckwaert's cellars are close to the Rhône and surrounded by fruit trees which are an important part of his estate. His vineyards are on higher ground near Uchaux, where he makes Côtes du Rhône and Côtes du Rhône-Villages. He does not make wines for keeping, but they are immediately attractive with perfumed violet flavours that spring out of the glass. He presses 20 percent of the crop and leaves the rest to ferment as whole fruit, giving very good colour and also softening out the tannins. More recently, he has been making a pure Syrah wine, Clos de l'Écu. *Open: By appointment only.*

A Gras et Fils (Domaine de St-Chétin)
84600 Valréas. Vineyards owned: 25ha. 130,000 bottles. VP-R

Red and white Côtes du Rhône are made here. The red comes in two styles, Domaine des Hauts de St-Pierre, a blend of Grenache, Mourvèdre, Cinsaut and Syrah, and Le Trésor de St-Chétin, which adds some Carignan. A white, La Gloire de St-André, is also made and has a tiny amount of Viognier in the blend. The wine is bottled for the owners by the local cooperative.
Open: By appointment only.

Jean-Marie Lombard (Brézème)
Quartier Piquet, 26250 Liuron.
Vineyards owned: 4.1ha. 22,000 bottles. VP-R

This small vineyard is one of the few to be found in the gap between the Northern and Southern Rhône. It is planted entirely with Syrah for the reds; Marsanne and Viognier have now been introduced for some whites. The wine is aged for up to two years in wood, which gives depth as well as a rich tannic fruit that matures into spicy, vanilla roundness after four or five years. It is good to see the vineyard being expanded. *Open: By appointment.*

Domaine Martin de Grangeneuve
84150 Jonquières. Vineyards owned: 50ha. 75,000 bottles. VP-R
Red, rosé and white Côtes du Rhône are produced here. The red is particularly attractive – rich and full bodied, it can age well. The white is one-third each Grenache Blanc, Bourboulenc and Clairette. The estate also produces a Vin de Pays de la Principauté d'Orange, a blend of Grenache and Syrah with ten percent Cabernet Sauvignon. *Open: During working hours.*

Clos de la Mure
Derboux 84430 Mondragon. 12ha. VP-R
A small producer of high-quality Côtes du Rhône and Gigondas. Eric Michel uses traditional techniques and combines these with low yields to achieve enormous concentration of fruit. He believes that wines should give pleasure, and both the Côtes du Rhône and the Gigondas (which he has made only since '94 when he acquired the vineyard in this appellation) do just that.
Open: Appointment preferred.

Domaine de la Réméjeanne
Cadignac, 30200 Sabran.
Vineyards owned: 25ha. 25,000 bottles. VP-R
A high proportion of Syrah (35 percent) in red Côtes du Rhône gives good depth and ageing ability. The white, which ferments for a month at a low temperature, is from Clairette, Bourboulenc and Ugni Blanc. Quality is good for both wines. Much of the wine is sold in bulk. *Open: Appointments preferred.*

Domaine de la Renjarde
84830 Sérignan du Comtat.
Vineyards owned: 52ha. 250,000 bottles. VP-R
Domaine de la Renjarde was one of the first estates to harvest entirely by machine. This does not seem to spoil the deep, peppery Côtes du Rhône Cuvée Henri Fabre (60 percent Syrah). There is also a Côtes du Rhône-Villages, Domaine de la Renjarde, (80 percent Grenache plus Syrah and Mourvèdre) made in a more traditional style for drinking younger. Under the same ownership as Château la Nerthe (*see* page 130). *Open: By appointment only.*

Domaine du Roure
St-Marcel d'Ardèche, 07700 Bourg St-Andeol.
Vineyards owned: 11ha. 12,000 bottles. VP-R
Vines of more than 50 years old produce superb wine: full, rich and slow to mature. The Grenache dominates, with smaller amounts of Syrah, Cinsaut and Carignan. While not all the wine is estate-bottled, there are plans to increase the amount up to around 80,000 bottles. *Open: Mon–Fri 8am–noon.*

Château de Ruth
84190 Gigondas.

The large estate of Château de Ruth is owned by the Meffre family, whose most famous wine is Gigondas from Château Raspail. The wine produced is characteristically good: it is commercial but enjoyably fruity and should be drunk young.
Open: Appointments preferred.

Domaine St-Apollinaire
84110 Puymeras.

A 100 percent biodynamic vineyard, owned by Frédéric Dumas, near the small village of Puymeras and not far from Rasteau. In addition to a blended Côtes du Rhône, there is also a wine made from 100 percent Syrah grapes. The wines have considerable intensity and depth of flavour, a result of the fact that they are only lightly filtered before they are bottled.
Open: Appointments preferred.

Château St-Estève d'Uchaux
Route de Sérignan, Uchaux 84100 Orange.
Vineyards owned: 49ha. 290,000 bottles. VP-R

An excellent estate on a sandy ridge north of Orange, producing a light style of wine. A full range of Côtes du Rhône wines is made by the Français family, including a rare 100 percent Viognier Blanc de Cépage and a classic-method sparkling *blanc de blancs*. Wines have both the Côtes du Rhône AC and the Villages AC – the Villages wines are 40 percent Syrah. There is a very fine Grande Réserve red containing 50 percent Syrah. In exceptional years, a Cuvée Prestige is also made with 60 percent Syrah: this is partly aged in new wood for 12 months.
Open: Mon–Fri 8am–noon, 2–6pm.

Coopérative Vinicole La Suzienne
26790 Suze-la-Rousse. Vineyards owned: 1,000ha. 1 million bottles. Coop (937 members).

A huge cooperative at the heart of the Côtes du Rhône plain, under the shadow of the Université du Vin. It makes Côtes du Rhône, Côtes du Rhône-Villages and Coteaux du Tricastin under the name of La Suzienne. Quality is variable but getting better. All the bottling is done by the Union des Vignerons at Tulette.
Open: By appointment only.

Domaine des Treilles
26770 Montbrison-sur-Lez.
Vineyards owned: 30ha. 45,000 bottles. VP-R

This is a traditional family estate and has been owned by Monsieur Rey-Mery's family since 1772. Sound reds are produced, with a high proportion of Grenache supplemented by Syrah; small quantities of white and a little rosé. The red has two years' ageing before being bottled. There is a small museum attached to the cellar with old viticultural implements on display.
Open: Mon–Sun, by appointment only.

La Vieille Ferme
Route de Jonquières, 84100 Orange. N

The *négociant* business is owned by the Perrin family of Château de Beaucastel in Châteauneuf-du-Pape. It produces both red and white Côtes du Rhônes of a good, consistent quality, from purchased grapes. It also produces red and white Côtes du Ventoux which again is of a high standard.

Domaine du Vieux Chêne
Rue Buisseron, 84850 Camaret.

Two wines are made here by the Bouche brothers. Cuvée des Capucines is in the forward, fruity style of Côtes du Rhône. Cuvée de la Haie aux Grives, with a greater proportion of Syrah in the blend, is more complex and should be given time to mature. Both are excellent examples of good-value Côtes du Rhône. There is also a white *vin de pays*.

CÔTES DU RHÔNE-VILLAGES AC

Domaine les Aussellons
84110 Villedieu.
Vineyards owned: 32ha. 200,000 bottles. VP-R

This Vinsobres estate produces both Villages wine and generic Côtes du Rhône. The Villages wine is made mainly from Grenache, but there is some Mourvèdre and Syrah in the blend. Ageing takes place in large wood barrels which gives the wine some good concentration. Small quantities of white are also made from Bourboulenc. *Open: Mon–Sun 8am–8pm.*

Domaine de Boissan
84110 Sablet.

Under the owner Hubert Bonfils, this estate makes a deeply coloured Côtes du Rhône-Villages Sablet that has ten percent Syrah and two percent Mourvèdre in its blend. It also makes a Gigondas, which has some wood-ageing.
Open: Appointments preferred.

Domaine Brusset
84290 Cairanne. Vineyards owned: 45ha.

Half this estate produces Côtes du Rhône-Villages Cairanne, while the other half comes under the generic Côtes du Rhône appellation. The Cairanne is made in rosé, white, and a red style which ages well. Monsieur Brusset also makes a powerful Gigondas and a rosé wine with some Mourvèdre in the blend.
Open: Appointments preferred.

Domaine de la Cantharide
84820 Visan. Vineyards owned: 16ha.

Good if uncomplicated red is made at this estate. The style is designed for ageing and the colour of the wines and the amount of tannin present would suggest it is successful.
Open: Appointments preferred.

Daniel et Jean Couston
Route de St-Roman, 26790 Tulette. Vineyards owned: Visan 50ha, Valréas 40ha. 500,000 bottles. VP-R

There are two estates belonging to this company. The Visan estate is Domaine du Garrigon, where red Villages and white and rosé Côtes du Rhône are made. The Valréas estate is Domaine de la Grande Bellane, producing red and rosé. A Côtes du Rhône Primeur is also produced. The company prefers to use organic methods in the vineyards and to stabilise the wine in the cellar with modern equipment rather than chemicals.
Open: By appointment only.

Union des Vignerons l'Enclave des Papes
84600 Valréas. Vineyards owned: 2,000ha. 3 million bottles. Coop (800 members).

This huge cooperative produces quick-maturing wine: mostly Côtes du Rhône, with some Coteaux du Tricastin. There is also some Côtes du Rhône-Villages Valréas. The members have increased their plantings of Grenache and Syrah and reduced the Carignan in their vineyards. The 'Enclave of the Popes' is a small area of land which remained Papal territory until the time of the Revolution and is now an enclave of the Vaucluse *département* in the middle of the Drôme. *Open: Mon–Fri 8am–noon, 2–6pm.*

Caves CN Jaume
26490 Vinsobres.

One of the few private producers in Vinsombres, Richard and Pascal Jaume run an immaculate cellar in the centre of the village. They produce Côtes du Rhône-Villages Vinsombre under the Domaine Jaume name as well as simpler Côtes du Rhône under the name of Cuvée Friande, which is designed for early drinking. The top wine is named after the Jaume parents, Claude and Nicole, who are still very much in evidence and obviously enjoying their sons' success. *Open: Mon–Sat during working hours.*

Domaine Martin
Plan de Dieu, 84150 Travaillan.
Vineyards owned: 48ha. 100,000 bottles. VP-R

Traditional techniques and stainless steel are used at this medium-sized estate. Reds are aged in wood, as is the Rasteau red *vin doux naturel* made from 100 percent Grenache. Other wines produced are red, white and rosé Côtes du Rhône and red Côtes du Rhône-Villages. *Open: Mon–Fri 8am–7pm.*

Domaine du Moulin
26110 Vinsobres.
Vineyards owned: Vinsobres 20ha. 40,000 bottles. VP-R

This traditional producer makes only Côtes du Rhône-Villages Vinsobres – and they are very good. The red is cherry-fresh, attractive when young, but with the ability to age for three or four years. A white and rosé are also made.
Open: Mon–Fri 8am–noon, 2–7pm.

Domaine Clos de l'Oratoire St-Martin
Route de St-Roman, 84290 Cairanne.
Vineyards owned: 25ha. 62,000 bottles. VP-R
A top-notch domaine making big, quite tannic wines with a
majority of Grenache but increasing amounts of Syrah and
Mourvèdre. A Cuvée Prestige Cairanne comes from old Grenache
and Mourvèdre; red and white Couvée Haut Coustins are aged in
wood. Frédéric and François Alary also make a lighter style red,
rosé and white Côtes du Rhône. *Open: Mon–Sat 8am–noon, 2–7pm.*

GAEC Pelaquié
St-Victor la Coste, 30290 Laudun.
Vineyards owned: 14ha. 20,000 bottles. VP-R
Red and white Côtes du Rhône-Villages Laudun are produced at
this small estate. Stainless-steel vats are used for the vinification,
giving a fruity, fresh red for drinking young. There is also a white
Côtes du Rhône and some red Lirac. The wines are all attractive
and well made. *Open: Mon–Sat 8am–noon, 2–6pm.*

Domaine Rabasse-Charavin
6 Font d'Estevenas, Coteaux St-Martin, 84290 Cairanne.
Vineyards owned: 23ha. 120,000 bottles. VP-R
A high-quality producer of Côtes du Rhône-Villages made from
Cairanne and Rasteau and generic Côtes du Rhône red and white.
The estate makes a 100 percent Syrah Côtes du Rhône, called
Cuvée d'Estevenas and aged in wood, which is very good. The
vineyards have a high proportion of 80-year-old vines. Mme
Corinne Couturier also makes two exciting *vins de pays*, one 100
percent Syrah, the other 100 percent Mourvèdre, as well as a
powerful 100 percent Syrah Cuvée Pigée Christophe, from grapes
trodden by foot. *Open: Mon–Sat 8am–12.30pm, 2–6pm.*

Cave des Vignerons de Rasteau
84110 Rasteau. Vineyards owned: 750ha. 2.2 million bottles.
Coop (180 members).
One of the best cooperatives in the Rhône Valley, producing Côtes
du Rhône and Côtes du Rhône-Villages Rasteau, including a
Cuvée Prestige which is matured in wood and a Côtes du Rhône
Primeur. The cooperative is also the biggest producer of sweet
Rasteau *vin doux naturel*, from 100 percent Grenache. One of the
reasons for its success is that it pays members on the quality of
the grapes, not the potential alcoholic content.
Open: Mon–Fri 8am–noon, 2–6pm.

Pierre Rosati
La Verrière, Route de Pegue, 84600 Valréas. Vineyards owned:
Valréas 18ha, St-Pantaléon-les-Vignes 2ha. 26,000 bottles. VP-R
Stainless-steel vinification and then wood-ageing for the reds
produces some smooth, clean-tasting Côtes du Rhônes – both
generic and Villages from Valréas. Monsieur Rosati also makes
white and rosé Côtes du Rhône. All the wines are sold under the
name Ferme La Verrière. *Open: Mon–Sun 8am–7pm.*

Cave Coopérative de Sablet Le Gravillas

84110 Sablet. Coop (200 members).

A somewhat old-fashioned cooperative, although efforts are being made to produce some good generic Côtes du Rhône. The Sablet and Gigondas wines which the coop also produces are less successful. *Open: Mon–Fri 9am–noon; 2.30–5.30pm.*

Château St-Maurice l'Ardoise

30290 Laudun. Vineyards owned: 96ha. 450,000 bottles. VP-R

Most of the production at this estate is of Côtes du Rhône-Villages or Côtes du Rhône, which is sold under a number of different names: Château St-Maurice l'Ardoise, Château St-Maurice, Domaine du Mont-Jupiter (there are ruins of an ancient temple on the site) and Clos de Rossignac. Monsieur Valat also makes a small amount of Lirac from vineyards in St-Laurent-les-Arbres, and Vin de Pays du Gard.

Open: During working hours.

Cave Coopérative St-Pantaléon-les-Vignes

26770 St-Pantaléon-les-Vignes.

Vineyards owned: Côtes du Rhône 635ha, Coteaux du Tricastin 56ha, Côtes du Rhône-Villages 13ha, Côtes du Rhône-Villages St-Pantaléon 47ha, Côtes du Rhône-Villages Rousset 35ha. 180,000 bottles. Coop (220 members).

Half the wine is sold in bulk to *négociants*, 20 percent is bottled for the cooperative at Tulette. The main wines are Côtes du Rhône-Villages St-Pantaléon and Rousset; some St-Pantaléon is aged in wood. *Open: Appointments preferred.*

Domaine Ste-Anne

30200 St-Gervais.

A wide range of red wines is made at this fine estate in St-Gervais. Cuvée Notre Dame des Cellettes has a high percentage of Syrah, while Cuvée St-Gervais also has a considerable amount of Mourvèdre (40 percent). The owner, Guy Steinmaier, also makes a Côtes du Rhône-Villages blend, and, most unusually, a 100 percent Viognier white wine, which has been compared favourable to Condrieu (at a much lower price).

Open: Appointments preferred.

Domaine la Soumade

Rasteau, 84110 Vaison la Romaine.

Vineyards owned: Rasteau 27ha. 80,000 bottles. VP-R

Côtes du Rhône-Villages Rasteau and Rasteau *vin doux naturel* are André Roméro's top AC wines; he also makes generic Côtes du Rhône and Vin de Pays de la Principauté d'Orange from Cabernet Sauvignon and Merlot. *Open: Mon–Sat 8am–noon, 2–7pm.*

Domaine du Val des Rois

Route de Vinsobres, 84600 Valréas, Vaucluse.

Vineyards owned: 4ha. 22,000 bottles.

The Bouchard family has been at this estate since 1681, and has commemorated the fact with a Cuvée de la 8ième Génération, a blend of Grenache and Gamay. The Côtes du Rhône-Villages Valréas 'Signature' is 75 percent Grenache and 20 percent Syrah, and can age up to ten years. Cuvée des Rois Côtes du Rhône red and rosé are also produced.

Open: Mon–Fri 9.30am–noon, 2.30–7pm.

Coopérative Vinicole la Suzienne *See* page 138.

Domaine de Verquière
84110 Sablet. Vineyards owned: 50ha. 100,000 bottles. VP-R
Monsieur Chamfort is a traditional producer who uses wood for maturing and is not afraid to leave the wine in cask for some time. He makes red Côtes du Rhône-Villages from Sablet, Vacqueyras AC and generic red and rosé Côtes du Rhône. There is also a high-quality Rasteau *vin doux naturel.*
Open: Appointments preferred.

CÔTES DU VENTOUX AC

Domaine des Anges
84570 Mormoiron. Vineyards owned: 20ha. 107,000 bottles. VP-R
English owner Malcolm Swann has planted Grenache, Syrah, Cinsaut and Carignan to make a full, fresh, easy-drinking Côtes du Ventoux which brings out all the attraction of this AC area. *Open: Mon–Sun 9am–12.30pm, 2–6.30pm; other times by appointment.*

GIGONDAS AC

Pierre Amadieu
84190 Gigondas. Vineyards owned: Gigondas 120ha, Côtes du Ventoux 35ha. 990,000 bottles. VP-R and N
A traditional firm with spectacular new cellars at the entrance to the village. Style is rather traditional, and none the worse for that. The principal wines are Gigondas and Côtes du Ventoux from the firm's own estates, but Châteauneuf-du-Pape and Côtes du Rhône are also made. *Open: During working hours.*

Edmond Burle
La Beaumette, 84190 Gigondas.
Vineyards owned: Gigondas 1.6ha, Vacqueyras 1ha, Côtes du Rhône 8ha, vin de table 5ha. 30,000 bottles. VP-R
This is a small, traditional firm which matures wine in wood, and whose pride and joy is their Gigondas Les Pallierondas, a rich and powerful wine. But Monsieur Burle also makes generic Côtes du Rhône, Vacqueyras and *vin de table.*
Open: During working hours.

Domaine du Cayron
84190 Gigondas. VP-R
High proportions of Syrah and Cinsaut produce wines which not only have great intensity and power, but which also age well.

Monsieur Faraud adopts traditional techniques, including long ageing in large wooden barrels, and minimum fining and filtration. *Open: Appointments preferred.*

Cave des Vignerons de Gigondas
84190 Gigondas.
Vineyards owned: 250ha. 500,000 bottles. Coop (93 members).
This cooperative uses carbonic maceration to soften the tannins and increase the fruit in its Gigondas. As a result it is soft and quite quick to mature. The brand names used are Cuvée du Président and Signeurie de Fontange. More traditionally made wines are sold under the names Signature and Tête de Cuvée. A smaller amount of Côtes du Rhône is also made. *Open: By appointment only.*

Domaine les Goubert (Jean-Pierre Cartier)
84190 Gigondas. Vineyards owned: 22ha. VP-R
This is a comparatively new estate, founded in 1973, producing red Côtes du Rhône-Villages (from Beaumes-de-Venise) and white (from Sablet) as well as the more significant Gigondas. A new interest is Côtes du Rhône from Beaumes-de-Venise. The style generally is elegant rather than too powerful, and the wines age well. A top *cuvée*, Cuvée Florence, aged in new wood, is made in small quantities in good years.
Open: Mon–Fri 9am–noon, 2–7pm; by appointment Sat and Sun.

Domaine de Longue-Toque
84190 Gigondas. Vineyards owned: 23ha. 55,000 bottles. VP-R
The Chapalain family has owned this domaine for many generations. It follows traditional methods for making its Gigondas, with some wines being aged in 400-litre wood casks. There is 20 percent Syrah and five percent Mourvèdre in the blend. *Open: Mon–Sun (winter) 9am–5pm, (summer) 9am–7pm.*

Domaine du Grand Montmirail
Gigondas, 84109 Beaumes-de-Venise.
Vineyards owned: 3ha. 66,000 bottles. VP-R
This estate is being revived by the energetic owner Denis Cheron. He has increased the proportion of Syrah in the wines and restricted yields to produce a concentrated blend with considerable ageing ability. Names used are Domaine du Roucas de St-Pierre, Domaine de St-Gens and Domaine du Pradas.
Open: By appointment only.

Le Mas des Collines
84190 Gigondas.
Vineyards owned: Gigondas 15ha, Côtes du Rhône 38ha.
60,000 bottles. VP-R
Mas des Collines is the name Monsieur Gorecki uses for his Gigondas. He calls his Côtes du Rhône 'La Bruissière'. Both are traditionally made wines, with good tannin and firm fruit. Much of the Gigondas vineyard is planted with old vines.
Open: Appointments preferred.

Gabriel Meffre

84190 Gigondas. Vineyards owned: Gigondas 92ha,
Châteauneuf-du-Pape 88ha, Côtes du Rhône 500ha, Côtes du
Provence 60ha. 2.5 million bottles. VP-R and N

The largest producer of Gigondas, Gabriel Meffre has maintained good quality and has done much to help the reputation of the AC area. Modern, large-scale techniques are used, with stainless steel much in evidence. Many famous names come under the Meffre banner: Château de Ruth in Ste-Cécile-les-Vignes, Château Raspail in Gigondas, and Château de Vaudieu in Châteauneuf. New plantations are currently under way to produce white Côtes du Rhône. *Open: By appointment only.*

Château de Montmirail

84190 Vacqueyras.

Both Vacqueyras and Gigondas are made at this estate in Montmirail. The style is light and quick-maturing, and there is a high proportion of Grenache in the blend.
Open: Appointments preferred.

Domaine de Pallières

84190 Gigondas. Vineyards owned: Gigondas 25ha.
113,000 bottles. VP-R

A long-established vineyard (founded 1765), still owned by the original family. There is a traditional approach to winemaking, with long fermentation and ageing for up to three years in wood. The result is a red Gigondas of immense power, considerable tannin and a very long life. The estate also produces a rosé.
Open: 8am–noon, 2–6pm.

Domaine du Pesquier

84190 Gigondas. Vineyards owned: 24ha. 60,000 bottles. VP-R

Solid wines from Gigondas and Côtes du Rhône, made in cement tanks and old wood. The wines age well.
Open: Mon–Fri 8am–noon, 2–7pm.

Domaine Raspail-Ay

Gigondas, 84190 Beaumes-de-Venise.
Vineyards owned: Gigondas 18ha. 50,000 bottles. VP-R

Red and rosé Gigondas are made by Dominique Ay in a traditional style, using large wood for fermentation and maturation. A blend of Grenache, Mourvèdre and Syrah grapes gives a big, complex, long-lasting wine, one of the best in the appellation.
Open: Mon–Sun 9am–noon, 2–6pm.

Domaine St-Gayan

84190 Gigondas. Vineyards owned: Gigondas 14ha, Côtes du
Rhône-Villages 16ha. 70,000 bottles. VP-R

Jean-Pierre Meffre produces firm, rich wines from his three estates. The Gigondas is powerfully tannic, a Côtes du Rhône Rasteau has a delightful perfumed flavour from the high proportion of Mourvèdre (35 percent). The generic Côtes du Rhône,

produced from vineyards in Sablet, is made in red, rosé and white.
Domaine St-Gayan has been in the family since 1400.
Open: Mon–Sat 9–11.45am, 2–7pm.

Domaine du Terme
Gigondas, 84190 Beaumes-de-Venise.
Vineyards owned: 26ha. 68,000 bottles. VP-R
A well-established estate that brings together a traditionally made
Gigondas, with a high proportion of Grenache, and Côte du
Rhône-Villages Sablet (red and white). Gigondas spends one year
in wood. *Open: During working hours.*

Château de Trignon
84190 Gigondas. Vineyards owned: 71ha. 250,000 bottles. VP-R
A large property, owned by the Roux family, with a holding in
Gigondas, vineyards in Rasteau and Sablet making Côtes du
Rhône-Villages, and more vineyards making generic Côtes du
Rhône. The family also has 25 hectares in Châteauneuf-du-Pape,
where it produces 100,000 bottles of Domaine des Sénéchaux.
Open: (Domaine du Trignon) Mon–Sat 9am–7pm; Sun by appointment.

LIRAC AC

Château de Clary
30126 Lirac.
Roman remains have been found on this estate and there is a
possibility that wines have been made here since then. The
current wine is red, powerful and strongly ripe.
Open: Appointments preferred.

Domaine de Castel-Oualou
30150 Roquemaure.
Vineyards owned: Lirac 93ha. 750,000 bottles. VP-R
There are three properties owned by the Assemat family, of
which Castel-Oualou is the largest. Here they make both Lirac
and Côtes du Rhône. Other estates under the same ownership are
Domaine des Garrigues and Domaine des Causses, which also
make both wines. Methods in this large undertaking are modern,
but the reds are aged for up to 12 months in new wood.
Open: Mon–Sat 8am–noon, 2–6pm; Sun by appointment.

Château le Devoy Martine
St-Laurent-des-Arbres, 30126 Tavel.
Vineyards owned: Lirac 41ha. 229,000 bottles. VP-R
Traditional and modern techniques mix, with stainless steel used
for fermentation and no wood-ageing. The Lombardo brothers
make red, rosé and white Lirac.
Open: Mon–Fri 9am–noon, 2–6pm; Sat 9am–noon.

Château de Ségriès
30126 Lirac. Vineyards owned: Lirac 20ha. 12,000 bottles. VP-R
The Comte de Régis, one of the pioneers of the Lirac AC, makes

traditional, quite tannic reds and rosés and a softer white at this estate, whose château dates from the 17th and 18th centuries. *Open: By appointment only.*

Domaines Verda (Château St-Roch)

30150 Roquemaure. Vineyards owned: Lirac and Côtes du Rhône 60ha. 250,000 bottles. VP-R
There are two Lirac estates owned by the Verda family. The original is Château St-Roch which produces red, rosé and white Lirac. The reds include a special *cuvée* which has two years in wood and two in bottle before sale. The other estate is Domaine Cantegril-Verda, acquired in 1983, where a lighter style of wine is made for more immediate drinking, and Côtes du Rhône. All the wines reach a high standard.
Open: Mon–Fri 8am–noon, 2–6.30pm.

TAVEL AC

Château d'Aquéria

30126 Tavel.
Vineyards owned: Tavel and Lirac 64ha. 350,000 bottles. VP-R
The Olivier family have owned this 17th-century property since 1920. The bulk of production here is of Tavel rosé, with smaller quantities of red Lirac. Traditional and modern techniques are combined to produce a classic Tavel, full of raspberry flavour and with a good balance of acidity and fruit. The vineyard is being expanded. *Open: Mon–Fri 8am–noon, 2–6pm.*

Domaine de la Genestière

30126 Tavel. Vineyards owned: Tavel 27ha, Lirac 11ha. 220,000 bottles. VP-R
The owner, Jean-Claude Garcin, produces mainly Tavel rosé here, but also some Lirac red and white. He uses traditional methods.
Open: Mon–Fri 8am–noon, 1.30–5.30pm.

Domaine Jean-Pierre Lafond

Route des Vignobles, 30126 Tavel. Vineyards owned: Tavel 30ha, Lirac 10ha, Côtes du Rhône 10ha. 150,000 bottles. VP-R
This old-established family estate works with modern methods to make a deliciously fruity, fresh Tavel. Monsieur Lafond also makes red Lirac and Côtes du Rhône. Brand names include Roc-Épine and Cuvée Lafond as well as Domaine Pierre Lafond.
Open: Mon–Fri 9am–noon, 2–6pm.

Domaine Maby

BP 8, 30126 Tavel. Vineyards owned: Tavel 42ha, Lirac 30ha, Côtes du Rhône 16ha, vin de pays 6ha. 500,000 bottles. VP-R
The Maby family has owned vineyards for several generations. It uses stainless steel for the Tavel and for a white Lirac, and wood for the red Lirac and Côtes du Rhône. The styles reflect the vinification, with fresh rosés and whites, and reds which need at least four years in bottle. *Open: Mon–Fri 8am–noon, 2–6pm.*

Les Vignerons de Tavel
Route de la Commanderie, BP 3, 30126 Tavel.
Vineyards owned: Tavel 400ha. 4 million bottles. Association of VP-R (135 members).
Modern techniques such as cold fermentation and centrifuging are employed by this group of producers, along with the traditional cold maceration on the grape skins. This avoids the problem of tannin which can affect some Tavel rosés. The wine is designed to be drunk young and fresh. This is not a cooperative but more of a marketing organisation. *Open: Mon–Sun 9am–noon, 2–6pm.*

Château de Trinquevedel
30126 Tavel. Vineyards owned: Tavel 30ha. 80,000 bottles. VP-R
Carbonic maceration for 72 hours is used to make this Tavel quite a deep rosé colour. It is fresh, attractively fruity and one of the most refreshing Tavels around. *Open: By appointment only.*

Le Vieux Moulin
30126 Tavel.
A modern, fresh Tavel Rosé is made from Grenache and Cinsaut to be drunk young. *Open: By appointment only.*

VACQUEYRAS AC

Clos des Cazeaux
84190 Vacqueyras.
This estate produces reasonable quantities of Vacqueyras and smaller quantities of Gigondas. Two *cuvées* of the Vacqueyras are made: Cuvée des Templiers and Cuvée St-Roch. The former is almost 100 percent Syrah, the latter has 75 percent Syrah and is lighter in style. *Open: Appointments preferred.*

Domaine de la Fourmone
Vacqueyras, 84190 Beaumes-de-Venise.
Vineyards owned: Gigondas 9ha, Vacqueyras 12ha, Côtes du Rhône 8ha. 38,000 bottles. VP-R
A traditional producer, Monsieur Combe makes a Vacqueyras full of deep fruit which sees at least eight months in wood. He also makes Gigondas under the brand name l'Oustau Fauquet: a big but elegant wine which needs seven years before it begins to mature. *Open: Appointments preferred.*

Domaine des Lambertins
Vacqueyras, 84190 Beaumes-de-Venise.
Vineyards owned: Vacqueyras 24ha. 70,000 bottles. VP-R
A traditional family firm run by the Lambert brothers producing Vacqueyras and Côtes du Rhône wines, both in red only.
Open: By appointment only.

Château des Roques
84260 Sarrians. Vineyards owned: 38ha. VP-R
Modern techniques operate here, although the red Vacqueyras (a

blend of Grenache, Mourvèdre and Syrah) does have some time in barrels. A top *cuvée* is called Cornelius, named after the Roman soldier whose offering to Mars was dug up near the estate house. The firm also makes a rare white Vacqueyras, from Marsanne and Bourboulenc. *Open: By appointment only.*

Domaine le Sang des Cailloux
Route de Vacqueyras, 84260 Sarrians.
Vineyards owned: Vacqueyras 18ha. 85,000 bottles. VP-R
Monsieur Jean Ricard makes a Vacqueyras which he ferments and matures in wood. The quality is high, with herby, spicy fruit and touches of wood tannin suggesting good ageing ability.
Open: Mon–Fri 8am–noon, 1–6pm.

CÔTES DU VIVARAIS VDQS

Domaine de Belvezet
07700 St-Remèze.
There is a little Cabernet Sauvignon and Merlot in this vineyard as well as the more usual Southern Rhône varieties. The wine style is fruity but powerful, and it can be drunk young.

Union des Producteurs
07150 Orgnac l'Aven.
Vineyards owned: 565ha. 350,000 bottles. Coop (183 members).
This cooperative dominates the VDQS of Côtes du Vivarais, producing red, rosé and white. The red has 30 percent Syrah and 40 percent Grenache, the white 50:50 Clairette and Grenache Blanc. The brand name is Vins d'Orgnac.
Open: Summer: everyday; winter: Mon–Fri and Sat morning.

Domaine de Vigier
Lagorce, 07150 Vallon Pont d'Arc.
Vineyards owned: 35ha. 70,000 bottles. VP-R
Côtes du Vivarais is made from 100 percent Syrah. The estate also produces varietal Merlot and Chardonnay Vin de Pays des Coteaux de l'Ardèche. *Open: Mon–Fri 8am–noon, 2–6pm.*

Provence

Provence was the first area of France to be planted with vines. They were already growing when Greek traders from Asia Minor arrived at the Phoenician city of Marseille in 600 BC. The Greeks set about consolidating what they found and when the Romans arrived in about 125 BC they continued the process. It was from Provence – the Roman Provincia – that vines were carried north up the Rhône Valley to the rest of France.

Provence is natural vine-growing country. Long, hot, dry summers and mild winters provide ideal conditions; the cool winds from the sea keep temperatures from soaring too high, while the mountains of the Lubéron protect the region from the worst effects of the Mistral wind.

It is a beautiful region to visit. Inland from the strip of resorts along the Mediterranean coast, the countryside is relatively unspoilt. The Massif des Maures and Monte Ste-Victorie loom huge over the vineyards of the Côtes de Provence and the Massif de Ste-Baume backs the coastal vineyards of Bandol. The vineyards of Les Baux are inside the spectacular circle of jagged mountains called Les Alpilles. The Alps stretch in a line along the north and east horizons.

There has always been a market here for the wines. The Mediterranean coast was colonised first by traders and, more recently, by holidaymakers. Vast quantities of local wine are drunk by visitors thronging the fashionable resorts of the Côte d'Azur every year.

Because it is so much a part of local society, wine is not treated very seriously in Provence. It is something to be enjoyed and not talked about too much. The general quality is adequate rather than inspiring, although there are a few pockets of vineyards producing higher quality, and standards are certainly improving. Out of the four million hectolitres made each year in

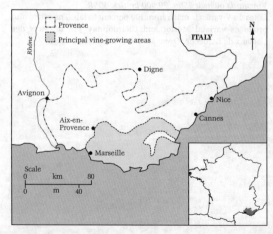

Provence about 20 percent is of Appellation Contrôlée status, that is less than the French average of 25 percent. The main concentration of vines is in the *département* of Var, the central part of Provence. Here vines cover over half the agricultural land, two-thirds producing rosé, the remainder almost all red. Provence is by far the biggest producer of rosé wine in France, traditionally much of it alcoholic, heady stuff with surprisingly little taste but quite a kick. More and more, however, the rosés are lighter and fresher, and there is greater emphasis on these wines as accompaniments to food rather than heady drinks.

Modern equipment has certainly helped to lighten the rosés, giving greater freshness and less risk of oxidation. The ability to control fermentation has also made possible an increase in the planting of vines for white wines, which most producers realise are more fashionable than rosés. But with 4,500 producers in the Côtes de Provence AC alone, it will take a while for the message to get through to everyone. It is still the case that the best wines of Provence come from much smaller areas in the west (Bandol, Cassis and Palette) and east (Bellet), with some decent producers also found around Aix-en-Provence and Les-Baux-en-Provence. Good wine still comes from these areas but, certainly in Bandol and Bellet, the prices can be unnecessarily high.

Much-needed improvements came with the creation of the Appellation Côtes de Provence in 1977. Tasting panels were introduced to check and control the wine quality, and these now taste upwards of 3,000 wines a year. New grape varieties from the north – Syrah and Cabernet Sauvignon – were planted to give the wines more taste, and more emphasis has been given to the Tibouren grape – one already grown in Provence – which gives a deliciously herby taste to otherwise dull rosés based on Grenache and Cinsaut.

Other areas of Provence are changing too. The two former VDQS areas of Coteaux d'Aix-en-Provence and Les Baux-en-Provence continue to be the best source of good Provençal reds. Apart from the products of one or two top estates, the wines are still not too expensive.

Between Aix-en-Provence and the Côtes de Provence the region of Coteaux Varois, newly promoted to Appellation Contrôlée, continues to show promise, especially for its red wines, for which Cabernet Sauvignon and Syrah grapes have been introduced. Production is huge – around 30 million bottles per year – and the price is good. While much of the wine comes from cooperatives, it is the few private estates that seem to be putting in the hard work.

The Appellations

APPELLATIONS CONTRÔLÉES

Bandol Red, white and rosé wines made in vineyards on the coast between Toulon and Marseille. The total production area is 1,000 hectares, on limestone soil. The approved grape varieties for the reds and rosés include Mourvèdre (about 50 percent of the red vineyards), Grenache, Cinsaut, Calitor, Carignan, Syrah and Tibouren. For whites, the grapes are Bourboulenc, Ugni Blanc, Clairette and Sauvignon. The red (by far the greatest production) and rosé wines are the more famous, often commanding high prices. Reds, which have to spend at least 18 months in wood, are deep, intense and spicy and peppery on the palate. Rosés are often aged before bottling and can develop a mature orange colour: they are an acquired taste, but are much appreciated in France. Whites are generally less interesting and, like rosés, should be drunk young. Reds can improve in bottle for six years or more.

Bellet A tiny AC to the north of Nice that seems to consume most of its wine. About 40 hectares of vines are planted. The wines can be red, rosé or white, but the white is best. The grapes used for the whites are the local Rolle with Roussanne, Chardonnay, Clairette and Bourboulenc, producing an attractive almondy wine. For reds and rosés, the grapes are the local Braquet (Italian Brachetto) and Folle Noire (Italian Fuella Nera) – this region being close to the Italian border – Cinsaut and Grenache. Prices for Bellet wines are high – undeservedly so. Drink young.

Cassis Not to be confused with blackcurrant liqueur. This is an area producing red, rosé and white wines, situated around the small port of Cassis between Marseille and Bandol. There are 150 hectares of vines producing 700,000 bottles each year. The most famous wine of the region is a white made from a blend of Marsanne, Ugni Blanc, Clairette, Grenache Blanc (locally known as Doucillon) and Sauvignon. The wine is dry, normally pale yellow in colour (because of slight oxidation), and quite tangy – like light *fino* sherry. Reds and rosés are made from Grenache, Cinsaut, Mourvèdre and Carignan. Drink whites young. Reds are capable of ageing, but drink sooner than Bandol (*see above*).

Coteaux d'Aix-en-Provence This is an area producing some of the best-value wines in Provence. Reds, rosés and whites are all made on 3,000 hectares of chalky soil lying mainly to the south and east of Aix-en-Provence. Red wines are made from Cinsaut, Grenache, Counoise, Carignan, Mourvèdre, Syrah and Cabernet Sauvignon. The Cabernet Sauvignon has an immense influence on the taste (it can comprise up to 60 percent of the blend) and produces a wine akin to a deep-coloured, intense-tasting Bordeaux. Other reds resemble Côtes du Rhône. The rosés are lighter in colour and taste than Côtes de Provence. Whites are made from Grenache Blanc, Clairette, Sémillon, Ugni Blanc and Sauvignon: the touch of Sauvignon gives these wines their class, style and freshness, even if they do tend to lack acidity. Age red wines for three to six years. Drink whites and rosés as young as possible.

Coteaux Varois A large area of vines around the town of Brignoles, making over 30 million bottles of wine a year. Red, rosé and white wines are made. For the reds the grapes used are: Cinsaut, Grenache, Mourvèdre, Carignan, Alicante and

Aramon (the grapes that have contributed most to the French portion of the European wine lake); Cabernet Sauvignon and Syrah are also used. These tend to be heavy, slightly too full and a little dull, but quality is improving. Whites come from Grenache Blanc, Ugni Blanc, Clairette and Malvoisie. It is the Malvoisie that gives them character and some fragrance and flavour, but on the whole they lack acidity.

Les Baux-en-Provence Smaller area than Coteaux d'Aix-en-Provence, lying within a circle of mountains near the hilltop resort of Les-Baux-en-Provence. Virtually all the wines are red, although rosé wines are permitted. Whites made here have the appellation Coteaux d'Aix-en-Provence. Quality is generally even higher than that of Aix-en-Provence although the style is similar and the grapes used are the same. This is partly due to the fact that production is smaller and controlled by private estates. The red wines can age for a little longer than those in Aix-en-Provence.

Côtes de Provence By far the largest AC in Provence, covering 18,000 hectares, producing red, rosé and white wines. This huge expanse is divided into three main areas: the coastal vineyards running from St-Tropez to Toulon; the valley north of the Massif des Maures around Les Arcs, and the vineyards around the Mont Ste-Victoire. By far the largest production is still of rosé wines. The old style was heavily alcoholic and full-bodied, made mainly from Carignan and Grenache grapes. Newer style rosés are lighter and include some Mourvèdre and Tibouren; they are lower in alcohol and cleaner and younger to taste. Reds are the next most important style in Provence. Made from Grenache, Cinsaut, Mourvèdre and Carignan, they now also include Syrah and Cabernet Sauvignon to an increasing degree. As with rosés, there has been a change of style and the introduction of these northern grape varieties has led to wines which are fresher and less prone to oxidisation. Tannic structure and a firmer spicy, stalky taste, have replaced the somewhat soft, heavy taste of old-style reds. Whites make up to 20 percent of production. Permitted grape varieties are Clairette, Ugni Blanc, Rolle and Sémillon. Early picking and temperature-controlled fermentation are improving these wines beyond all recognition. Reds can age well: try them at two to five years old. Drink rosés and whites as young as possible.

Palette A tiny AC area, just to the east of Aix-en-Provence, that consists of two properties. Here old vines, on 15 hectares of limestone soil, produce red, rosé and white wines. The reds are the finest: made from Mourvèdre, Grenache and Cinsaut they are aged in wood, which makes them austere, lean and quite tannic, needing to be kept for some time before they are drunk. The rosés are made from the same grape varieties. White wines are made from Clairette, Grenache Blanc and Ugni Blanc and despite the use of these traditional 'southern' grapes, they are surprisingly lively and steely to taste. Drink as young as possible.

VDQS

Coteaux de Pierrevert Often referred to as the highest vineyard in France – certainly the scenery is Alpine and remote – this is a small area of 400 hectares in the Alpes-de-Haute-Provence *département* on the River Durance, north of Aix-en-Provence. Red, rosé and white wines are produced here. The rosé is the best of them: made from Cinsaut, Carignan and Grenache it is fresh, acidic and good when drunk within two years of the vintage. White wines are made from Clairette, Marsanne and Roussanne grapes.

VINS DE PAYS

Departmental *vins de pays*

Vin de Pays des Alpes-de-Haute-Provence Full-bodied reds and rosés from the valley of the Durance, made from the usual mix of southern grapes: Carignan, Grenache, Cinsaut, Syrah and Mourvèdre. There is a small production of white wines, mainly from Clairette and Muscat à Petits Grains.

Vin de Pays des Bouches-du-Rhône One of the largest *vin de pays*-producing areas in Provence. The wines come from three distinct zones: the Aix-en-Provence area, the main Côtes de Provence vineyards in the east of the *département*, and the Camargue. Eighty percent of production is of red wine, made from the southern grape varieties and some Cabernet Sauvignon.

Vin de Pays du Var This is the most important *vin de pays* region in Provence, covering the whole of the Var *département*. Côtes de Provence AC is also produced in this region, although half the rosés made here are classified as *vin de pays* rather than AC. Grape varieties used for rosé wines are: Grenache, Cinsaut and Syrah, with some Roussanne du Var. The red wines are made from the Carignan, Grenache, Cinsaut, Syrah, Mourvèdre and Cabernet Sauvignon grape varieties. Very little white wine is made.

Vin de Pays du Vaucluse Another large *vin de pays* area, producing wines from the Côtes du Rhône, Côtes du Ventoux and Côtes du Lubéron regions north and east of Avignon. The red wines are very much in the style of Côtes du Rhône, although Cabernet Sauvignon is also found in the blend. A considerable amount of white wine is produced from Ugni Blanc grapes.

Other departmental *vins de pays*:

Vin de Pays des Alpes-Maritimes

Vin de Pays des Hautes-Alpes

Zonal *vins de pays*

Vin de Pays d'Argens Wines from 17 communes in the Var *département*, in the valleys of the Issole and Argens. Production is mainly of rosé wines from local grape varieties; red wines are from the Cabernet Sauvignon, and a small proportion of white, from the Ugni Blanc, Clairette, Bourboulenc and Rolle, is also made.

Vin de Pays des Maures Wines from the region of the Massif des Maures, west of St-Tropez in the Var *département*. The *vin de pays* region stretches inland from the coast as far as Fréjus. Reds and rosés account for almost all the production though a tiny amount of white is also made. All the usual local varieties are permitted, and Cabernet Sauvignon may also be used.

Vin de Pays du Mont-Caume A zone producing a small amount of wine, situated on the coast west of Toulon around the AC area of Bandol. The majority of production is of powerful red wines and the rest is of rosé. Very little white is made.

Vin de Pays de la Petite Crau A small area between Avignon and Les Alpilles of Baux-en-Provence. Its stony vineyards produce fruity red wines and smaller amounts of rosé and white wine. The area is dominated by one cooperative.

Provence Producers

BANDOL AC

La Bastide Blanche
83330 Ste-Anne-du-Castellet.
White wines are best, though the red wines can have good weight and tannin. A high proportion of the grapes planted are Grenache.

Domaine de Frégate
Domaines Notre-Dame de Port d'Alon, Route de Bandol, 83270 St-Cyr-sur-Mer. Vineyards owned: Domaine de Frégate 30ha. 120,000 bottles. VP-R
Red wines make up half of the production here. They are aged for the statutory 18 months, but not sold until three years old – and at their best after five to six years. Whites and rosés are sold the year after harvest. The estate is situated next to the sea, with its cellar cut into the rock.
Open: Mon–Fri 8am–noon, 2–6pm; Sat 10am–noon, 3–6pm.

Domaine le Galantin
83330 Le Plan du Castellet.
Vineyards owned: 20ha. 80,000 bottles. VP-R
Monsieur Pascal is only a part-time *vigneron* but produces a fragrant red wine from 60 percent Mourvèdre, 20 percent Grenache and 20 percent Cinsaut (which he buys in) and white and rosé wines too. The latter are vinified in stainless-steel vats, from free-run juice only; the red is made in stainless steel, then aged in wood for the 18-month minimum. While the white and rosé are light and fresh, the red, made traditionally, is one of the weightier wines of the appellation, and can be long lived.
Open: Mon–Sun 9am–noon, 2–6pm.

Domaine de l'Hermitage
Le Rouve, 83330 Le Beausset.
Vineyards owned: 36ha. 180,000 bottles. VP-R
Owner Gérard Duffort has completed a thorough restoration since

acquiring the estate in 1974. Half his production is of red wines (including a small amount of Syrah), with about 45 percent rosé and five percent white wine (made from Ugni Blanc and Clairette). The equipment used is modern, and the reds are vinified in stainless steel before being wood-aged in an air-conditioned cellar for 18 months. The whole operation is highly professional and the results are expensive.

Open: Mon–Fri 8am–noon, 2–6pm.

Domaine la Laidière

GAEC Estiènne, Ste-Anne d'Évenos, 83330 Le Beausset.
Vineyards owned: 24ha. 90,000 bottles. VP-R

Among the secrets behind the very fine wines from this estate are the carefully carried out destalking and long slow fermentation processes. Stainless steel is used for vinification, but reds (60 percent of production) are then aged in oak. The red wines last well, and the whites and rosés often have more fruit than the average Bandol. The Estiènne family was involved in the creation of the Bandol AC in 1941. *Open: Mon–Fri 9am–6pm.*

Moulin des Costes

Mas de la Rouvière, 83740 La Cadière d'Azur.
Vineyards owned: 75ha. 350,000 bottles. VP-R

The Bunan family have owned this estate since 1962 when they returned from Algeria. Red and rosé Bandol is made in equal quantities, with a smaller amount of white. The wines are made using modern and traditional methods and some are superb. A high percentage of Mourvèdre is used for the red and, unlike many estates in Bandol, a little Cabernet Sauvignon is grown. This is used to make Vin de Pays de Mont-Caume.

Open: Summer: 8am–noon, 2–7pm; winter: 8am–noon, 2–5.30pm.

Domaine de la Noblesse

Chemin de l'Argile, 83740 La Cadière d'Azur.
Vineyards owned: 25ha. 131,000 bottles. VP-R

Jean-Pierre Gaussen, the owner of this small estate, makes powerful red wines and also a little rosé and white. Stainless steel is used for fermentation, producing wines which are modern in style. *Open: Mon–Sat 8am–noon, 2–8pm.*

Domaines Ott

22 Boulevard d'Aguillon, 06601 Antibes.
Vineyards owned: 140ha. 550,000 bottles. VP-R

One of the largest producers in Provence, founded in 1896. Domaines Ott owns estates in Côtes de Provence (Château de Selle and Clos Mireille) as well as Bandol (Château Romassan). It is most famous for its highly sought after Bandol Rosé Coeur de Grain, which is fermented and aged in wood. This is an orange-coloured wine which may lack freshness but compensates with a wide range of flavours. Small amounts of red and white Bandol are also made. The Clos Mireille estate produces a white Côtes de Provence from Ugni Blanc and Sémillon; Château de Selle produces rosé and red from a high proportion of Cabernet Sauvignon; its white is dominated by Sémillon.

Open: Each estate Mon-Fri 8am-noon, 2-6pm.

Château de Pibarnon
83740 La Cadière d'Azur.
Vineyards owned: 48ha. 180,000 bottles. VP-R

The vineyards of Comte Henri de St-Victor at Château de Pibarnon are situated on limestone soil and cover a wide area of the Bandol region. Both modern and traditional winemaking techniques are used, including stainless steel for the vinification. The red wine (60 percent of production) is aged for a maximum of two years in wood and has the typical Bandol richness and tannin. It needs seven to eight years' ageing before it reaches maturity. The rosé, too, is a wine for keeping. The white wine – with 40 percent of its blend from the rare Bourboulenc grape – needs to be drunk young.

Open: Mon-Sat 9am-12.30pm, 2.30-6.30pm; appointments preferred.

Château Pradeaux
83270 St-Cyr-sur-Mer.
Vineyards owned: 19ha (Mourvèdre). 38,000 bottles.

Wine from this property is made from 95 percent Mourvèdre and is aged for anything up to eight years in large wooden barrels. The result is sometimes just too woody, but may also reveal great staying power. *Not open.*

Château Ray-Jane
83330 Le Plan du Castellet. Vineyards owned: 14ha. 56,000 bottles.

Very traditional wines are made here, full of tannin and powerful fruit. The grapes are not destalked before pressing, and the wines are neither fined nor filtered. They need many years to mature. A small estate by Bandol standards.

Open: Mon-Sat 8am-noon, 2-7pm.

Château Romassan *See Domaines Ott, page 156*

Château Ste-Anne
Ste-Anne d'Évenos, 83330 Le Beausset.
Vineyards owned: 25ha. 103,000 bottles. VP-R

François Dutheil de la Rochère owns two estates: the 20 hectares and 16th-century building of Château Ste-Anne, producing Bandol, and five hectares producing Côtes de Provence. Winemaking methods are traditional and the use of chemicals for vinification is avoided. The red wines are wood-aged for up to 22 months. Bandol wines also include a light rosé and some white. The Côtes de Provence is all rosé. *Open: Mon-Fri 8am-noon, 2-7pm.*

Domaine des Salettes
83740 La Cadière d'Azur.
Vineyards owned: 29ha. 150,000 bottles. VP-R

Half the production of Jean-Pierre Boyer's Domaine des Salettes, on the slopes of Mal Passe, is of Bandol rosé, a light fresh style of wine. About 45 percent is of a full, smooth red with less Mourvèdre than some others of the area. This is a solid, reliable producer, even if dazzling wines are not achieved. The vineyard has recently been expanded by 15 hectares. *Open: By appointment only.*

Domaine Tempier

EARL Peyraud, 83330 Le Plan du Castellet, Var.
Vineyards owned: 28ha. 100,000 bottles. VP-R

Use of chemicals is minimal in this vineyard, which was established in 1834. Owner Lucien Peyraud works hard to support the wines of Bandol, and makes his wines using traditional methods: wood for some of the fermentation, and also for maturing the red wines for up to 30 months. The results are tannic wines that need plenty of time but mature well, with complex flavours. Red and rosé are made. *Open: Mon–Fri 9am– noon, 2–6pm; Sat 9am–noon.*

Domaine de Terrebrune

Ollioules, 83330 Ste-Anne d'Évenos.

One of the hallmarks of this showpiece estate is the fact that the wines are kept in bottle for two years (after two years in wood) before release. They are put on the market only a year or two before they are mature. The cellars used for ageing these wines are carved out of the surrounding rock.

Château Vannières

83740 La Cadière d'Azur.
Vineyards owned: 29ha. 160,000 bottles. VP-R

The vineyard of Vannières dates back to the 16th century, when it was the property of André de Lombard, Seigneur de Castellet. Today the Boisseaux family run the property using traditional methods, vinifying in wood. The firm produces a red Bandol and a red Côtes de Provence, both with the same *cépages*, including six percent Syrah. The red Bandol, one of the best in the appellation, can be very long-lasting with splendid rich, ripe fruit. *Open: Mon–Sat 8am–noon, 2–6pm.*

Domaines Walter Gilpin

3345 Montée du Château, 83330 Le Castellet.
Vineyards owned: 22ha. VP-R

One of the leading lights in the Bandol appellation, Walter Gilpin makes robust wines in a traditional way. He owns 15 hectares in Bandol, making red and rosé, and seven hectares of red, rosé and white Côtes de Provence. *Open: Mon–Sat 9am–noon, 2.30–6pm.*

BELLET AC

Château de Bellet

St-Roman de Bellet, 06200 Nice.
Vineyards owned: 9ha. 30,000 bottles. VP-R

Ghislain de Charnacé makes white, red and rosé wines at the historic castle of Bellet in the hills above Nice. The white wines he produces are made from Rolle and Chardonnay grapes; the reds and rosés from Braquet, Folle Noire, Cinsaut and Grenache. Vinification methods are all traditional. The white is to my mind the most interesting of the three wines: the Chardonnay giving it considerable depth and balancing the simple, rather bland freshness of the Rolle grape. The rosé is fruitier than many other of the Côtes de Provence rosés – but is also more expensive.

Open: By appointment only.

Clot dou Baille

277 Chemin de Saquier, 06200 Nice.
Vineyards owned: 10ha. 25,000 bottles. VP-R

Perched dramatically above a sheer drop down to the valley of the Var, the cellars of Ludovic Cambillau are in the middle of his small terraced vineyard. He makes immediately attractive wines: a crisp, appley white from Rolle; a soft, mandarin-scented rosé from Braquet and light, spicy red from Folle Noire, Grenache and Cinsaut. *Open: Appointments preferred.*

Château de Crémat

442 Chemin de Crémat, 06200 Nice.
Vineyards owned: 8ha. 35,000 bottles.

The tiny Crémat estate is owned by the Bagnis family who have much larger holdings in Côtes de Provence. Vinification is modern, but most reds go into large wood for three years.

Open: Appointments preferred.

CASSIS AC

Domaine du Bagnol

12 Avenue de Provence, 13260 Cassis.
Vineyards owned: 7ha. 35,000 bottles. VP-R

High-quality white and rosé wines are made at this tiny domaine, under the Marquis de Fesques name. The white is particularly typical: full-flavoured Cassis, aged for two years in tank before bottling. Techniques are traditional and Madame Lefèvre intends to keep it that way. *Open: Mon-Sun 9am-noon, 2-7pm.*

La Ferme Blanche

13260 Cassis. Vineyards owned: 27ha. 150,000 bottles. VP-R

The appellation's largest estate, established in 1715, produces mainly white wines, which tend towards lightness and freshness. The blend includes ten percent Sauvignon Blanc grapes. Red and rosé are also made. *Open: Mon-Fri 9am-noon, 2-5.30pm.*

Château de Fontcreuse

13 Route de la Ciotat, 13260 Cassis.
Vineyards owned: 20ha. 110,000 bottles. VP-R

Mainly white wine, with a little rosé, is made at this estate, owned by Monsieur Brando. Stainless steel is used, and whites are kept for one year in tank, rosés for six months, before bottling.

Open: Mon-Fri 8.30am-noon, 2.30-5pm.

Clos Ste-Magdelaine
Avenue du Revestel, 13260 Cassis.
Vineyards owned: 12ha. 50,000 bottles. VP-R
Three-quarters of production is of a straw-coloured white with a nutty bouquet and a tinge of greenness from the Sauvignon in the blend; the remainder is of a rosé made from Cinsaut, Grenache and Mourvèdre. The vineyard lies on a narrow spit of land jutting into the bay of Cassis. *Open: Mon–Fri 10am–noon, 3–7pm.*

COTEAUX D'AIX-EN-PROVENCE AC

Château Bas
13116 Vernègues. Vineyards owned: 80ha. 530,000 bottles. VP-R
All styles, including a sparkling wine, are made at this estate which is based around a 17th-century château. Most is red and rosé, a blend of Grenache, Cabernet Sauvignon, Syrah and Cinsaut. The crisp white has a touch of Sauvignon Blanc, the sparkling Vin Mousseux blends Ugni Blanc and Sauvignon Blanc. The best *cuvées*, both white and red, are called Cuvée du Temple. *Open: Mon–Fri 8.30am–noon, 2–6pm; Sat 9am–noon, 2–5pm.*

Domaine les Bastides
St-Canadet, 13610 Le Puy-Ste-Réparade.
Vineyards owned: 20ha. 130,000 bottles. VP-R
Organic methods are used in this vineyard, which produces red and rosé Coteaux d'Aix using traditional grape varieties. The red, Rouge Tradition, is a blend of Grenache, Mourvèdre and Cinsaut. There is also a Cuvée Spéciale made from 50 percent Cabernet Sauvignon. *Open: Mon–Sun 8am–noon, 2–7pm.*

Château de Beaulieu
13840 Rognes. Vineyards owned: 300ha. 1.8 million bottles. VP-R
The largest estate in this AC, owned by the Touzet family. A modern winery produces red, white and rosé wines from vines to the east of Aix grown on volcanic soil. The red is Grenache, Cabernet Sauvignon, Syrah and Mourvèdre; the rosé from Cinsaut and Carignan; and the white from Sauvignon Blanc, Clairette, Ugni Blanc and Sémillon. The Touzet family built up this estate during the past decade and now live in the well-restored house. *Open: Mon–Sun 8.30am–noon, 2–6pm, by appointment.*

Château de Beaupré
13760 St-Cannat. Vineyards owned: 30ha. 202,000 bottles. VP-R
Christian Double is owner of this 18th-century house and estate on the edge of the town of St-Cannat. He makes red, white and rosé in standard *cuvées*, and a red and white Collection du Château. *Open: Mon–Sun.*

Commanderie de la Bargemone
RN7, 13760 St-Cannat.
Vineyards owned: 60ha. 400,000 bottles. VP-R
High standards have been achieved since the estate was bought

(1977) and spectacularly restored by wealthy northern French industrialists, the Rozan family. Winemaking techniques rely on tradition, but some carbonic maceration is used for reds and stainless-steel fermentation for the whites. The best red, Cuvée Tournebride, made with 50 percent Cabernet Sauvignon, spends some time in wood, and the more standard red, Commanderie de la Bargemone, is a blend of Grenache (45 percent), Cinsaut, Syrah, Cabernet and Carignan. Rosé is made from Grenache and Cinsaut; white from Sauvignon, Grenache Blanc and Ugni Blanc. *Open: Mon–Sat 8am–noon, 1.30–6pm.*

Château La Coste
13610 Puy-Ste-Réparade.
Vineyards owned: 180ha. 1.3 million bottles. VP-R
One of the largest estates in Provence. The Bordonado family owns Château La Coste and two associated estates: Domaine de la Grand Séouve and Domaine de la Boulangère. Winemaking techniques are modern for rosés and whites but traditional for reds. Nearly half the production is of red, with 40 percent rosé and 15 percent white. For such large-scale production, the quality of the wines is very high – especially for the reds. The Bordonado family also owns the 30-hectare estate, Château de Costefriede, whose first vintage was the '87. *Open: By appointment only.*

Château de Fonscolombe
13610 Puy-Ste-Réparade.
Vineyards owned: 160ha. 1 million bottles. VP-R
The Marquises de Saporta have owned this estate since 1720. Modern equipment is used to produce some of the best-value Coteaux d'Aix wines. The red Château de Fonscolombe makes up the bulk of production; it is fruity, aromatic and can be drunk young, although it will age for some years. Other brands used are Domaine de la Crémade and Marquis de Saporta. Fonscolombe also makes a Vin de Pays des Bouches-du-Rhône, called Domaine de Boullery. *Open: Mon–Fri 8am–noon, 2–6pm.*

Château des Gavelles
13540 Puyricard. Vineyards owned: 23ha. 78,000 bottles. VP-R
New owners at this estate (1992) have made improvements to the vineyard and are making rosé in stainless steel and reds with four months in small oak *barriques*. The archbishops of Aix-en-Provence used to live in the house.
Open: Mon–Sun 9.30am–12.30pm, 3.30–7pm.

Château St-Jean
1415 Chemin Rocaille-Celony, 13090 Aix-en-Provence.
Vineyards owned: 80ha. VP-R
Red, white and rosé are all made on this large estate. Techniques are relatively old-fashioned, but the wines, especially the reds, seem to win plenty of local awards. The owner, Charles Sedou, also owns Château Vignerolles (*see* page 162). The top *cuvée* is called Natacha. *Open: Tues–Fri 3–7pm; Sat 9am–noon, 3–7pm.*

Château Vignelaure

Route de Jouques, 83560 Rians.
Vineyards owned: Coteaux d'Aix-en-Provence 62ha, Côtes de
Provence 65ha. 810,000 bottles. VP-R

This estate is widely seen as making the best wine in Coteaux d'Aix-en-Provence. A decline in quality during the late 1980s and early 1990s has now been overcome as new owners, the Irish O'Brien family, make use of the latest advice and technology from Bordeaux-based Michel Rolland and Hugh Ryman. The '95 Château Vignelaure is the first of these new wines to be released: lovers of the estate can buy the *vin de pays* Domaine de Vignelaure as a foretaste. *Open: Mon–Sun 9.30am–6pm.*

Château Vignerolles

13700 Gignac-la-Nerthe.
Vineyards owned: 80ha. 500,000 bottles. VP-R

This property, owned by Charles Sardou, is to the west of Aix-en-Provence and operates using modern technology and stainless steel for vinification. Production is of 65 percent red wine, 30 percent rosé and five percent white. The brand names used are Château St-Jean de l'Hôpital and Cuvée Margot. White and rosé wines are better than the red – the white, with its touch of Sauvignon, is especially attractive. *Open: By appointment only.*

LES BAUX-EN-PROVENCE AC

Mas de la Dame

13520 Les Baux-en-Provence.
Vineyards owned: 55ha. 300,000 bottles. VP-R

Rosé and red wine is made here, one of the best Baux-en-Provence estates, and the oldest. Stainless steel is used. Three red wines are made: Gourmande, Réserve and Cuvée de la Stèle. The high proportion (14 percent) of Syrah in the red wine, Rouge Réserve, gives it good ageing ability, and the introduction of 23 percent Cabernet Sauvignon gives considerable elegance.
Open: By appointment only.

Mas de Gourgonnier

Le Destet, 13890 Mouries.
Vineyards owned: 35ha. 200,000 bottles. VP-R

A new vineyard on an old family estate, run organically by Nicolas Cartier. Red, rosé and white are produced – his best wine is the Reserve du Mas, a blend of Grenache (40 percent), Cabernet Sauvignon (30 percent) and Syrah (30 percent). His other red, called Tradition, introduces ten percent Mourvèdre. The white, a wine fresh in character, comprises 40 percent Sauvignon Blanc. A very serious estate. *Open: Mon–Fri 8am–noon, 2–6pm.*

Château Romanin

13210 St-Rémy-de-Provence. VP-R

A biodynamic estate whose first vintage was the '90. Two whites – one oaked, the other fresh and unoaked – are made, as well as a

red which is aged in large *foudres*. A curiosity of the estate is the Vin Cuit, a desert wine made from heated must.
Open: By appointment only.

Mas de Ste-Berthe
13520 Les Baux-en-Provence.
Vineyards owned: 33ha. 25,000 bottles. VP-R

Carbonic maceration and stainless-steel vats enable production of easy-drinking, fruity wines at this estate, which is situated in a spectacular position under the cliff-top village of Les Baux. Almost two-thirds of the production is of red wine, one-third rosé, and a few thousand bottles of white are also made. The brand Cuvée Louis David is the best quality wine, and is designed for some ageing. *Open: Mon-Sun 9am-noon, 2-6pm.*

Domaine des Terres Blanches
RN99, 13210 St-Rémy-de-Provence.
Vineyards owned: 36ha. 158,000 bottles. VP-R

Organic farming methods are adopted on this model estate and few chemicals are used in the making of the wine. Noël Michelin, the owner, is a strong advocate of this method of winemaking which is gaining ground at other Baux-en-Provence estates. The firm produces a white, a rosé and a red. The red is sometimes described as austere and it certainly needs time; with ageing it becomes very poised and elegant. Two special *cuvées* are also produced: Cuvée Aurelia, mainly from Cabernet Sauvignon and Cuvée Bérangère, a classic southern blend of Mourvèdre and Syrah or Grenache. *Open: Mon-Sat 8.30am-12.30pm, 2.30-6.30pm, (reservations required for groups).*

Domaine de Trévallon
13103 St-Étienne-du-Grès.
Vineyards owned: 16ha. 65,000 bottles. VP-R

Domaine de Trévallon's vineyards are on the north side of the Alpilles Mountains. This is another of the estates in Les Baux that practises organic methods. In the winery, stainless steel is used, but the wine is aged in wood. The red – the sole wine from this estate – is a blend of 60 percent Cabernet Sauvignon and 40 percent Syrah, a splendid combination, producing a wine that is well structured, and has considerable ageing ability.
Open: By appointment only.

Domaine de la Vallongue
13810 Eygalières. Vineyards owned: 38ha. 252,000 bottles. VP-R
Red and rosé production has been supplemented by small quantities of white, based on Rolle, Sémillon, Grenache Blanc and Clairette. The wines are based mainly on the traditional varieties of the area – Carignan, Cinsaut and Grenache – with only a little amelioration from Cabernet Sauvignon and Syrah. The red is full-bodied, southern-tasting and traditional. The rosé tends to mature quickly and needs to be drunk young.
Open: Mon-Sat 9.30am-noon, 2.30-6pm.

CÔTES DE PROVENCE AC

Domaine de l'Aumerade
83390 Pierrefeu-du-Var.
Vineyards owned: 525ha. 2.5 million bottles. VP-R
This huge landholding is run as part of Domaine Fabre by Louis
Fabre. He has six estates, of which the largest by far is Domaine
de l'Aumerade at 350 hectares. Here red, white and rosé are made.
Other estates are: Domaine de la Clapière, Domaine de la
Deidière, Domaine de St-Honoré, Château la Fôret and Domaine
du Jas de Cape. Top *cuvées* include a *blanc de blancs*, Cuvée Sully.
Open: Mon–Sat 8am–noon, 2–6pm.

Château Barbeyrolles
83580 Gassin. Vineyards owned: 12ha. 62,000 bottles. VP-R
Organic methods are used in this small vineyard owned by
Régine Sumeire. Sumeire, who has a PhD in history, has been
researching the history of viticulture in this region. She makes
very fine red and rosé wines; the red a blend of a third each
Grenache, Mourvèdre and Syrah which spends ten to 18 months
in wood. Two rosés are made, one standard *cuvée*, although very
light and refreshing, and a delicate Rosé Petal Cuvée, made with
very light pressing. *Open: Mon–Sat 9am–6pm.*

La Bastide Neuve
Le Cannet des Maures, 83340 Le Luc.
Vineyards owned: 17ha. 100,000 bottles. VP-R
The reds – from Syrah, Mourvèdre and Grenache – are made
traditionally, before being aged for a year in large barrels. A
Tibouren-based rosé of great character and a white from Ugni
Blanc are made in enamel-lined tanks. The rosés are called
Cuvée des Anges and Perle de Rosé, and the reds Cuvée Anton
and Beau Sarment. *Open: Mon–Sat 8am–noon, 2–7pm.*

La Bernarde
83340 Le Luc. Vineyards owned: 33ha. 200,000 bottles. VP-R
M and the late Mme Meulnart bought this vineyard in 1974 and
invested considerable sums to produce top-quality wines. The
vineyard is situated at an altitude of 300 metres, north of Les
Maures. Reds include the special *cuvée*, Clos Bernarde St-
Germain, made from 55 percent Syrah, 40 percent Cabernet
Sauvignon and five percent Grenache, and Clos de la Bernarde,
which contains 30 percent Grenache. Both reds are matured in
bottle rather than wood. The estate produces a delicate rosé made
with 30 percent Tibouren plus Grenache and Cinsaut, and white
wines made from Ugni Blanc and Sémillon.
Open: By appointment only.

Château de Berne
Route de Berne, 83510 Lorgues.
Vineyards owned: 50ha. 300,000 bottles. VP-R
Despite the initial appearance of Hollywood among the Provençal

pine trees, this estate, which is owned by a British company, is producing some good-quality, modern-style wines. Côtes de Provence white, red (which contains Syrah, Grenache and Cabernet) and rosé (made from Cinsaut) are made here in a brand new cellar. Two styles of red – a standard *cuvée* and a Cuvée Special – are made. A Roman-style amphitheatre in the grounds is intended for plays – and presumably the audience drinks the wines. *Open: Every day.*

Domaine de Bertaud-Belieu

83580 Gassin. Vineyards owned: 51ha. 238,000 bottles. VP-R

The exotic *chai* – designed like a Roman temple or classical church – suggests that this is an estate where money is no object. It makes 40 percent red, 50 percent white, and ten percent rosé. The white, from Rolle with Sémillon and Ugni Blanc, is crisply perfumed. The red is a blend of Cabernet Sauvignon and Syrah, rich and very elegant. *Open: Mon–Sat 10am–1pm, 2–7pm.*

Château Commanderie de Peyrassol

SCEA Rigord, Flassans, 83340 Le Luc.
Vineyards owned: 62ha. 331,000 bottles. VP-R

Modern technology is used at this large estate to vinify reds, whites and rosés. The red is aged in new wood, the time varying according to vintage. There are two ranges, a Commanderie de Peyrassol and a Château de Peyrassol. The special *cuvée*, Cuvée Marie Estelle, is from lower-yielding vines, the red comprising 60 percent Cabernet Sauvignon. The rosé is called Le Rosé d'Art. *Open: Mon–Sun 9am–noon, 2–5pm. Appointments necessary for groups.*

Vignobles Crocé-Spinelli

Château des Clarettes, 83460 Les Arcs.
Vineyards owned: 34ha. 60,000 bottles. VP-R

Monsieur Crocé-Spinelli owns three estates: Château des Clarettes near Les Arcs, Domaine du St-Esprit and Domaine de Fontselves near Draguignan. The wine from St-Esprit has a high percentage of Syrah, while the Clarettes relies more on Mourvèdre. At Fontselves some Cabernet Sauvignon is used. Rosé wines are also made. *Open: By appointment only.*

Domaine de Curebeasse

KM 4, Route de Bagnols, 83600 Fréjus.
Vineyards owned: 18ha. 80,000 bottles. VP-R

Low-temperature fermentation is used here for rosés and whites: the whites stay on their lees after this to retain their freshness. There are three styles of red and two of rosé. The best red is Roches Noires, from vines on volcanic soil; it is matured in wood and made from 50 percent Mourvèdre, 30 percent Cabernet and 20 percent Syrah. Other reds use Cinsaut, Carignan and Grenache. The white is a blend of Rolle and Ugni Blanc: attractive and fresh, it needs to be drunk young.
Open: Mon–Sat 9am–12.30pm, 3–6.30pm.

Domaines et Château Élie Sumeire
38 Grand'Rue, La Croix Rouge, 13013 Marseille.
Vineyards owned: Château Cussin Ste-Victoire, 13530 Trets,
56ha, Château des Anglades, 83400 Hyères, 24.5ha, Château
l'Afrique, 83390 Cuers, 70ha.

The Sumeire family owns these three estates in different parts of
the Côtes de Provence AC, making it one of the appellation's
largest landowners. All the vineyards are worked without the use
of chemicals. Whites and reds are sold young, but the family
makes a practice of ageing reds for a period of between six
months and two years.
Open: Each estate every day 9am–noon, 2–6pm.

Domaine des Féraud
Route de la Garde Freinet, 83550 Vidauban.
Vineyards owned: 60ha. 190,000 bottles. VP-R

High-quality winemaking is carried out at this large estate. The
red, a blend of 60 percent Cabernet Sauvignon, 25 percent Syrah
and 15 percent Grenache, is a strange Bordeaux creature in the
middle of Provence, big and tannic and requiring some ageing.
The rosé and white are well made if less unusual. The vineyard
has been owned by the Laudon-Rival family for three generations.
Open: By appointment only.

Château de Gairoird
83390 Cuers. Vineyards owned: 30ha. 80,000 bottles. VP-R

Half Monsieur Pierrefeu's production is of rosé, for which there is
a good export market. It is made in small refrigerated tanks of
epoxy-lined resin, and is held together by the 30 percent of
Mourvèdre in the blend, which also gives some elegance. The
white contains 40 percent Clairette, plus Rolle and Ugni Blanc.
Reds contain Syrah and Grenache. A second label is called
Domaine St-Jean. *Open: Mon–Fri 8am–noon, 2–6pm.*

Château du Galoupet
St-Nicholas, 83250 La Londe. Vineyards owned: 72ha. VP-R

The British-owned Château du Galoupet aims to combine traditional grape varieties of the region with modern winemaking
techniques. The vineyard has been modernised and new equipment installed since its current owners bought the estate in 1993.
But, more traditionally, reds are aged in 500-litre vats for up to 18
months, while the actual château dates back to Louis XIV and the
older part of the cellar is Roman. Wines made here include red,
white and rosé Côtes de Provence and a special *cuvée* of rosé
produced mainly from Tibouren. There are also two Vins de Pays
des Maures, made from Chardonnay and Cabernet Sauvignon.
Open: Mon–Sat 9am–7pm, and Sun morning.

Vignobles Gasperini
42 Avenue de la Libération, 83260 La Crau.
Vineyards owned: 15ha. 85,000 bottles. VP-R

The estate has been in the Gasperini family since 1834 and is now run by Alain and Guy who preserve traditional methods. The red wine, Cuvée des Commandeurs, is matured in wood, which enhances the ageing potential of the Cabernet Sauvignon in the blend. There is also a rosé made from Grenache and Cinsaut called Cuvée Dame Jardin. *Open: Mon–Fri 8am–noon, 2–7pm.*

Domaines Gavoty
Le Grand Campdumy, 83340 Cabasse.
Vineyards owned: 109ha. VP-R
There are two vineyards owned by the Gavoty family: Le Grand and Le Petit Campdumy. Fruit is the predominant characteristic of all the wines. The main part of production is of rosé, but the youthful, fresh white wines and the red, made partly by carbonic maceration, are excellent examples of the fresher style of the new Côtes de Provence. *Open: Mon–Sat 8am–noon, 2–6pm.*

Château Grand'Boise
BP No 2, 13530 Trets.
Vineyards owned: 40ha. 165,000 bottles. VP-R
This well-maintained, 17th-century estate lying southeast of Aix-en-Provence has been in the Gruey family since 1879. A combination of techniques is used: cement tanks for white and rosé and carbonic maceration for reds, followed by some wood-ageing. The red is meaty, savoury on the palate and quite soft, despite its blend of Cabernet Sauvignon, Syrah and Grenache. Some of the grapes used for the white wine are bought in.
Open: Mon–Sat 8am–noon, 1.30–5.30pm.

Château de Jasson
Route de Collobrières, 83250 La Londe.
Vineyards owned: 15ha. 90,000 bottles. VP-R
The de Fresne family bought this estate five years ago in a run-down state, but have considerably improved the quality of the wines and winemaking. In '96, all three styles of Côtes de Provence – red, white and rosé – won awards. The attractive countryside between Hyères and St-Tropez was enough to tempt Queen Victoria to picnic under an oak tree on the domaine. *Open: Every day 9.30am–noon, 3.30–5.30pm. Closed Sun afternoon.*

Les Maîtres Vignerons de la Presqu'Île de St-Tropez
Carrefour de la Foux, 83580 Gassin. Vineyards owned: 617ha.
2.5 million bottles. Coop (12 members).
The cooperative selects from its members only wines that it wishes to bottle and sell, hence the high quality. Stainless steel is used for whites and rosés, the white (Ugni Blanc and Rolle) is particularly attractive. The brand name Carte Noire is used, and Château de Pampelonne's and St-Martin-la-Roche's wines are bottled separately. There is also a top-quality range of reds called Cuvée de Chasseur and a Vin de Pays du Var – the red is particularly good value. Distinctive marketing tactics include an association with local Michelin three-star chef Roger Vergé and painted bottles. *Open: Mon–Fri 8am–noon, 2–6pm, by appointment.*

Domaine de la Malherbe
83230 Bormes-les-Mimosas.
Vineyards owned: 25ha. 100,000 bottles. VP-R
The vineyard lies in a spectacular setting by the sea, facing the Fort de Bregançon, an island castle residence of the French President. Madame Serge Ferrari, the owner, has invested considerable sums to create a modern winery which produces wines benefiting from the cool air of the coast. Three brand names are used: Reine Jeanne, Pointe du Diable and, for the top *cuvées*, Domaine de la Malherbe. Rosé is especially fine.
Open: By appointment only.

Mas de Cadenet
13530 Trets. Vineyards owned: 50ha. 100,000 bottles. VP-R
The Negrel family have owned this pretty estate since 1813. Syrah, Cabernet Sauvignon and Grenache are used for the red, while rosé wines are made from Cinsaut and Grenache. Techniques are a combination of traditional and modern. The red is the best wine: it is spicy and rich, has ageing ability and also comes through well when young.
Open: By appointment only.

Château de Mentone
St-Antonin du Var, 83510 Lorgues.
Vineyards owned: 29ha. 35,000 bottles. VP-R
Much of the produce from this estate goes in bulk to Lyon and Paris, but a small amount is bottled on the premises. Traditional methods are used by Madame Perrot de Gasquet, whose family has owned Château de Mentone for 150 years. The estate has grown rapidly over recent years.
Open: By appointment only.

Château Minuty
83580 Gassin. Vineyards owned: 100ha. 600,000 bottles. VP-R
Owned by the Matton family, this large estate makes mainly traditional Provence rosé from Grenache and Cinsaut: the Cuvée de l'Oratoire is the top wine. The other wine of which they are proud is their white, Blanc Prestige, made from Rolle and Sémillon. *Open: Mon–Sat 9am–noon, 2–6pm.*

Clos Mireille *See Domaines Ott, page 156*

Domaine de Peissonnel
Route de la Garde Freiner, 83550 Vidauban.
Vineyards owned: 15ha. 60,000 bottles. VP-R
Unusually for Côtes de Provence, this estate produces only red wines. Even more unusually, it makes a wine from 80 percent Merlot with 15 percent Cabernet Franc: best in cooler years, when the wine's structure shows through. The Domaine de Peissonnel red *cuvée* is a blend of 50 percent Syrah and 50 percent Cabernet Sauvignon: a strongly tannic wine which needs at least four years before it is ready to drink. *Open: By appointment only.*

Domaine des Planes
83520 Roquebrune sur Argens.
Vineyards owned: 35ha. 150,000 bottles. VP-R
The Rieders, he German, she Swiss, own this immaculate estate
which produces top-quality wines. The couple believe that the
best rosés can be made from the rare Tíbouren grape. For reds,
they blend Cabernet Sauvignon and Syrah, but their finest wines
are single varietals, one from Mourvèdre which puts many a
Bandol in the shade, and one from Cabernet Sauvignon.
Open: By appointment only.

Pradel
06270 Villeneuve Loubet.
Vineyards owned: none. 15.6 million bottles. N
This *négociant* is a large-scale merchant, making large-scale Côtes
de Provence, Bellet and Bandol. *Open: By appointment only.*

Domaine de la Pugette
Le Thoronet, 83340 Le Luc. Vineyards owned: 23ha. VP-R
Monsieur Petit makes a red, rosé and white at his estate near
Brignoles in the central Côtes de Provence. The vineyards stretch
up to the ruins of the Abbey of Thoronet, which was a Cistercian
monastery. The red, made from Grenache, Syrah and Cabernet
Sauvignon, is the best: aged in wood, it has firm tannin when
young and needs time to mellow. *Open: By appointment only.*

Vignobles F Ravel (Château Montaud)
83390 Pierrefeu.
Vineyards owned: 404ha. 2 million bottles. VP-R
M Ravel has built up this, one of Provence's largest estates, since
the 1960s. Château Montaud is the estate name for Côtes de
Provence: red, rosé and white is made as well as Vin de Pays des
Maures, using Cabernet Sauvignon for the red and Tíbouren for
the rosé. Rosé forms the bulk of production and is light with
plenty of acidity. The attractive red is from Syrah and Mourvèdre
and needs some ageing. The white is less interesting. *Open:
Mon–Thur 8am–noon, 1.30–5.30pm; Fri 8am–noon, 1.30–4.30pm.*

Domaine Richeaume
13114 Puyloubier.
Vineyards owned: 26ha. 100,000 bottles. VP-R
Monsieur Hoesch's vineyards are on the slopes of Mt Ste-Victoire
in the east of the Côtes de Provence. He makes a red from
Cabernet Sauvignon and Syrah, which is aged for two years in
wood, and maintains that even his rosé and white are wines for
keeping. A *blanc de blancs* from Clairette is certainly well made in
a traditional way. *Open: Mon–Fri 9am–noon, 1.30–5.30pm.*

Domaine de Rimauresq
Route de Notre-Dame des Anges, 83790 Pignans.
Vineyards owned: 32ha. 180,000 bottles. VP-R
A new cellar has been completed at this old estate, and this has

resulted in the production of fresh rosé, mainly produced from Tibouren, and white from Rolle. The principal production, however, is of red, a blend with a high proportion of Cabernet Sauvignon and Syrah, which spends up to two years in wood.
Open: Mon–Fri 8.30am–12.30pm, 1.30–6pm.

St-André de Figuière
83250 La Londe les Maures.
Vineyards owned: 15ha. 60,000 bottles. VP-R
An organically run vineyard with modern equipment in the winery, producing some deliciously refreshing wines. The white is light and fresh, a blend of Sémillon, Ugni Blanc and Rolle. The red Cuvée Spéciale is a soft, rich wine, a blend of Mourvèdre and Carignan, which needs three to four years' ageing. The estate also produces a Vin de Pays du Var.
Open: Mon–Fri 9am–noon, 2–6pm.

Château St-Baillon
83340 Flassans-sur-Issole.
Vineyards owned: 25ha. 147,000 bottles. VP-R
Stainless steel for vinification and wood for maturing the reds sit side by side in this new winery, owned by Hervé Goudard since 1974. As much as 60 percent of the vineyard is devoted to Cabernet Sauvignon and Syrah, which are blended into the spicy, peppery Cuvée de Roudaò, and are joined by Cinsaut and Grenache in the Rouge Tradition. Rosé is also made, and a *blanc de blancs* of Rolle and Ugni Blanc.
Open: Mon–Sat 8am–noon, 1–7pm; Sun by appointment.

Château St-Maur
Route de Collobrières, 83310 Cogolin.
Vineyards owned: 39ha. 160,000 bottles. VP-R
Close to the pretty hilltop villages of Cogolin and Grimaud, this estate boasts splendid buildings, including its own church, which dates back to the 16th century. In the cellars, recently equipped with stainless steel, it makes the usual range of wines, rosé being the most important. *Open: Mon–Sat 9am–noon, 2–7pm.*

Château Ste-Roseline
83460 Les Arcs-sur-Argens
The red is the best wine made at this estate, based around an ancient monastery. It is made from 60 percent Mourvèdre, 30 percent Cabernet Sauvignon and ten percent Syrah, a potent combination which gives considerable power, good structure and longevity. *Open: By appointment only.*

Château de Selle *See Domaines Ott, page 156*

Domaine de la Source Ste-Marguerite
Le Haut Pansard, 83250 La Londe les Maures.
Vineyards owned: 25ha. 65,000 bottles. VP-R
Monsieur Fayard produces red, rosé and white wine from his

estate, which was acquired in 1977. Techniques have been modernised and the rosé and whites particularly have benefited.
Open: Mon–Sat 8am–noon, 2–7pm.

PALETTE AC

Château Simone
13590 Meyreuil. Vineyards owned: 17ha. 75,000 bottles. VP-R
By owning three-quarters of the vineyards of the AC area, the Rougier family are entitled to regard themselves as synonymous with Palette. They make red, rosé and white wines. To my mind – on the rare occasions when I have tasted them – the wood-aged red (from Grenache, Mourvèdre, Cinsaut, and local varieties Manosquan, Caster, Brun-Fourca and Teoulier) needs six or seven years before being ready. The white is herbily aromatic.
Open: By appointment only.

COTEAUX VAROIS AC

Domaine du Deffends
83470 St-Maximin. Vineyards owned: 10ha. 40,000 bottles. VP-R
Two reds and a rosé – all AC Coteaux Varois – are produced from this small estate. Clos de la Truffière (made from 40 percent Cabernet Sauvignon, 45 percent Syrah, 15 percent Grenache and Cinsaut) and Rouge du Deffends (20 percent Cabernet and Syrah, 80 percent Grenache and Cinsaut) are the two reds. The Rosé de la Nuit is made from 80 percent Cinsaut and 20 percent Grenache. A form of carbonic maceration is used to bring out colour in the red. The rosé is almost blush pink in colour.
Open: By appointment only.

Domaine de St-Jean de Villecroze
83690 Villecroze.
Vineyards owned: 43ha. 200,000 bottles. VP-R
This modern winery, founded in 1975, produces Coteaux Varois and Vin de Pays du Var from a large vineyard containing a considerable proportion of Cabernet Sauvignon and Syrah as well as the more usual Cinsaut (used for rosé) and Grenache. A sparkling *blanc de blancs* is made from Ugni Blanc, using the classic method. The Vins de Pays du Var are 100 percent varietals (from Syrah and Cabernet Sauvignon). The Coteaux Varois red is a blend of Cabernet Sauvignon, Syrah and Grenache. Red and rosé wines are also sold in bulk. The vineyard is unusual because of the training system on wires and the use of California T-budding techniques for the Cabernet Sauvignon vines.
Open: Oct to April: Mon–Fri 8am–noon, 1–5pm; Sat/Sun 10am–noon, 3–5pm; May to Sept 8am–noon, 1–7pm; Sat/Sun 10am–noon, 3–7pm.

The Midi

Languedoc – the land of the French wine lake – and Roussillon occupy the stretch of Mediterranean coast that sweeps in a great arc from Marseille down to the Spanish frontier. A wide coastal plain in Languedoc is bounded by the mountains of the Massif Central to the north. In Roussillon, the mountains are closer to the sea. What is not harsh, rugged hill country is flat alluvial plain interspersed with marshy tracts.

From the mountains, small rivers run down to the sea. Torrents in winter and virtually dry in the long, hot summers, they have long ago carved out valleys on whose slopes vineyards are the natural form of agriculture.

This is the hottest part of France. The heat is dry, tempered with the Mistral and Tramontane winds which blow for days on end across the wide open spaces of the plains. Although the coastal strip is now becoming built up with the growth of tourism, inland the landscape is empty, scattered with red-roofed villages and a few larger, often walled, towns commanding the heights.

Nearly 40 percent of all French wines comes from these two regions. Much of it was once virtually undrinkable plonk – all red – which went to quench the thirst of the French farm or factory worker or to increase the EC surplus of industrial alcohol.

But increasingly this region has become the driving force behind the innovations and developments in French wine: from *vins de cépages*, wines made from a single grape variety and labelled as such, to modern techniques in the huge cooperatives, the Midi has become the source of much that is good value and much that is of excellent quality.

The previous period in the Midi's viticultural history was not so exciting. The hillside vineyards – those now being replanted and producing the best wines – were ravaged by phylloxera and it was not judged to be worth replanting them.

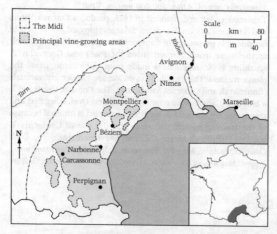

Vinous activity was transferred to the plain, where enormous yields were possible and cash returns were greater. Alicanté and Aramon as well as Carignan were planted – giving yields of up to 200 hectolitres per hectare of thin, watery wine which sold well to the less affluent of the industrial towns of the north.

Fashions change and the traditional industries have waned in France as elsewhere. The thirst for cheap wine after a day's work in a dusty steel mill or coal mine has gone. The French want better quality wine – and are drinking less of it. The call has gone out for a return to the hill vineyards and the abandonment of those on the plains. And this is what is happening.

The authorities are now trying to encourage quality rather than quantity. One way of doing this is to create AC and VDQS zones in the hills, which has the effect of pushing up prices. The government has also paid the farmers on the plains to uproot their vineyards and plant other crops such as cereals. The authorities have through various incentives encouraged local traditional vineyards, especially those in Roussillon, where there is a long history of quality winemaking. And in Languedoc it has promoted the introduction of the noble grape varieties such as Cabernet Sauvignon, Syrah, Mourvèdre – even Chardonnay – to blend with local grapes to give more flavour, style and aroma or to be made as wines in their own right, using the regional *vins de pays* that have been created such as Vin de Pays d'Oc.

The authorities are also awarding grants for new equipment in the wineries. Temperature-controlled vinification and stainless steel have arrived in Languedoc and Roussillon, where they are at last creating the possibility of decent white wines and unoxidised reds. The techniques of carbonic maceration, which bring out colour and flavour, have been introduced and encouraged.

The message is reaching the conservative French farmers in a number of ways. Cooperatives are important. Some 60 percent of the region's wines go through cooperatives. Most farmers have tiny holdings on which they can scarcely survive, let alone become involved in the high-tech of quality winemaking. A few big *négociant* firms – Nicolas and Chantovent among them – are also buying wine from small-holders, the best of which they bottle under individual domaine names. And increasingly, individual estates are leading their areas by example.

What this means for the wine drinker is that, over the past five years this area has blossomed, producing a range of good-quality, inexpensive wines. There is rarely anything of startling quality – the region needs time for that – but there are certainly pockets of very good quality and larger areas where standards are improving all the time.

Happily, this does not just mean that what is now being offered is simply well-made 'modern' wines. Some of the new AC and VDQS areas recognise long traditions. There have been vines here since the second century BC, and Narbonne was one of the first major cities of Roman Gaul. The French are good at recognising local character, and small vineyard areas have been given separate ACs in cognisance of their differences in style and quality.

The region also produces a range of sweet, fortified wines which, though popular in France, are virtually unknown outside the country. These are potentially high-alcohol wines whose fermentation is stopped by the addition of about ten percent *eau-de-vie*, leaving a strong, rich, sweet wine. They can be either *vins doux naturels* (made from grape brandy from any French source) or *vins de liqueur* (made with spirit from the region of production) and can be red or white. Those made from the Muscat grape are most attractive, those from the Grenache most distinctive.

The Appellations

GARD AC

Clairette de Bellegarde White wine only, made from the Clairette grape in two small areas within the larger Costières de Nîmes. Up to 3,000 hectolitres are produced on red, pebbly soil. The wines are often fragrant, if full, and have a pale gold colour. They lack acidity and tend towards flabbiness unless made with care.

Costières de Nîmes Red, white and rosé wines from a large area southeast of Nîmes and north of the Camargue marshes. The 4,000 hectares of vineyard are on flat land, much of it quite barren, some of it sandy, partly also planted with olive, lemon and orange groves. Red wines form around 80 percent of production, rosé about 15 percent and white around five percent. Red and rosé wines are made from Carignan (which can constitute up to 50 percent of the wine, although better producers use less), Cinsaut, Grenache, Mourvèdre, Syrah, Counoise and Terret Noir grapes. Syrah or Mourvèdre must make up at least 15 percent of the blend. The reds can be attractively simple, with southern warmth and nuttiness topped up with a Rhône-like spicy pepperiness. Whites are made from Clairette, Bourboulenc, Grenache Blanc and Ugni Blanc. Modern vinification and the picking of underripe grapes is helping to improve their quality and make fresh if undistinguished wines. This was formerly the Costières du Gard region.

GARD VINS DE PAYS

Departmental *vin de pays*

Vin de Pays du Gard Production is large and consists mainly of standard red wines from local grape varieties. A small amount of rosé, and an even smaller amount of white, are also made.

Zonal *vins de pays*

Vin de Pays des Coteaux Flaviens Near Aïgues-Mortes, this zone is mainly for reds from southern French and Bordeaux grapes.

Vin de Pays des Coteaux du Pont du Gard Mainly reds from local grape varieties, though Cabernet Sauvignon may also be used. The wines are from 19 communes around the famous Pont du Gard.

Vin de Pays des Coteaux de Cèze Production of a small amount of red wine and an even smaller amount of white from a large area in the north of the *département*.

Vin de Pays des Coteaux du Salavès Red and rosé wines produced here from a variety of grapes, including Merlot, Cabernet Sauvignon and Cabernet Franc, in the region west of Nîmes.

Vin de Pays des Coteaux du Vidourle On the western edge of the *département*, in the valley of the Vidourle around Sommières. The production of this zone is mainly of red wines from a mixture of local southern and Bordeaux grape varieties. A small amount of white, using Ugni Blanc, Grenache Blanc and Clairette, is also made. Some Cabernet wines are produced as 100 percent varietals.

Vin de Pays du Mont Bouquet Situated southeast of Alès, this is another *vin de pays* mostly for reds. A high percentage of Syrah is introduced to the blend to give well-coloured, characterful wines.

Vin de Pays des Sables du Golfe du Lion A virtually single-company vin de pays, dominated by the huge Salins du Midi firm, under the brand name of Listel. A wide range of wines is made from local grapes, though a considerable proportion of Chardonnay, Sauvignon Blanc and Cabernet Sauvignon are also used.

Vin de Pays de l'Uzège Around the town of Uzès, 26 communes produce red, rosé and some white wines. The usual southern grape varieties are used.

Other zonal *vins de pays*:

Vin de Pays des Coteaux Cévenols
Vin de Pays des Côtes du Líbac
Vin de Pays de la Vaunage
Vin de Pays de la Vistrenque

HÉRAULT AC

Clairette du Languedoc Dry, medium and sweet white wines made exclusively from the Clairette grape in communes around Cabrières, Aspiran and Clermont l'Hérault in the valley of the Hérault. Much of the 10,000 hectolitres produced is sold for vermouth, but other wines are aged to produce Rancio – what some might call an oxidised wine, but which others describe as maderized and profess to enjoy. High in alcohol, Clairette du Languedoc is best drunk on its own or before or after a meal.

Coteaux du Languedoc A highly complicated region producing red and rosé wines throughout Hérault. The grapes used are Carignan, Cinsaut, Counoise, Grenache, Mourvèdre, Syrah and Terret Noir. White wines are not permitted in the basic Coteaux du Languedoc AC, although certain communes (*see below*) also produce dry white wines using Clairette, Picpoul and Bourboulenc (locally known as Malvoisie). Standards are improving right across the region and one or two producers are outstanding. Twelve communes are allowed to add their name to the general AC. Two – La Clape and Quatourze – are in the Aude *département*, the rest are in Hérault. They are also allowed to use the village name without the Coteaux du Languedoc prefix – just to confuse us all!

Coteaux du Languedoc-Cabrières Rosé wines from vineyards just outside Béziers, mainly from Carignan and Cinsaut with a little Grenache.

Coteaux du Languedoc-La Clape In the Aude *département*, on the edge of the Corbières AC area, a large mound-shaped hill supports the vineyards of La Clape. Red, dry white and rosé wines are made on chalk soil. Red and rosés are made from Carignan, Grenache, Cinsaut and Terret Noir, whites from Clairette, Picpoul and Bourboulenc.

Coteaux du Languedoc-Coteaux de la Méjanelle or **La Méjanelle** Red wines from Carignan, Cinsaut and Grenache from near Montpellier. A small amount of dry white is also made.

Coteaux du Languedoc-Coteaux de St-Christol Vineyards northeast of Montpellier producing simple red wines from Carignan, Cinsaut and Grenache.

Coteaux du Languedoc-Coteaux de Vérargues Red and rosé wines, from vineyards northeast of Montpellier. Carignan, Cinsaut, Grenache and some Aramon are used.

Coteaux du Languedoc-Montpeyroux Red and rosé from schist soil north of Béziers. The reds include some Syrah in the *cépage*, which gives them some style.

Coteaux du Languedoc-Picpoul de Pinet Dry white wines made from Picpoul, Clairette and Terret Blanc in a small vineyard area just inland from the Bassin de Thau. The wines tend to flabbiness quite quickly and need to be drunk when young and very fresh.

Coteaux du Languedoc-Pic-St-Loup Red, rosé and dry white from north of Montpellier. These are fairly ordinary, straightforward wines.

Coteaux du Languedoc-Quatourze Vineyards around Narbonne in the Aude *département* producing red, dry white and rosé wines on stony soil. The red is particularly powerful and traditionally was used to strengthen weaker brews. Now generally bottled in its own right.

Coteaux du Languedoc-St-Drézéry West of St-Christol, vineyards producing red and a small amount of rosé. The usual grapes are used, but often with a higher proportion of Carignan.

Coteaux du Languedoc-St-Georges d'Orques Red and rosé wines from northwest of Montpellier. A high proportion of Cinsaut is used and the wines age well.

Coteaux du Languedoc-St-Saturnin Stylish wines made from Grenache, Cinsaut, Carignan and Mourvèdre, with Syrah to give the extra quality. Red and rosé are made in the hills north of the Hérault River.

Faugères Red, rosé and dry white wines coming from seven communes in the foothills of the Cevennes north of Béziers.

The vineyards are on steep hillsides and are difficult to work. Between 40,000 and 50,000 hectolitres are made each year. Grapes for the red wines are principally Carignan and, increasingly, Grenache and Cinsaut. Full-bodied, with intense colour and best described as hearty, the wines need the accompaniment of rich food. A little white is made from the Clairette grape.

Minervois A large area of vineyards, in 61 communes, which crosses the departmental boundary between Hérault and Aude. The best vineyards are in the Hérault around Minerve and St-Jean-de-Minervois. Red and rosé are produced from Carignan (over 50 percent), Grenache and Cinsaut with some Syrah and Mourvèdre. A small amount of white is also made. The reds are characterised by spicy, ripe, southern fruit which makes them attractive young, although producers who use some wood make wines that can age.

St-Chinian One of the most promising AC areas in the Hérault, producing red and rosé wines in a large area to the southwest of the Faugères AC. The vineyards, on slate soil with limestone, cover the hillsides on both banks of the Orb river. 80,000 hectolitres are made each year. The grapes are Carignan, Grenache, Cinsaut, Mourvèdre and Syrah, with the better producers having only a small proportion of Carignan. The wines are lighter and more elegant than other reds from Languedoc and the growth of prestigious single-domaine wines is encouraging.

HÉRAULT VINS DOUX NATURELS (VDN) VINS DE LIQUEUR

Clairette du Languedoc Made from the same grapes that produce the dry white Clairette du Languedoc.

Frontignan Red VDN made from Grenache, north of Sète. Also known as Vin de Frontignan. Can be a VDN or *vin de liqueur*.

Muscat de Frontignan In the same area as Frontignan, this is a white wine, and one of the best VDNs from the Muscat grape. Can be either a *vin doux naturel* or a *vin de liqueur*.

Muscat de Lunel From the Muscat grape in the area around St-Christol northeast of Montpellier.

Muscat de Mireval A small area just north of Frontignan.

Muscat de St-Jean-de-Minervois A small area at the northern extremity of the Minervois.

HÉRAULT VINS DE PAYS

Departmental *vin de pays*

Vin de Pays de l'Hérault One of the biggest *vin de pays*-producing regions in France (1.1 million hectolitres on average). The inclusion of one of the Midi's top estates – Mas de Daumas Gassac – shows that this is not just an area of inexpensive wines. Red wines are 85 percent of production here, made from Carignan, Grenache Noir, Cinsaut and Syrah, with Cabernet Sauvignon and Merlot also permitted. Small amounts of white and rosé are also made.

Zonal *vins de pays*

Vin de Pays de l'Ardailhou Carignan, Grenache and Cinsaut are
the principal grapes used in this area on the coast southeast of
Béziers. Once again, the production is predominantly of red
wines.

Vin de Pays de la Bénovie A region of 15 communes around St-
Christol producing red, rosé and white wines from the usual
southern grape varieties.

Vin de Pays du Bérange Red and rosé are predominant among
the wines of this *vin de pays*, with only six percent of white;
production is small. Some Bordeaux grape varieties may be
used. This zone is situated northwest of Montpellier.

Vin de Pays de Bessan Another small area which, unusually, is
dominated by rosé and white wine production. Local grape
varieties are used, although the small amount of red produced
may also include Cabernet Sauvignon.

Vin de Pays de Cassan An increasing amount of white wine is
made in this small area in the centre of the *département*,
although the majority continues to be of red. Cabernet
Sauvignon and Merlot may be added to the blend.

Vin de Pays de Caux The wines of this *vin de pays* are mostly
rosés, with some reds produced in a small area in the centre
of the *département*. Syrah is used to give some character.

Vin de Pays des Collines de la Maure A large area along the
coast between Sète and Montpellier. Reds and rosés make up
the main proportion of production and Syrah is used in the
blend, along with the southern grape varieties. Cabernet
Sauvignon and Merlot are made into 100 percent varietal
wines.

Vin de Pays des Coteaux de Bessilles Another small zone
in the centre of the *département*, producing red and rosé
wines. There has been an increase in the proportion of white
wines made – an indication that some interest is being taken
in the wines of this area.

Vin de Pays des Coteaux d'Enserune The wines from 13
communes near Béziers: red and some rosé. The grape varieties used are standard for the region.

Vin de Pays des Coteaux de Fontcaude Situated west of
Béziers, this *vin de pays* zone covers six communes which
make small quantities of white and rosé wines, and larger
quantities of red.

Vin de Pays des Coteaux du Libron Predominantly red wines
from the Béziers region. Technical specifications for production help to keep the standards reasonably high.

Vin de Pays des Coteaux de Murviel A *vin de pays* of the
valleys of the Libron and Orb, northwest of Béziers; the wines
are mostly red, either including Bordeaux grape varieties in
their blend or as single varietal wines.

Vin de Pays des Côtes du Brian Red wine *vin de pays* of the
Minervois region. Many AC Minervois producers also make
this wine, usually adding some of the permitted Cabernet
Sauvignon grape.

Vin de Pays des Côtes de Thau *Vin de pays* produced from around the shores of the Bassin de Thau in the south of the *département*. The production here is divided almost equally between red, rosé and white wines. Traditionally the area's principal concern was to supply base wine for vermouth, but the local cooperatives have lately developed an interest in bottling their own wine.

Vin de Pays des Côtes de Thongue Situated in the basin of Thongue, east of Béziers, this is predominantly a red wine area, although white is becoming increasingly important. Single varietal wines are also made here, with Cabernet Sauvignon and Chardonnay both planted specifically for this purpose.

Vin de Pays des Gorges de l'Hérault *Vin de pays* made in an area south of the popular tourist destination of St-Guilhem-le-Desert. A large proportion of the production is red wine but quantities are small.

Vin de Pays du Mont Baudile Found on the slopes of Mont Baudile, this is principally red wine country, but production of whites is increasing.

Vin de Pays de Pézenas Small production from one commune. This area specialises in 100 percent varietal wines from Cabernet Sauvignon and Merlot, while also making blends from the normal southern varieties.

Vin de Pays du Val de Montferrand Wines from a large stretch of the northern Hérault (and one commune in the Gard *département*); production is mainly of red wines. There is also a local speciality known as Vins de Café; red wines made using a short maceration to give a fruity style.

Vin de Pays de la Vicomté d'Aumelas Wines from 13 communes in the Valley of the Hérault, producing a fairly standard mixture of 85 percent red, 12 percent rosé, three percent white wines.

Other zonal *vins de pays*:

Vin de Pays de Cessenon
Vin de Pays des Coteaux du Salagou
Vin de Pays des Côtes du Ceressou
Vin de Pays de la Haute Vallée de l'Orb
Vin de Pays des Monts de la Grage

AUDE AC

Corbières The largest AC area in Languedoc and Roussillon, covering 92 communes from the coast right back to the high land of the Hautes-Corbières. Up to 600,000 hectolitres of wine are produced in an average year, of which 90 percent is red, one percent rosé, the rest white. Grapes for the red and rosé are Carignan, Cinsaut, Grenache, Mourvèdre, Terret Noir and Syrah with a little white Picpoul. For the white, the grapes are Clairette and Bourboulenc. Similar in style to Minervois (*see under* Hérault), the wines are possibly softer and heavier with less ability to age, but the range of quality from good to bad is enormous. However, new equipment and better practices in the vineyards are improving quality all the time, and today many estates are capable of making very fine wines using new wood for ageing special *cuvées*.

Crémant de Limoux This hilly region southwest of Carcassonne is centred on the winter carnival town of Limoux. Classic-method sparkling white wine is produced from Mauzac Blanc, Clairette and Chardonnay. The area's producers – dominated by a cooperative – claim that their sparkling wine used the classic method before Dom Pérignon introduced it in Champagne. Whether or not that is true, the Crémant de Limoux is one of the best sparklers in France outside Champagne. The wine used to be called Blanquette de Limoux – 'Blanquette' coming not from the colour of the wine but from the white film that covers the underside of the leaves of the Mauzac.

Fitou Two areas of vineyards within the larger Corbières AC, by the coastal lagoon of Salses. The AC applies to red wine only, made from a minimum of 70 percent Carignan with Grenache and Cinsaut. The result is a powerful, full-bodied red which has to be aged for a minimum of nine months in wood. The wines have recently achieved some popularity on the export market. The AC is one of the oldest in the Aude, having been established in 1948.

AUDE VDQS

Cabardès or **Côtes du Cabardès et de l'Orbiel** Red and rosé from north of Carcassonne on the slopes of the Minervois. Grapes are Carignan, Cinsaut, Grenache, Mourvèdre and Syrah with Cabernet Sauvignon, Cot, Fer and Merlot from the Southwest region just across the hills. Reds, quite tannic in their youth, are better.

Côtes de la Malepère Vineyards to the southwest of Carcassonne on the western side of the Aude Valley. Red and rosé wines are made principally from Cinsaut, Cot and Merlot with smaller amounts of Cabernet Sauvignon, Cabernet Franc, Grenache and Syrah: a heady brew which actually produces some comparatively sophisticated wines. Rosés are from Grenache and Cinsaut and are better than many rosés from surrounding areas.

AUDE VINS DE PAYS
Departmental *vin de pays*
Vin de Pays de l'Aude Wines mainly from the centre and east of the *département*. Production is of 90 percent red, made from Carignan, Grenache, Cinsaut and Syrah. A small amount of white wine uses Sémillon, Chardonnay and Chenin Blanc grapes. This is classic supermarket wine.

Zonal *vins de pays*
Vin de Pays de la Cité de Carcassonne Wines made in 11 communes scattered around the lovely medieval city of Carcassonne; most of these are red, and of a higher quality

than many other *vin de pays* in the region. This *vin de pays* also benefits from the touristic associations of Carcassonne.

Vin de Pays des Coteaux de la Cabrerisse This zone covers three communes in the centre of Corbières. Grapes are strictly controlled, in contrast to AC Corbières; the main varieties are Bordeaux *cépage nobles*: Cabernet Sauvignon, Cabernet Franc and Merlot; southern French varieties also appear.

Vin de Pays des Coteaux du Littoral Audois On the coast to the east of the Corbières hills, this is an area producing almost entirely red wines. They are mainly sold by cooperatives in bulk on the French internal market.

Vin de Pays des Coteaux de Miramont Wines from nine communes around Capendu in the east of the *département*, between Minervois and Corbières. Distribution is largely in the hands of a group of independent producers.

Vin de Pays des Coteaux de Narbonne A *vin de pays* producing a comparatively small amount of red wine in the region around Narbonne. Merlot and Cabernet Sauvignon are permitted, as are the usual southern varieties.

Vin de Pays des Coteaux de Peyriac Wines from the centre of the Minervois region, from 17 communes in the Aude and two in Hérault, producing red and rosé from both Bordeaux and southern grape varieties. About 90 percent is made by local cooperatives.

Vin de Pays des Côtes de Lastours Northwest of Carcassonne, on the edge of the Minervois, this zone combines characteristics of the mediterranean and atlantic climates. The dual influence is also reflected by the grape varieties: Jurançon Noir, Mauzac and the other mediterranean grapes.

Vin de Pays des Côtes de Lézignan Another zone in the heart of Corbières. The soil is stony and most of the production is of red grapes – some from Gascony and some from the mediterranean. Formerly known as Coteaux du Lézignanais.

Vin de Pays des Côtes de Pérignan Part of the Massif of La Clape (*see* Coteaux du Languedoc AC). Production is almost entirely of red wine, from three local cooperatives.

Vin de Pays de Cucugnan Found on the southern edge of the *département*, this zone covers a small area within the commune of Cucugnan. Production is controlled by the cooperative of Tuchan, and most of the wine produced is red.

Vin de Pays de la Haute Vallée de l'Aude Centred on the sparkling-wine town of Limoux, this is one of the rare *vin de pays* zones where the predominant production is of white wine. Varietal wines of 100 percent Chardonnay, Merlot and Cabernet Sauvignon grapes are also important.

Vin de Pays d'Hauterive en Pays d'Aude Wines from a straggling zone which extends southwest of Narbonne between the Aude and the plateau of Corbières. Eight communes are entitled to make this wine.

Vin de Pays du Torgan Formerly known as Vin de Pays des Coteaux Cathares, this zone extends over ten communes in the Hautes-Corbières. Production is almost entirely red.

Vin de Pays du Val de Cesse In the north of the *département*, this zone is based around the canton of Ginestas in the Minervois. Merlot and Cabernet Sauvignon are among the permitted grape varieties. Some whites are made from a blend which includes Macabeo.

Vin de Pays du Val de Dagne A range of varieties is permitted for the mainly red wines produced in this zone, which is in the centre of the *département*.

Vin de Pays du Val d'Orbieu Twelve communes between Narbonne and Lézignan are permitted to make this *vin de pays* which is 96 percent red. Marketing is controlled by an efficient central organisation, which has ensured wide distribution of the wine.

Vin de Pays de la Vallée du Paradis Wines from ten communes around Durban. This is one of the most widely exported *vins de pays* of the *département* – its popularity probably enhanced by its name. Some 95 percent is red wine; grapes include Cabernet Sauvignon and Merlot.

Other zonal *vins de pays*:

Vin de Pays des Coteaux du Termenès
Vin de Pays des Côtes de Prouille
Vin de Pays des Hauts de Badens

PYRÉNÉES-ORIENTALES AC

Collioure Tiny AC area right by the Spanish border, covering the same area as the Banyuls *vin doux naturel* AC (*see below*). Red wine from Grenache, Carignan, Mourvèdre, Syrah and Cinsaut are made in baking hot vineyards on the slopes of the Monts Albères as they drop down to the sea. Potentially a fine wine, especially from the old-established vineyards, it is a declining area, now with only about 50 hectares.

Côtes du Roussillon Red, rosé and dry white wine are produced from a large area of the Pyrénées-Orientales. The Côtes du Roussillon spread south from Perpignan and vines grow on the coast and inland to the foothills of the Pyrenees. Reds and rosés are made from Carignan, Cinsaut, Grenache and Mourvèdre grapes and the local Ladoner Pelut plus the white Spanish Macabeo in small amounts. Whites are from Macabeo and Malvoisie.

Côtes du Roussillon-Villages The area north of Perpignan in the Valley of the Agly is regarded as producing superior wine. The soil is gravelly with some granite and schist which gives the wines a backbone and elegance as well as a range of styles. Only red wines are covered by this appellation. Two villages – Caramany and Latour-de-France – are allowed to add their name to the Villages AC.

PYRÉNÉES-ORIENTALES VINS DOUX NATURELS (VDN), VINS DE LIQUEUR

Banyuls Red and tawny *vin doux naturel* (VDN) from the same area as the red wine Collioure, stretching down to the Spanish frontier. These VDNs are made from Grenache Noir, Grenache

Gris, Grenache Blanc, Macabeo, Malvoisie and Muscat grape
varieties. The greater the proportion of Grenache used, the
better the wine seems to age.

Banyuls Rancio Banyuls VDN which has been aged in barrels in
the open air under the sun to concentrate the wine. The best
Banyuls Rancio is called Banyuls *Grand Cru*, and is considered
by some to rival tawny port.

Grand Roussillon VDN red wine from the general area of the
Pyrénées-Orientales. Can also be made as Rancio.

Maury Red and rosé VDN from the north bank of the River Agly.
It is made only from Grenache Noir. Lighter than Banyuls, it
can also be aged in wood to produce Rancio.

Muscat de Rivesaltes A Muscat-based VDN from just north of
Perpignan. In the same area as Rivesaltes (*see below*).

Rivesaltes Red, white and rosé VDN made from Grenache Noir,
Macabeo, Malvoisie and Muscat. Only 100 percent Muscat
wines can be called Muscat de Rivesaltes. If aged in wood, this
is called Rivesaltes Rancio.

PYRÉNÉES-ORIENTALES VINS DE PAYS

Departmental *vin de pays*

Vin de Pays des Pyrénées-Orientales Mostly red wines, produced all around the *département* except in the southeast.

Zonal *vins de pays*

Vin de Pays Catalan The most important *vin de pays* zone in
the *département*, stretching from the Mediterranean to the
western boundary. About 70 percent of production is of red
and 20 percent is of rosé wine, from a range of grapes
including Cabernet Sauvignon, Mourvèdre and Syrah. Whites
are made from Muscat, Macabeo, Chardonnay and Grenache
Blanc.

Vin de Pays des Coteaux des Fenouillèdes Mountain vineyards
in the northwest of the *département*, producing mainly red
wines from the usual grape varieties. Smaller amounts of rosé
and a tiny amount of white wine is also made.

Vin de Pays des Côtes Catalanes Not to be confused with Vin de
Pays Catalan (*see above*), these wines come from the northeast
of the *département*, around Rivesaltes and along the coast. Of
the wine produced, 80 percent is red, made from a mixture
that includes Syrah, Merlot and Cabernet Sauvignon.

Vin de Pays Val d'Agly Wines from 16 communes in the area of
Haut-Agly. These are mainly traditional reds, but there is an
increasing production of whites and rosés.

One other zonal *vin de pays*:

Vin de Pays des Côtes Vermeilles

THE MIDI

Regional *vin de pays*

Vin de Pays d'Oc Covering the whole of Languedoc-Roussillon,
this *vin de pays* is used for wines made from grape varieties
not traditional to the region. Thus there are Vin de Pays d'Oc

made from Cabernet Sauvignon, Cabernet Franc, Merlot, Syrah and Mourvèdre, with whites from Chardonnay, Sauvignon Blanc, Chenin Blanc, Viognier and Vermentino. Seventy percent of production is of single varietal wines. Many of the most interesting of the new wave of southern French wines are being made using this *vin de pays*.

Gard Producers

CLAIRETTE DE BELLEGARDE AC

Domaine de l'Amarine
30127 Bellegarde.
Vineyards owned: 37ha. 225,000 bottles. VP-R
Costières de Nîmes and Clairette de Bellegarde are the two styles of wine produced on this large estate. The Costières de Nîmes comes in red, rosé and white from a standard range and special *cuvées* of red (Cuvée des Bernis) and rosé (Cuvée Royal). Grenache predominates in the red with Cinsaut, Carignan and Syrah; the white is 100 percent Grenache Blanc. Clairette de Bellegarde is 100 percent Clairette. Some rosé classic-method sparkling wine is also made (Cour de Bernis).
Open: By appointment only.

COSTIÈRES DE NÎMES AC

Château de Belle-Coste
30132 Caissargues. Vineyards owned: 53ha. 333,000 bottles. VP-R
Bertrand du Tremblay's family has run this estate for more than a century. The firm makes red, rosé and white Costières de Nîmes. The red (matured in wood) uses Syrah and Mourvèdre with Grenache Noir, and the rosé 100 percent Grenache Noir. There are two whites, one with Ugni Blanc and Grenache Blanc, the other Grenache Blanc alone. *Open: Mon–Sat 9am–noon, 2–6pm.*

Château Roubaud
Gallician, 30600 Vauvert. Vineyards owned: Costières de Nîmes 80ha. 573,000 bottles. VP-R
This estate has been owned by the Molinier-Thomas family since 1927. While some of the wine is sold in bulk, bottled red, white and rosé Costières de Nîmes are also made using modern techniques. The usual *cépage* includes some Syrah for red wines and Ugni Blanc for whites.
Open: Mon–Sat 8am–noon, 1.30–7pm.

Château de St-Vincent
Jonquières St-Vincent, 30300 Beaucaire.
Vineyards owned: 41ha. 250,000 bottles. VP-R
This is a traditional estate in the birth village of the writer Daudet. The firm makes red and rosé, using wood for ageing the reds. The grapes for both styles are Grenache, Cinsaut, Carignan and some Merlot. *Open: Mon–Fri.*

Domaines Viticoles des Salins du Midi
68 Cours Gambetta, 34063 Montpellier.
Vineyards owned: Côtes de Provence 123ha, Coteaux Varois 139ha, vin de pays 1,750ha. 25.4 million bottles. VP-R
France's largest wine producer, with vineyards in the Côtes de Provence (Château La Gordonne, Domaine de St-Hilaire), a *négociant* business (Bernard Camp Romain) and a huge vineyard area in the sand-dunes of the Gard *département* making Vins de Pays des Sables du Golfe du Lion. Quality for such vast production is high. The brand name is Listel. The firm is now part of the Val d'Orbieu cooperative (*see* page 197).
Open: Visits to the Côtes de Provence vineyards only.

Château de la Tuilerie
Route de St-Gilles, 30900 Nîmes.
Vineyards owned: 100ha. 533,000 bottles. VP-R
An immaculately maintained and go-ahead estate owned by Madame Chantal Comte. The property, which she inherited from her husband, includes another 200 hectares of fruit trees. She makes red, rosé and white Costières de Nîmes, the white with 100 percent Grenache Blanc, the red a blend of Grenache, Syrah and Cinsaut and the rosé 100 percent Cinsaut. The red is the best of the three and ages well. *Open: Mon–Sat 8am–1pm, 2–7pm.*

Hérault Producers

COTEAUX DU LANGUEDOC AC

Georges Bonfils
20 Quai d'Alger, 34200 Sète. VP-R and N
This firm is mainly a *négociant* for wines from the Coteaux du Languedoc and the Vin de Pays de l'Hérault. It also has a Coteaux du Languedoc estate, Domaine de Lavabre, which produces a fairly standard red from Cinsaut, Grenache, Syrah and Carignan. Other Coteaux du Languedoc wines are estates for which the firm has exclusive rights: Château de Beauregard and Château de St-Series. The *vins de pays* – especially Chardonnay Vin de Pays d'Oc – are better than the AC wines. *Open: By appointment only.*

J Boscary (Château Rouquette-sur-Mer)
11100 Narbonne. VP-R
A white from 100 percent Bourboulenc and a rosé from Grenache are made here. There is also a wood-aged red, made using some Syrah, which has a high reputation. The vineyard is planted on the steep slopes of the mountain of La Clape, overlooking the sea.

Château La Condamine Bertrand
34230 Paulhan. Vineyards owned: 64ha. 87,000 bottles. VP-R
Stainless steel has been installed at this family-owned estate and whites and rosés are vinified at controlled temperatures. Reds – the bulk of production – go through carbonic maceration which brings out the fruit and colour. Red and rosé are made under the

Coteaux du Languedoc AC, the white has the Clairette du Languedoc AC. A range of wines in the interesting Vin de Pays des Côtes de Thongue includes reds from Syrah, Mourvèdre, Merlot and Cabernet Sauvignon.
Open: Mon–Fri 9am–noon, 2–8pm; appointments preferred.

Château de l'Engarran
34880 Laverune. Vineyards owned: 40.5ha. 118,000 bottles. VP-R
The estate of Château de l'Engarran makes red and rosé Coteaux du Languedoc from Carignan, Grenache, Syrah and Cinsaut. This is aged in wood for 18 months and produces rich, slightly spicy wine which takes some ageing. The second label, Domaine de l'Engarran, produces a Vin de Pays d'Oc Blanc from Sauvignon and Ugni Blanc, while there are red Vin de Pays des Collines de la Maure from Carignan and Grenache. Housed in the historic château is a small wine museum. *Open: Mon–Sun 10am–noon, 2–7pm.*

Château des Hospitaliers
Place Général-Chafford, St-Christol, 34400 Lunel.
Vineyards owned: 20.5ha. 69,500 bottles. VP-R
Red and rosé Coteaux du Languedoc-St-Christol are produced at this small estate, using traditional methods. The red is a rich, smooth wine aged in wood. Some Syrah is used in the blends, including a Cuvée Spéciale. The estate also produces a white Vin de Pays de la Bénovie from Chardonnay, Grenache Blanc and Ugni Blanc. *Open: Mon–Sun 8am–8pm.*

Château de Nizas
34320 Roujan. Vineyards owned: 43ha. 180,000 bottles. VP-R
Red Coteaux du Languedoc Château Carrion-Nizas is produced using carbonic maceration and some wood-ageing, resulting in a typical southern taste which is improved with a touch of Syrah. Perhaps more interesting is the estate's Vin de Pays de Caux: the red is made from ten percent Cabernet Sauvignon and 15 percent Merlot, plus the usual local varieties. Small amounts of rosé and white *vin de pays* are also made. *Open: Mon–Fri 8am–noon, 2–7pm.*

Château Notre Dame du Quatourze
11100 Narbonne.
Vineyards owned: 80ha. 500,000 bottles. VP-R
One of the bigger private producers from the small Quatourze area near Narbonne. Monsieur Yvon Ortola makes red, white and rosé Coteaux du Languedoc using some stainless steel for vinification and aiming for highly aromatic wines. He has been planting Mourvèdre, Syrah and Grenache to replace the Carignan. The white Coteaux du Languedoc is made from Macabeo.
Open: Mon–Sun 9am–7pm.

Château Pech-Céleyran
Salles d'Aude, 11110 Coursan.
Vineyards owned: 93ha. 350,000 bottles. VP-R
The vineyard is owned by the Comte de St-Exupéry and produces

red and rosé Coteaux du Languedoc-La Clape, some of which has up to two years in wood. Plantings of Cabernet Sauvignon, Merlot, Viognier and Chardonnay are used as part of the blend for red, rosé and white Vin de Pays des Côtes de Pérignan. Both the Chardonnay and Cabernet wines are aged in wood. This producer obviously takes trouble with the wines.

Open: Mon–Sun 9am–6pm.

Château Pech-Redon
11100 Narbonne. Vineyards owned: 40ha. 100,000 bottles. VP-R
Cabernet Sauvignon and Merlot form 15 percent of this vineyard, and it shows in the red Coteaux du Languedoc-La Clape. In addition to the reds, Monsieur Demolombe makes a rosé, La Clape, using 25 percent Syrah and 25 percent Grenache. He also makes a *blanc de blancs* Vin de Pays des Coteaux de Narbonne from Chardonnay and a *blanc de noirs* from Cinsaut. Because the vineyard is high on the slopes, the vines get a slower, longer growing season than those on the plain.

Open: Mon–Sun 9am–noon, 1–7pm.

Domaine du Poujol
34570 Vailhauques.
Vineyards owned: 16.5ha. 100,000 bottles. VP-R
A newly-acquired British-owned property which produces both Coteaux du Languedoc in red and rosé and *vin de pays*. Investment includes the halving of yields in the vineyards as well as new equipment in the cellars and new plantings. The Coteaux du Languedoc red is aged for ten months in wood. Vin de Pays de l'Hérault wines include a red which is a blend of Merlot, Cinsaut and Carignan.

Open: Sat–Sun 10am–6pm. Weekdays by appointment.

Château de Ricardelle
Route de Gruissan, 11104 Narbonne.
Vineyards owned: 47ha. 400,000 bottles. VP-R
Organic methods only in the vineyard – no chemical sprays – and modern equipment in the winery produce some attractive Coteaux du Languedoc-La Clape wines. The vineyard is on the western slopes of the hill of La Clape facing out over the city of Narbonne. The red is a blend of Carignan, Grenache, Syrah and Cinsaut. The rosé (or *gris*) omits the Syrah. Vin de Pays de l'Aude red and rosé, which include some Merlot, are also made.

Open: Mon–Fri 8am–noon, 2–6pm.

Château St-Jean d'Aumières
34150 Gignac. Vineyards owned: 27ha. 30,000 bottles. VP-R
While the bulk of Daniel Delclaud's production is of *vin de pays*, he also produces some Coteaux du Languedoc from Grenache, Cinsaut and Syrah. Modern vinification in stainless steel is used, but Monsieur Delclaud's aim, he says, is to produce red wines for keeping and a new ageing cellar has just been built for this purpose. His wines include Vin de Pays de l'Hérault made from 50 percent

Cabernet Sauvignon, plus Grenache, Cinsaut and Syrah. Probably
his most interesting wine is a 100 percent Cabernet Sauvignon Vin
de Pays des Gorges de l'Hérault, which is matured in wood.
Open: Mon–Sun 9am–noon, 1–6pm; closed Sun in winter.

Les Vins de St-Saturnin
34725 St-Saturnin-de-Lucian. Vineyards owned: 780ha.
4 million bottles. Coop (192 members).
The main cooperative in the Coteaux du Languedoc-St-Saturnin
AC area, specialising in the rosé Vin d'Une Nuit brand (a blend of
Carignan, Cinsaut, Grenache and Syrah), so called because the
skins remain on the must for only one night. The cooperative also
makes a large number of brands of red Coteaux du Languedoc –
the best is the Cuvée Spéciale – Vin de Pays de l'Hérault and *vin
de table. Open: Mon–Fri 8am–noon, 2–6pm; Sat 8am–noon, 2–7pm.*

Château de Salles
Salles d'Aude, 11110 Coursan.
Vineyards owned: 28ha. 200,000 bottles. VP-R
The Château de Salles has been in the Hue-Bellaud family since
the 18th century. The firm is now making a range of wines
including Coteaux du Languedoc-La Clape. The Grenache dominates the blend for this wine which is made partly by carbonic
maceration. There is a small proportion of Syrah, Terret Noir and
Carignan as well as Cinsaut. A Vin de Pays des Côtes de Pérignan
is also produced; the red version has 80 percent Merlot and ten
percent Syrah in the blend and is an interesting and successful
wine. *Open: By appointment only.*

FAUGÈRES AC

Domaine du Fraïsse
1 bis, Rue du Chemin de Ronde, Autignac, 34480 Magalas.
Vineyards owned: 24.5ha. 75,000 bottles. VP-R
Jacques Pons uses carbonic maceration for his red Faugères, they
are made from Carignan, Grenache, Syrah and Cinsaut grapes. He
vinifies the different *cépages* separately, then blends them before
bottling. He now makes white Coteaux du Languedoc wines as
well as red AC Faugères with plantings of Bourboulenc, and *vin de
pays* from Chardonnay. *Open: By appointment only.*

Domaine de la Grange des Aires
Cabrerolles, 34480 Magalas. VP-R
The classic regional grape varieties – Carignan, Grenache, Syrah
and Cinsaut – are planted here to make Madame Platelle's long-
lived reds. The estate, which has passed through the female line
for generations, was established in the last century.

Bernard et Claude Vidal
La Liquière, Cabrerolles, 34480 Magalas.
Vineyards owned: 29ha. VP-R
Carbonic maceration techniques are used here to gain maximum

fruit from the usual blend of grape varieties. Both a red and a rosé
are made, the red soft and well balanced, the rosé somewhat
muted and less interesting.

MINERVOIS AC

Château Canet
11800 Rustiques. Vineyards owned: 40ha. 240,000 bottles. VP-R
A Minervois vineyard owned since 1992 by the Alsace producer
Dopff et Irion (*see* page 87). The red, made from Carignan, Syrah,
Grenache and Cinsaut, is aged for six months in wood; the white,
from Roussanne, Bourboulenc and Terret, for three months.
Open: By appointment only.

Domaine Daniel Domergue
Trausse-Minervois, 11160 Caunes.
Vineyards owned: 5ha. 25,000 bottles. VP-R
A small producer who is producing interesting wines. Over half
the vineyard is planted with Syrah, which dominates three of
Monsieur Domergue's wines: Cuvée Noire (100 percent Syrah),
Cuvée d'Or (75 percent Syrah) and Cuvée Chanteperdrix (80
percent Syrah). Another Minervois, Cuvée des Clos du Bosc, is
100 percent Mourvèdre. Although the quantities are small, the
quality is high. *Open: By appointment only.*

Château de Fabas
Laure-Minervois, 11800 Trèbes.
Vineyards owned: 44ha. 260,000 bottles. VP-R
There is a fairly high percentage of Syrah and Mourvèdre in this
vineyard – with more being planted. But the red Minervois is
dominated at present by Grenache, giving a typical southern
taste and warm, rounded finish. Jean-Pierre Ormières uses
temperature-controlled fermentation and a long maceration, and
his Cuvée Spéciale receives some wood-ageing. Rosé and a small
amount of white wine are also made. *Open: Mon–Fri 8am–6pm;
Sat 8am–noon, 1–7pm; Sun by appointment.*

Château Gibalaux-Bonnet
Laure-Minervois, 11800 Trèbes.
Vineyards owned: 76.5ha. 60,000 bottles. VP-R
Monsieur Bonnet makes Minervois red from Carignan and
Grenache with 20 percent Syrah; rosé has 50 percent Carignan
and 50 percent Mourvèdre. Vin de Pays des Coteaux de
Peyriac red and white are also made (the white has 50 percent
Chardonnay). The second wine of the estate is called Château
Bonnet; there is also a top Cuvée Prieuré. The use of stainless
steel produces very clean wines.
Open: Mon–Fri 8am–noon, 2–6pm; Sat/Sun by appointment.

Château la Grave
11800 Trèbes. Vineyards owned: 80ha. 200,000 bottles. VP-R
A new barrel-ageing cellar sets the scene for this estate, whose

top red Minervois, Privilège, based on Syrah, Grenache, Carignan and Mourvèdre, is aged for up to 12 months in wood. There is a lighter style of red known as Expression, which is matured in bottle before its release. A white *vin de pays*, which includes Chardonnay in the blend, provides the other half of the firm's production.

Open: Every day from June to Sept. Other times by appointment.

Château de Gourgazaud
La Livinière, 34210 Olonzac.
Vineyards owned: 68ha. 500,000 bottles. VP-R

This is the showplace vineyard of the giant Chantovent organisation, a major *négociant* in Languedoc and Roussillon. It is planted with a considerable proportion of Syrah, which is blended with Carignan, Merlot and Cabernet Sauvignon to produce a highly drinkable red, good young but able to age. Minervois Blanc (Sauvignon, Macabeo and Marsanne) is well made but much less interesting. Plantings of Cabernet, Syrah and Chardonnay are now producing *vin de pays*.

Open: Mon–Sat 9am–noon, 3–6pm.

Cave Coopérative des Coteaux du Haut-Minervois
34120 La Livinière.
Vineyards owned: 650ha. 300,000 bottles. Coop (180 members).

A variety of vinification techniques are used at this cooperative (established 1924) including carbonic maceration, must heating and de-stalking before fermentation. The best wine – Cuvée Jacques de la Jugie AC Minervois – is made by carbonic maceration, then given some ageing in wood. No whites are made, but about a third of production is of *vin de pays*.

Open: By appointment only.

Domaine de l'Herbe Sainte
Mirepeisset, 11120 Ginestas.
Vineyards owned: 40ha. 60,000 bottles. VP-R

Guy Rancoule has owned this vineyard since 1965 and has installed stainless steel and planted some Cabernet Sauvignon, Cot and Merlot to add to his Minervois and Vin de Pays du Val de Cesse. He uses organic methods both in the vineyard and the winery, vinifying in stainless steel but cutting the use of sulphur to a minimum. Although only a small production is bottled at the domaine at present, Monsieur Rancoule is planning to bring the figure up to 400,000 bottles soon.

Open: June–Sept 9am–noon, 3–7pm; otherwise by appointment only.

Paul Herpe et Fils (Château de Vergel)
11120 Ginestas. Vineyards owned: 22ha. 220,000 bottles. VP-R

Red Minervois is produced here, with 30 percent Syrah giving it attractive, firm fruit. Techniques are traditional, with wood maturation. The estate also makes a *vin de pays*. The firm also owns vineyards in Corbières and Coteaux du Languedoc-La Clape.

Open: Appointments preferred.

Domaine Jacques Maris

34210 La Livinière. Vineyards owned: 52ha. 190,000 bottles. VP-R
Red, rosé and white Minervois are the main production at this
large estate in the heart of the Minervois AC, northwest of
Olonzac. Wine is still sold in bulk but the proportion of bottled
wine has gone up in the past five years. Some carbonic
maceration is used for the Carignan which forms 70 percent of
the red and 50 percent of the rosé. Syrah is used in the Cuvée
Spéciale, giving a distinct perfume to the wine. Whites are made
from 100 percent Macabeo. *Open: By appointment only.*

Château de Paraza

Paraza, 11200 Lézignan.
Vineyards owned: 130ha. 44,000 bottles. VP-R
Two styles of Minervois are made on this large, much-praised
estate: a Rouge Tradition, which is vinified traditionally, and a
Cuvée Spéciale, made by carbonic maceration and containing
some Syrah. The Cuvée Spéciale is a more attractive style – with
a deep colour and intense, concentrated fruit and a perfumed
taste. Madame de Girard also makes a rosé, which is designed for
drinking young. *Open: By appointment only.*

Domaine du Pech d'André

Azillanet, 34210 Olonzac.
Vineyards owned: 19ha. 18,000 bottles. VP-R
The estate, at the base of the hill in the town of Minerve, produces
two red Minervois: one based on 50 percent Mourvèdre with
Carignan and Grenache, the other replacing the Mourvèdre with
Syrah. Both are excellent examples of the quality that Minervois
can now produce, the Syrah wine perfumed and peppery, the
Mourvèdre softer, warmer and ready to drink younger. Smaller
amounts of rosé and white are also made.
Open: Mon–Sun 8am–8pm.

Cave Coopérative de la Région de Peyriac-Minervois

11160 Peyriac-Minervois.
Vineyards owned: 320ha. 50,000 bottles. Coop (250 members).
Only a small amount of Minervois is bottled at this cooperative,
the rest being sold in bulk. The wines are dominated by the
traditional Carignan, but carbonic maceration gives freshness and
colour. Tour St-Martin is the cooperative's top Minervois *cuvée*,
which has 50 percent Carignan, and the remaining 50 percent is
made up of a blend of Syrah, Grenache and Mourvèdre. Vin de
Pays des Coteaux de Peyriac is also made by the cooperative.
Much of the wine sold in bulk goes to the big *négociant* firm of
Chantovent. *Open: By appointment only.*

Château de Pouzols

Pouzols Minervois, 11120 Ginestas. Vineyards owned: 78ha. VP-R
While the bulk of production at this estate is of Vin de Pays du Val
de Cesse, with reds made from Merlot, Grenache, Carignan and
Cinsaut and whites from Mauzac, the top wine of the estate is a

Minervois. Both Syrah and Mourvèdre are used in the blend, which is aged for up to two years in tank and for nine months in wood. *Barrique* ageing now takes place in a brand new cellar. *Open: By appointment only.*

Jean de Thelin
Château de Blomac, Blomac, 11700 Capendu.
Vineyards owned: 102ha. VP-R
A well-established estate which makes Minervois (using ten percent Syrah in the blend), Vin de Pays d'Oc and *vin de table*, using 'foreign' varieties – Cabernet Sauvignon, Merlot and the Spanish red variety used in Rioja, Tempranillo.

Les Vignerons du Haut-Minervois
34210 Azillanet.
Vineyards owned: 301ha. 35,000 bottles. Coop (250 members).
The members at this long-established cooperative have vineyards in Azillanet, Cesseras and Minerve and produce mainly Carignan, with a smaller amount of Syrah, Grenache, Cinsaut and Terret Noir. Most of the production here is of Vin de Pays des Côtes du Brian and Vin de Pays de l'Hérault, much of which is sold in bulk. Winemaking is modern, with temperature control and carbonic maceration. *Open: By appointment only.*

Château de Villerambert-Julien
11160 Caunes-Minervois.
Vineyards owned: 60ha. 373,000 bottles. VP-R
At this château (founded in Roman times) Michel Julien uses both traditional vinification and carbonic maceration to make his red Minervois. His top *cuvée*, Cuvée Trianon, has 50 percent Carignan, 25 percent Syrah and 25 percent Grenache and Mourvèdre, giving a wine with plenty of raspberry fruit which should be drunk within three years. The other red wine is Cuvée Opéra. Monsieur Julien also makes a rosé wine.
Open: Mon–Sun 9am–7pm.

Château de Villerambert Moreau
11160 Caunes-Minervois.
Vineyards owned: 120ha. 300,000 bottles. VP-R
There are two Minervois estates owned by the Moreau family: the Château de Villerambert and the Château Villegly. The Villegly wines have more character and depth but both are well made. The firm also makes red and rosé Vin de Pays des Coteaux de Peyriac and a Cabernet Sauvignon/Syrah *vin de pays*, Domaine Moreau. *Open: Mon–Sun 2–7pm.*

PICPOUL DE PINET AC

Claude Gaujal
BP No 1, 34850 Pinet.
Vineyards owned: 44ha. 85,000 bottles. VP-R
The firm has been in Gaujal family hands since 1791. Most of the

wines are citrus-like Picpoul de Pinet, made using modern techniques. Other bottled wines include a Sauvignon Blanc and red Merlot Vin de Pays des Côtes de Thau.

Open: Mon–Fri 9am–noon, 2–6pm.

ST-CHINIAN AC

Château Coujan

34490 Murviel lès Béziers.

Vineyards owned: 100ha. 120,000 bottles. VP-R

The Guy family has run this model estate since 1868, producing one of the best St-Chinian reds from Syrah, Grenache and Cinsaut. This top *cuvée* is named after Gabrielle de Spinola who bought wine from this estate in the 18th century. An elegant wine, it is aged for a while in 200-litre barrels which add a layer of complexity. Another *cuvée* is Cuvée Bois Joli, based on 60 percent Mourvèdre. The estate also produces red and white, sold as Vin de Pays des Coteaux de Murviel.

Open: Mon–Sat 9am–noon, 3–7pm; Sun by appointment.

Pierre et Henri Petit

Villepassans, 34360 St-Chinian.

Vineyards owned: 21.5ha. 15,000 bottles. VP-R

Red and rosé St-Chinian are produced on this small family estate, mainly from Carignan and Cinsaut, but with a little Mourvèdre, Syrah and Merlot. Carbonic maceration is used for the reds.

Open: By appointment only.

Les Coteaux du Rieu Berlou

343 Avenue des Vignerons, Berlou, 34360 St-Chinian.

Vineyards owned: 600ha. 300,000 bottles. Coop (100 members).

St-Chinian AC Berlou Prestige, the top red wine from this cooperative, is made from Carignan, Grenache and Syrah using carbonic maceration. It needs three years in bottle before drinking. There is also a standard red St-Chinian and rosé and white wine. Seventy percent of production here is of *vin de pays* and *vin de table*, sold in bulk. New plantings of Mourvèdre and Syrah seem to have improved in quality.

Open: Mon–Sat 9am–noon, 2–6pm.

VIN DOUX NATUREL

Frontignan Coopérative

34112 Frontignan. Vineyards owned: 600ha. 2 million bottles. Coop (350 members).

This is by far the biggest producer of sweet Muscat de Frontignan, the only wine the firm makes. It operates traditionally, with some ageing of the wine in wood, and the result is a good commercial wine which preserves the grapey taste of Muscat and adds a touch of honeyed sweetness. *Open: Mon–Sun March: 8.45am–12.15pm, 1.45–6.30pm; April 8.45am–7pm; May–Aug 8.45am–7.30pm, Sept to 7pm; Oct–Dec 8.45am–12.15pm, 1.45–6pm.*

Cave de Rabelais
BP 14, 34840 Mireval.
Vineyards owned: 150ha. 300,000 bottles. Coop (80 members).
Muscat de Mireval is the product from this appropriately named cooperative. Vinification is in stainless steel, but the rest of the production is traditional. Mireval is one of the smaller, less publicised Muscat areas, but its production is just as good as that of the better-known appellations.
Open: Mon–Fri 8am–noon, 2–6pm; closed March.

VIN DE PAYS D'OC

Domaine de la Baume
RN113, 34290 Servian VP-R and N
An Australian-owned winery set in an ancient farmhouse which hides a state-of-the art vinification plant. Varietally-labelled wines such as the estate Merlot and whites such as the Chardonnay continually win awards. For the local producers, the appearance of an Australian winery on their doorstep has proved both a great surprise and an education.
Open: By appointment only.

Vignobles James Herrick
Domaine de la Motte, Chemin de Bougna, 11100 Narbonne.VP-R
The Briton James Herrick, who learned his craft in Champagne, Australia and California, owns three vineyards in the Aude Valley from which he produces Chardonnay wines and, more recently, a red. The produce of each estate – La Boulandière, Les Garrigues de Truilhas and Domaine de la Motte – is bottled separately as well as blended. *Open: By appointment only.*

Skalli – Fortant de France
278 Avenue du Maréchal Juin, 34204 Sète. N
One of the most important producers of varietally-labelled Vin de Pays d'Oc, using the Fortant de France brand and extensive marketing, which includes great emphasis on a mediterranean lifestyle. The wines are correct, well made, occasionally very good, and certainly, for their price, excellent examples of what the Languedoc can produce in the new wave of winemaking.
Open: Mon–Fri 8am–noon; 2–5.30pm.

Aude Producers

CORBIÈRES AC

Château de la Baronne/Domaine des Lanes
11700 Fontcouverte.
Vineyards owned: 40ha. 150,000 bottles. VP-R
Temperature-controlled carbonic maceration is used for reds at both these estates. The Château de la Baronne also produces a rosé, while Domaine des Lanes makes a white (Vin de Pays d'Hauterive). *Open: Appointments preferred.*

Château de Cabriac
11600 Douzens. Vineyards owned: 85ha. 518,000 bottles. VP-R
Corbières red and white are made here at this estate which has a
minority shareholding from Château Chasse-Spleen in Bordeaux.
The wines are not aged in wood and are designed for relatively
early drinking. *Open: By appointment only.*

Cave Coopérative Embres et Castelmaure
11360 Durban Corbières.
Vineyards owned: 276ha. 410,000 bottles. Coop (123 members).
Most of the production here is of Corbières, although there is also
Vin de Pays de l'Aude. This is one of the better cooperatives of the
many in the Corbières region: its production of white wines is
especially good. The château of Castelmaure was the home of the
Pompadour family.

Château du Grand Caumont
11200 Lezignan. Vineyards owned: 105ha. 773,000 bottles. VP-R
Corbières and Vin de Pays d'Oc are the wines produced at this
estate which is owned by the Rigal family. The firm vinifies in
traditional cement tanks and does not use wood, so emphasising
fruit. The top *cuvée* of Corbières is Cuvée Tradition. *Vin de pays* is
made from Merlot, Cabernet Sauvignon, Carignan and Cinsaut.
Open: Mon-Fri 8am-6pm; Sat/Sun by appointment.

Château Haut-Gléon
Villesque-des-Corbières, 11360 Durban.
Vineyards owned: 29ha. 110,000 bottles. VP-R
Modern cellars produce an especially attractive white Corbières
at this estate. Both this wine and the red are aged in barrels, some
of which are new, for eight to nine months. The estate buildings
include a 12th-century chapel.
Open: Mon-Sat 9am-noon; 2-6pm

Château de Lastours
*11490 Portel des Corbières. Vineyards owned: 99ha. 450,000
bottles. VP-R*
Red, *gris de gris* rosé and white Corbières are made on this estate.
The red is the best of the three, with the top *cuvée*, Simone
Descamps, an interesting blend of Carignan, Grenache and
Cinsaut, plus a little Syrah and Merlot. This particular wine needs
around five years before it is ready, but a new *cuvée*, Arnaud de
Berre, is made to be drunk young. The *gris de gris* is 100 percent
Grenache, the white 100 percent Malvoisie – a very attractive
wine. *Open: Mon-Fri 8am-4pm.*

Château de Luc/Château Gasparets
11200 Luc-sur-Orbieu.
Vineyards owned: 176ha. 600,000 bottles. VP-R
The Fabre family is an important landowner in Corbières. It runs
three estates: Château de Luc, Château Gasparets and Domaine
de l'Ancien Courrier. It also makes Vin de Pays des Coteaux

d'Enserune from Merlot, Cabernet Sauvignon and Sauvignon Blanc, using the name Domaine de la Grande Courtade. Top wines from the Corbières estates are matured in *barriques*. Château Gasparets, a blend of Mourvèdre and Grenache, is a particularly fine wine.

Open: Mon–Sun 9–11.30am, 1.30am–5.30pm.

Château de Mandourelle

11360 Villèsque-des-Corbières.
Vineyards owned: 43ha. 233,000 bottles. VP-R

Red and rosé Corbières are made here; carbonic maceration is used for the reds. This château also produces a top Cuvée: Henri de Monfroid, named after the present owner's grandfather.

Open: By appointment only.

Château de Mattes

11130 Sigean. Vineyards owned: 94ha. 150,000 bottles. VP-R

Corbières and *vin de pays* are both produced on this estate. The Corbières comes in a number of different *cuvées*: Anne Laure, Bacchus and Anne Josephine de Sabran. None has wood vinification, although the top wines are aged in large wood for six months. The domaine has been in the Brouillat-Arnould family since 1731. *Open: Mon–Fri during working hours.*

Château les Ollieux

Montséret, 11200 Lézignan.
Vineyards owned: 55ha. 360,000 bottles. VP-R

Madame Surbézy-Cartier, who owns this vineyard, makes wine the modern way. She has modernised part of the vineyard as well, introducing Syrah and Grenache where previously there were only Cinsaut and Carignan. Red and rosé are made under the name of the château and under the Domaine Surbézy-Cartier name. The château itself is old: a Cistercian monastery from medieval times, it came into the family in 1855. The estate also makes Les Aigletierres des Ollieux Vin de Pays des Coteaux de la Cabrerisse, from a blend of Alicante, Merlot, Cinsaut and Carignan. *Open: By appointment only.*

Château les Palais

St-Laurent-de-la-Cabrerisse, 11220 Lagrasse.
Vineyards owned: 100ha. 162,000 bottles. VP-R

This estate made a name for itself when it pioneered the use of carbonic maceration for red wines in Corbières back in the 1960s. It continues to make soft, fresh, fruity wines which have made it one of the most familiar Corbières names.

Domaine des Pensées Sauvages

11360 Albas. Vineyards owned: 70ha. 20,000 bottles. VP-R

Owned by the English Bradford family, the estate concentrates on one wine: a red Corbières which is aged in *barriques* and larger wood. More Syrah has recently been planted, and Viognier to make a white wine. *Open: July and Aug Mon–Fri 11am–6pm.*

Domaine du Révérend/Domaine du Trillol
Cucugnan, 11350 Tuchan.
Vineyards owned: 61ha. 270,000 bottles. VP-R and N
Owned by Peter Sichel, the Bordeaux *négociant* and château owner. Domaine du Révérend, the larger estate, is in Cucugnan; Domaine du Trillol is in remote country at Rouffiac. The wines are made in the Bordeaux manner, with considerable wood-ageing. Both estates make white and red Corbières; Révérend also makes small amounts of rosé. *Open: Domaine du Révérend only: Mon–Sat during working hours; closed 31 Dec–15 Feb.*

Château St-Auriol
11220 Lagrasse. Vineyards owned: 40ha. 235,000 bottles. VP-R
Red Corbières is the principal wine from this highly regarded estate run by Claude Vialade and Jean-Paul Salvagnac. They are great proponents of the different *terroirs* of Corbières, believing the region of Lagrasse gives a particularly mild climate for grape growing. Their wines certainly are generous, the reds aged for six months in *barriques*, the white for three months. The firm also makes a red Vin de Pays de l'Aude. *Open: By appointment only.*

Château du Vieux Parc
Avenue des Vignerons, 11200 Conilhac-Corbières.
Vineyards owned: 48ha. 333,000 bottles. VP-R
Carbonic maceration is used to make the reds at this medium-sized estate, although the wines are also aged in wood for eight months. Whites are made in stainless steel.
Open: Mon–Sun 9am–8pm.

Les Vignerons du Val d'Orbieu
Route de Moussan, 11100 Narbonne. Coop.
Certainly the largest producer in the Corbières and Minervois regions, combining under a sales and marketing umbrella the production of a number of cooperatives. It makes a huge range of extremely high quality Vin de Pays d'Oc varietal wines from grapes such as Merlot, Cabernet Sauvignon and Chardonnay, to a number of AC wines. These wines appear under a variety of names. The most recent venture is a *vin de pays* made jointly with the Australian firm Penfolds.

Château Villemagne
11220 Lagrasse. Vineyards owned: 14ha. 6,000 bottles. VP-R
A small estate owned by the Carbonneau family and making mainly red, with some rosé Corbières plus *vin de pays* and *vin de table*. Methods are traditional, and the reds can stay in wood for up to ten years. Rooms are also available at the estate for holiday lettings. *Open: Appointments preferred.*

Château de la Voulte-Gasparets
Boutenac, 11200 Lézignan-Corbières.
Vineyards owned: 41ha. 266,000 bottles. VP-R
Two *cuvées* of red Corbières are the main production from this

family-owned estate. The vines are old, with low yields and consequent high quality. The standard *cuvée* comes from Carignan, Grenache, Cinsaut and Syrah. For the Cuvée Réserve, the proportion of Syrah is increased and there is no Cinsaut: the wine is deeper, more perfumed and one to keep. A rosé and a white are also made. This is one of the few estates in the area where exports are more important than local sales.

Open: Mon–Sun 9am–noon, 2–4pm.

FITOU AC

Paul Colomer

11350 Tuchan. Vineyards owned: 19ha. 40,000 bottles. VP-R

This small property produces both Fitou and Rivesaltes *vins doux naturels*. The Fitou is made in stainless steel, using some carbonic maceration, giving a powerful wine which is better drunk within three years of the vintage. The sweet Rivesaltes Rouge is 100 percent Grenache. Monsieur Colomer, whose family have owned the estate for generations, also produces a white, honeyed Muscat de Rivesaltes. *Open: By appointment only.*

Cave Coopérative de Fitou

11510 Fitou. Vineyards owned: 444ha. 300,000 bottles.
Coop (185 members).

Fitou is the main production here, made using carbonic maceration and stainless steel. The Fitou Terre Natale is an attractively spicy wine, benefiting from a dash of Mourvèdre and Syrah. Other wines produced are Rivesaltes Rouge *vin doux naturel*, much of which is sold in bulk, and a good example of a Muscat de Rivesaltes. Corbières red, white and rosé are also produced.

Open: Mon–Fri 8am–noon, 2–7pm.

Château de Nouvelles

11350 Tuchan. Vineyards owned: 88ha. 150,000 bottles. VP-R

One of the few private producers in the Fitou appellation, the property has been in the family since 1834. The wines are made in stainless steel without any wood-ageing and are intended for drinking young – and they are none the worse for that. Apart from the Fitou, there is a range of Corbières wines and Rivesaltes (including an aged Royal Rancio, which is a very attractive aperitif). Vineyard plantings include the Mourvèdre grape variety, which is added to the *cépages* of the Fitou region.

Open: Mon–Sat 8am–noon, 2–5pm.

Les Producteurs du Mont Tauch

11350 Tuchan. Vineyards owned: 1,015ha. 3.5 million bottles.
Coop (550 members).

The largest cooperative in the Fitou region producing Fitou, Corbières and Rivesaltes wines. It is a highly mechanised operation, with controlled-temperature fermentation and carbonic maceration. Various brands are produced, d'Aguilar and Don Neuve being the best known. The cooperative has been developed over the past few years so that now 80 percent of its production is bottled. Vin de Pays du Torgan and *vin de table* are also produced. *Open: Mon–Fri 8am–noon, 2–6pm.*

Cave Coopérative des Viticulteurs de Paziols
11530 Paziols.
Vineyards owned: 750ha. 600,000 bottles. Coop (215 members).
Fitou and Corbières are the main production at this cooperative, which takes in virtually all the producers in the commune of Paziols. Some carbonic maceration is practised, but methods are traditional. An interesting touch with the Fitou is the use of ten percent white Macabeo to lighten the wine. Red and Muscat Rivesaltes are also made. *Open: By appointment only.*

CABARDÈS VDQS

Château Rivals
11600 Villemoustaussou.
Vineyards owned: 19.4ha. 30,000 bottles. VP-R
Red and rosé Cabardès are made from Grenache, Merlot and Cabernet Sauvignon (for the red) and Grenache and Carignan (for the rosé). Despite the blend, the red is made to be drunk young. White *vin de pays* is made from 100 percent Macabeo. The owner at this interesting estate, Madame Charlotte Tronçin-Capdevila, is experimenting with Bordeaux-style wines.
Open: By appointment only.

Pyrénées-Orientales Producers

BANYULS AC, COLLIOURE AC

Groupement Interproducteurs du Cru Banyuls
Route de Mas Reig, 66650 Banyuls-sur-Mer. Vineyards owned: 4,305ha. 3.9 million bottles. N and Coop (1,200 members).
This large-scale operation is a group of three cooperatives which also acts as a *négociant*. It dominates the Collioure and Banyuls AC areas (with 2,600 hectares in Banyuls). There has been consid-erable investment in equipment and the general quality is good. Brand names used include Templiers and Cellier des Templiers. The group makes considerable quantities of Rivesaltes red, Muscat (under the name Aphrodis) and Côtes du Roussillon. *Open: Mon–Fri 9.30am–noon, 2–6pm; all day in summer.*

Cave Coopérative Les Dominicains
66190 Collioure. Vineyards owned: 2,800ha. 26,660 bottles.
Coop (287 members).
Despite the address, most of the land belonging to this co-operative produces Banyuls, with a small area making Collioure. Most of the wine is sold to *négociants* but some is bottled under the Le Dominicain name and there is an attractive Collioure Cuvée Matisse. *Open: By appointment only.*

Société Coopérative Agricole l'Étoile
26 Avenue du Puig del Mas, 66650 Banyuls-sur-Mer.
Vineyards owned: 170ha. 290,000 bottles. Coop (70 members).
Virtually all the production here is of Banyuls *vin doux naturel*,
made principally from Grenache Noir and Carignan grapes. A
range of these wines is produced: *Grand Cru* Select Vieux, Grande
Réserve, Doux Paille, Extra Vieux, a Muscat-based Tuile and drier
styles, and a small amount of Collioure which is made in stainless
steel. *Open: By appointment only.*

Domaine du Mas Blanc
9 Avenue Général de Gaulle, 66650 Banyuls-sur-Mer.
Vineyards owned: 13ha. 38,000 bottles. VP-R
Production from this 17th-century estate is split evenly between
Banyuls *vin doux naturel* and red Collioure, which sport some
particularly lurid labels. The Banyuls is made with the usual
cépages of Grenache Noir, Mourvèdre and Carignan with the
addition of some Syrah. The Collioure is made with 40 percent
Mourvèdre, 40 percent Syrah and 20 percent Grenache grapes: it
can take considerable ageing. *Open: By appointment only.*

CÔTES DU ROUSSILLON AC,
CÔTES DU ROUSSILLON-VILLAGES AC

Domaines de Canterrane
66300 Trouillas. Vineyards owned: 160ha. 380,000 bottles. VP-R
The estates of the Conte family include Château de Canterrane
and its associated La Tour de Canterrane. The firm makes a range
of Roussillon wines including Côtes du Roussillon, Rivesaltes *vin
doux naturel* red and Muscat de Rivesaltes. Large-scale production
does not seem to harm quality and indeed wines are aged for up
to six years before release.
Open: Château de Canterrane Mon–Sun 8am–noon, 2–6pm.

Les Vignerons Catalans
66000 Perpignan. 25 million bottles. Coop.
A huge operation, which buys in finished wines from cooperatives throughout the region and blends them into a large
range of generally good quality. It makes *vins de pays* as well as
Côtes du Roussillon and many other appellations. A shop at the
cellars in Perpignan sells many of the wines.
Open: Mon–Fri 8am–noon, 2–6pm.

Domaine Cazes
4 Rue Francisco Ferrer, 66602 Rivesaltes.
Vineyards owned: 127.5ha. 775,000 bottles. VP-R
A dynamic private firm producing a range of 15 wines from Côtes
du Roussillon and Côtes du Roussillon-Villages, through *vins doux
naturels* to Vin de Pays Catalan. In '93 it produced Credo, a
Cabernet Sauvignon and Merlot wine, designed – successfully –
to show how well the Bordeaux grapes worked in the region.
Open: Mon–Sun 8am–noon, 2–6pm, by appointment.

Château de Corneilla
66200 Corneilla-del-Vercol.
Vineyards owned: 60ha. 235,000 bottles. VP-R
Red Côtes du Roussillon is the most important wine to come from
this ancient estate (the château dates from the 15th century).
Philippe Jonquères d'Oriola, the owner, makes a top *cuvée* of the
red which he ages in wood – a full-bodied wine with a touch of
spice. He also makes white and rosé Côtes du Roussillon. Other
wines from the estate include Rivesaltes *vin doux naturel*, Muscat
de Rivesaltes and a red *vin de pays* called Domaine du Paradis
made entirely from Cabernet Sauvignon: a surprisingly sophisticated wine from the French deep south. *Open: Summer: Mon–Sat
10am–noon, 5–7.30pm; winter: Mon, Weds, Sat 10am–noon.*

Château de l'Esparrou
Canet-Plage, St-Nazaire, 66140 Canet.
Vineyards owned: 99ha. 18,000 bottles. VP-R
Côtes du Roussillon, made using a high percentage of Mourvèdre
and Syrah and some carbonic maceration, is the top wine from
this estate. It receives some barrel maturation which adds to the
complexity. Other wines made here are Rivesaltes, Muscat de
Rivesaltes and *vin de pays*.

Domaine Força-Réal
Mas de la Garrigue, 66170 Millas. Vineyards owned: 40ha. VP-R
In a spectacular mountain-side setting, JP Henriques produces
red and white Côtes du Roussillon and Rivesaltes from a vineyard
which he is in the process of restoring and replanting. The second
wine of the estate is Mas de la Garrigue, while the Domaine Força-
Réal is a wood-aged Côtes du Roussillon. His pride is a caramel-
and-coffee-flavoured Rivesaltes Hors d'Age.
Open: Mon–Fri 8–11am, 1–4pm.

Domaine Gauby
Le Faradjal, 66600 Calce. VP-R
A small family-owned domaine where Gérard Gauby produces a
fascinating collection of wines – Côtes du Roussillon red and
white in various blends, a number of *vin de pays* – the Blanc *vin
de pays* (a blend of Carignan Blanc, Grenache Blanc and Macabeo)
sells for more than the Côtes du Roussillon. Fifty-year old vines
produce Vieilles Vignes. wood-ageing is a serious consideration
here. *Open: By appointment only.*

Château de Jau/Les Clos de Paulilles
*Cases de Pène, 66600 Rivesaltes. Vineyards owned: 201ha.
830,000 bottles. VP-R*
While Château de Jau produces Côtes du Roussillon, the principal
production of Les Clos de Paulilles is of Collioure. A restaurant
and art exhibitions make a visit to Château de Jau, in whose
grounds are the ruins of a Cistercian monastery, more than just a
visit to another wine cellar. Apart from Appellation Contrôlée
wines, Les Clos de Paulilles also produces quantities of *vin de*

pays. Another property, which produces Rivesaltes, is called Mas Christine. *Open: Château de Jau: Sept–May Mon–Fri 8am–5pm; June–end Sept Mon–Sun 10am–7pm (and restaurant); Les Clos de Paulilles: 15 June–15 Sept Mon–Sun 10am–7pm.*

Société Coopérative Vinicole Lesquerde
66220 St-Paul de Fenouillet.
Vineyards owned: 434ha. 275,000 bottles. Coop (70 members).
A well-run cooperative producing Côtes du Roussillon red, white and rosé and Côtes du Roussillon-Villages. Most of the production is now bottled at the cooperative. The wines are sound but break few viticultural records. *Vins doux naturels* – both red and Muscat-based – are also made.

Cave les Vignerons de Pezilla-la-Rivière
66370 Pezilla-la-Rivière. Vineyards owned: 500ha. Coop.
One of the most go-ahead cooperatives in the region, producing a fascinating selection of *vins de pays* (including a Chardonnay) as well as Côtes du Roussillon wines from separate domaines (Château de Blanes is vinified in wood) and a range of Rivesaltes. *Open: Mon–Sat 8am–noon, 2–6pm; Sun 10am–noon, 3–6pm.*

Domaine Piquemal
1 Rue Pierre Lefranc, 66600 Espira-l'Aigly. VP-R
In a series of cellars in the centre of Espira-l'Aigly, Pierre Piquemal makes a range of wines including a Merlot-dominated red, rosé and a white from Muscat Sec. Recent vintages of Côtes du Roussillon have been vinified in wood and emphasise soft tannins and ripe fruit. Rivesaltes is also made. *Open: Mon–Sat 9am–noon; 2–6pm.*

Château Planères
66300 St-Lasseille. Vineyards owned: 90ha. VP-R
A reliable range of Côtes du Roussillon is made at this estate, of which the best is the Château Planères Prestige. Other wines include single varietal Macabeo and Vermentino whites. The cellars are housed in an 18th-century typical Catalan *mas*.
Open: Mon–Sat 9.30am–noon; 2–5pm. Sat by appointment.

Sarda-Malet
Mas St-Michel, 12 Chemin de Ste-Barbe, 66000 Perpignan.
Vineyards owned: 50ha. 140,000 bottles.
The bulk of this estate produces AC Côtes du Roussillon and Rivesaltes *vin doux naturel*. There are also two Côtes du Roussillon whites from a blend of Grenache, Roussanne, Marsanne, Malvoisie and Macabeo grapes, one tank-fermented, the other vinified in wood, and a range of red Côtes du Roussillon wines including a wood-aged Étiquette Noire which requires ageing for four or five years. The top wine is a Syrah/Mourvèdre blend called Terroir Mailloles. The *vins doux naturels* include red Rivesaltes and Muscat de Rivesaltes. The Sarda-Malet estate also produces Vin de Pays Catalan.
Open: Mon–Fri 8am–12.30pm, 2–6.30pm; Sat/Sun by appointment.

VIN DOUX NATUREL

Mas Péchot
66600 Rivesaltes. Vineyards owned: 139ha. 199,500 bottles. VP-R
The Muscat de Rivesaltes made on this estate is produced from
the higher quality Muscat à Petits Grains (as opposed to Muscat
d'Alexandria) and has a deservedly high reputation. The estate
also makes a red Côtes du Roussillon.

Les Maîtres Vignerons de Tautavel
24 Avenue Jean-Badia, 66720 Tautavel. Vineyards owned:
440ha. 150,000 bottles. Coop (110 members).
This cooperative specialises in Rivesaltes wines, both the Muscat
and the *vin doux naturel*. The unusual labels celebrate the discovery of the remains of ancient man in caves in the region, these
are displayed in the town's interesting museum.
Open: Mon–Sat 8am–noon, 2–6pm; Sun 10am–noon, 3–6pm.

Cave Coopérative Vinicole Les Vignerons de Maury
128 Avenue Jean Jaurès, 66460 Maury. Vineyards owned:
1,712ha. 6.7 million bottles. Coop (282 members).
The *vin doux naturel* of Maury in all its forms is what matters at
this cooperative. It makes aged Rancio as well as the younger
styles and wines like Maury Vieille Réserve. It also makes a small
amount of Muscat de Rivesaltes, plus Côtes du Roussillon-Villages
and Côtes du Roussillon white. *Open: By appointment only.*

Les Vignerons de Rivesaltes
2 Rue de la Roussillonnaise, 66602 Rivesaltes. Vineyards
owned: 1,600ha. 3 million bottles. Coop (540 members).
The largest cooperative in the region and the largest producer of
Côtes du Roussillon as well as Rivesaltes. The top *cuvée* of Côtes
du Roussillon is Arnaud de Villeneuve, which is aged in wood.
The cooperative is also increasingly producing *vins de cépage*: Vin
de Pays d'Oc made from single grape varieties such as Malvoisie,
Cabernet Sauvignon, Sauvignon Blanc and Chardonnay.
Open: Mon–Fri 8am–noon, 2–6pm; Sat 8am–noon.

Corsica

The best vines in this land of mountains and rugged splendour are on the difficult terrain of the west coast, the north tip and the south. The finest wines are heady reds and full-bodied rosés. On the eastern plain, large vineyards produce basic blending wines and whites tend to be either over-oxidised or nondescript. Some *vin doux naturels* are also made. Southern French grape varieties: Carignan, Cinsaut, Grenache and Mourvèdre, produce much of the wine, mostly as Vin de Pays de l'Île de Beauté. Native Corsican varieties, Vermentino and Malvoisie for whites, Nielluccio and Sciacarello for reds and rosés, are used in the AC wines. Noble varieties Cabernet Sauvignon, Merlot, Chardonnay and Chenin Blanc, are made into varietal wines under a *vin de pays* label.

The new technology of southern France has been slow to arrive, but major producers and some top estates have improved vinification and selection and are making some acceptable wines, the most interesting from traditional Corsican varieties.

The Appellations

APPELLATIONS CONTRÔLÉES

Of 28,000 hectares planted, 4,000 are Appellations Contrôlées. There are eight AC zones and all can produce red, dry white or rosé: Vin de Corse, Vin de Corse Calvi, Vin de Corse Coteaux du Cap Corse and Patrimonio can also make semi-sweet whites. Best vintages: (reds) '88, '89, '90, '91, '93; (rosés) '93; (whites) '93.

VIN DE PAYS

Regional *vin de pays*

Vin de Pays de l'Île de Beauté A *vin de pays* classification covering the whole island, this is designed to enable the production of wines from 'foreign' grape varieties, including Cabernet Sauvignon and Chardonnay, as well as local varieties grown outside AC areas. Production is of 58 percent red, 26 rosé and 16 percent white wine.

Corsica Producers

Clos Capitoro
Bianchetti Frères et Fils, Pisciatella, 20166 Porticcio.
Vineyards owned: 50ha. 270,000 bottles. VP-R
Producing wines under the Clos Capitoro (AC Coteaux d'Ajaccio) and Leitizia (AC Vin de Corse) names. Clos Capitoro red is full-bodied and heady (13per cent alcohol); the rosé and white are in a modern style. Much new planting has taken place in recent years. *Open: Mon-Sat 8am-noon, 2-7pm; Sun by appointment.*

Orenga de Gaffory
20253 Patrimonio. Vineyards owned: 55ha. 245,000 bottles. VP-R
Mostly red and rosé Patrimonio is produced, but the interesting wines are white: a Cuvée des Gouverneurs, matured in new

wood, and a sweet Muscat du Cap Corse. The firm also owns Domaine San Quilico. *Open: Mon–Fri 9am–noon, 1.30–6.30pm.*

Domaine Peraldi
Chemin du Stiletto, 20167 Mezzavia.
Vineyards owned: Ajaccio 40ha. 175,000 bottles. VP-R

An old firm and the largest producer in the Ajaccio AC. Modern vinification for all wines is followed by ageing in new wood *barriques* for reds, giving them a general life span of around ten years. Whites and rosés are bottled quickly for freshness. *Open: Mon–Sat 8am–noon, 2–6pm; appointments necessary for groups.*

Domaine de Torraccia (Christian Imbert)
20137 Lecci de Porto Vecchio.
Vineyards owned: Lecci 43ha. 200,000 bottles. VP-R

A large estate outside Porto Vecchio on the east coast. The tower in the name dates back to 1500 BC. The vineyard is treated biologically, giving low yields. Local grapes are supplemented by Grenache, Cinsaut and some Syrah to give a red with generous ripe herby fruit which takes some ageing. Top red *cuvée* is a Réserve Oriu. White and rosé are produced in a more modern fruity style. *Open: Mon–Sat 8am–noon, 2–6pm; by appointment only.*

Union des Vignerons Associés du Levant
Rasignani, 20290 Borgo. Vineyards owned: St-Florent, Marana, Bravone, Aghione 2,100ha. 600,000 bottles. Coop.

This cooperative specialises in varietal wines. Under the AC Vin de Corse it makes a 100 percent Nielluccio. *Vins de pays* include 100 percent Cabernet Sauvignon, Pinot Noir and Chardonnay. Particular emphasis is put on whites and new equipment has been installed. The resulting wines are full of fruit but lack regional character. Brand names include L'Île aux Pièves and St-Florent. *Open: Mon–Fri 9am–noon, 3–7pm; Sat morning only.*

The Southwest

The Southwest's vineyards, wedged between the great expanses of Bordeaux and the Midi, are tiny by comparison with most. Not so long ago they were still struggling to survive the effects of phylloxera, which almost wiped out the whole area. What was left was disappearing through indifference. Yet, gradually, the Southwest has been rejuvenated through the efforts of cooperatives, which have performed a vital role, bringing together tiny plots of land, which makes more commercial sense. The determination of a few private estates, some new, others ancient, has also helped by providing a quality standard to emulate. An important contribution has also been made by travellers who went on wine-buying trips to the Southwest and came back with tales – and samples – of the wines.

There are two distinct wine traditions here. Historically, the northern vineyards of the region, Bergerac, Côtes du Marmandais, Côtes de Duras and Cahors, were closely linked to Bordeaux. At one time their wine was more famous than the wines of Bordeaux itself; later they were used to strengthen insipid wine from the vineyards of the Gironde. Some of these areas today make Bordeaux taste-alikes sold at lesser prices, while Cahors, for example, has moved along a distinct path of its own. But even now, they all have a recognisable link with Bordeaux.

That is not true of the wines from further south. This is strange territory indeed. Grape varieties from a dim, almost mythical past, with difficult Basque names, yield wines with a range of tastes that are found nowhere else. There are sweet whites and impenetrable reds, sparkling wines made by methods unique to the area, and increasingly there are some excellent dry white wines. In this 'secret countryside' there are quiet valleys, deep rivers, miles of woods, and small, ancient towns and villages perched on hilltops or clinging to river valleys. The part of the

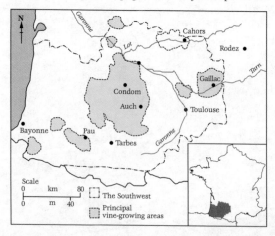

Southwest called Gascony is home of one of France's richest gastronomic traditions – home, too, to armagnac brandy. The region enjoys an Atlantic rather than a mediterranean climate, but one protected from the ocean storms by the vast pine forests of the Landes, which stretch from the edge of the Bordeaux vineyards to the Pyrenees. The summers are cooler than in Languedoc and Roussillon, the rainfall higher and the winters often harsh. The consequence for the wines is immediately apparent: they are lower in alcohol than the wines of the Midi, and tend to have more complex, varied flavours. The whites, are full-bodied and often have good acidity; the reds, when deep and tannic, can age well while lighter reds, made to be drunk chilled, can be as fresh as Loire reds. As for vintages: most dry whites and rosés should be drunk young, as should many reds.

Bergerac, astride the River Dordogne, is the first area a traveller coming from the north would reach. This is a gentle landscape, an extension of the Bordelais regions of St-Émilion and the smaller Côtes de Castillon. The complex of ACs here covers three basic styles – a red normally in the style of a light Bordeaux, fresh, dry whites, and a range of sweet white wines, none of which quite achieve the greatness of Sauternes.

Just to the south, attached to the eastern end of the Bordeaux Entre-Deux-Mers, is the tiny Côtes de Duras. Once it was simply another satellite of Bordeaux. Today its reds are similar in style to Bergerac, while its whites are inspired by Entre-Deux-Mers. Further south, another small area, the Côtes du Marmandais which acquired AC status in 1990, makes attractive reds which can compare with many a lesser Bordeaux red.

To the east, we come to one of the most important of these southwestern ACs: Cahors. Its reputation for black wines used to bolster Bordeaux has not helped it to revive its fortunes after phylloxera, and today there seem to be two distinct styles of wine emerging from the area: high-quality, long-lived reds from the traditional vineyards on the slopes and lighter, early drinking wines from new vineyards on the valley floor.

Further east again, the beautiful valley of the Tarn is home to the vineyards of Gaillac, perhaps the most widely known AC in the Southwest, especially for its occasionally exciting sparkling and *perlé* wines. Sweet whites are made, too, from local grapes, and some producers are making light, peppery reds which can have immense charm.

Going back west, the small Côtes du Fronton AC makes some of the Southwest's most enjoyable red wine. Much of it is drunk in Toulouse, but what escapes is good quality and good value. That is also true of Buzet, an area lying along the southern banks of the Garonne River, whose reds are certainly more full of life than the average basic Bordeaux. Between Côtes du Fronton and Buzet are the two small VDQS areas of Côtes du Brulhois and Lavilledieu.

South of these red wine areas lie the vineyards whose white wines go to make armagnac: the rolling country of Gascony at its most luscious and remote. South again are two AC areas which almost disappeared. Madiran was reduced to five hectares 30 years ago, now it is up to over 800 and producing a complex, tannic, sometimes unforgiving wine that you either love or hate, but at least, with its excellent ageing ability, you cannot ignore. The companion white in the same area is Pacherenc du Vic-Bilh, another distinctive taste. Tucked around these two AC areas are two VDQS zones – Tursan and Côtes de St-Mont – and the general local AC of Béarn.

Then comes Basque country, the foothills of the Pyrenees. From here originates the intriguing-sounding Irouléguy, from an area making red, white and rosé wines only of local interest; and the potentially superb sweet wines of the Jurançon appellation. Sadly, these are rare: much of the production is of less exciting dry white – a concession, we must assume, to modern taste.

With these two small areas, the wines of the Southwest stop beneath the high ridges of the Pyrenees. Over the mountains, in Spain, a completely different wine culture takes over.

The Appellations

APPELLATIONS CONTRÔLÉES

Béarn Red, rosé and dry white wines are produced here from a large area of the *département* Pyrénées-Atlantiques. The Béarn AC surrounds the smaller, superior ACs of Madiran and Pacherenc du Vic-Bilh as well as Irouléguy and Jurançon. Reds and rosés are made from up to 60 percent Tannat, Courbu Noir, Fer, Manseng Noir, Pinenc, Cabernet Sauvignon and Cabernet Franc. Whites are a similar mix of local and Bordeaux varieties including Gros Manseng, Petit Manseng, Courbu, Baroque, Lauzat, plus Sémillon and Sauvignon Blanc.

Béarn-Bellocq A new, small appellation within the Béarn AC where the same grape varieties are planted. The AC covers the communes of Orthez and Sallies-de-Béarn.

Bergerac The area-wide AC for the Bergerac region. Red and rosé are made from Cabernet Sauvignon, Cabernet Franc, Merlot, Malbec and the local Fer. Light wines, which should be drunk young. Vintages: '89, '90, '92, '93, '94, '95.

Bergerac Sec The white equivalent of Bergerac. Wines can be made from Sémillon, Sauvignon, Muscadelle, Chenin Blanc and the local Ondenc. A number of new-style wines, made with Sauvignon, are of high quality.

Buzet Vineyards on the left bank of the Garonne between Agen and Aiguillon, producing red, rosé and dry white wines. Reds are produced from Cabernet Franc, Cabernet Sauvignon, Merlot and Malbec. The small amount of white made comes from Sémillon, Sauvignon and Muscadelle. Most of the wine is produced by the cooperative, which maintains high standards. Previously known as Côtes de Buzet. Vintages: '89, '90, '93, '94, '95.

Cahors Red wine is produced only from vineyards on the slopes and the valley floor of the River Lot between Puy l'Evêque and Cahors. Winemaking in this area was established before

Roman times, and the wines highly regarded by Avignon Popes and Russian Tsars. The grapes cultivated now are Malbec (known locally as Auxerrois) up to 70 percent, then Merlot, Tannat and Jurançon Noir. The wine at its best is deep-coloured with high tannins, but also has strong fruit that needs a good four years before it softens. Some producers make a lighter style of wine for more immediate drinking. Vintages: '86, '88, '89, '90, '93, '94, '95.

Côtes de Bergerac Red wine from the Bergerac region. Higher alcoholic content than straight Bergerac. Two million bottles are produced. Grapes are the same as for Bergerac: Cabernet Franc, Cabernet Sauvignon, Merlot, Malbec and Fer. Vintages: *see* Bergerac.

Côtes de Bergerac Moelleux Sweet white wine from the general Bergerac AC made from Sémillon, Sauvignon and Muscadelle. Soft, at best clean and fruity.

Côtes de Duras Dry and sweet white and some red wine from an area immediately adjacent to the Bordeaux Entre-Deux-Mers AC area. Whites are from Sémillon, Sauvignon, Muscadelle, Mauzac and Ondenc, plus Ugni Blanc. Dry whites are better than sweet, which tend to be sulphured. Reds are from Cabernet Franc, Cabernet Sauvignon, Merlot and Malbec, and have attractive fruit and depth.

Côtes du Frontonnais Red and rosé wines from a small area north of Toulouse on the east bank of the River Garonne. The grapes are up to 70 percent Négrette, plus Cabernet Sauvignon, Cabernet Franc, Cinsaut, Malbec, Merlot, Syrah and Gamay. Excellent wines at good prices with fresh, soft fruit. The commune of Villaudric is allowed to add its name to the AC. Vintages: '89, '90, '93, '94, '95.

Côtes du Marmandais Soft, attractive reds and less interesting whites from vineyards adjoining the Bordeaux region on both sides of the Garonne. The grapes include Bordeaux varieties – Cabernet Franc, Cabernet Sauvignon and Merlot – local Fer, Abouriou and Malbec, Syrah from the south of France and Gamay. The small production of white wine comes from Sémillon, Ugni Blanc and Sauvignon.

Côtes de Montravel Small amounts of sweet white wine from within the general Bergerac area. Certain hillside slopes in certain communes are allowed to use the Côtes de Montravel AC, whose wines are generally of higher quality than simple Montravel (*see* page 211). Sémillon, Sauvignon Blanc and Muscadelle are the permitted grape varieties.

Gaillac A range of white, medium white, red, rosé and sparkling wines from the valley of Tarn, between Albi and Rabastens. Over half the production is white, from Mauzac Blanc and Len de l'El or Loin de l'Oeil (so called because the grapes appear hidden to the eyes of the pickers), with Ondenc, Sauvignon, Sémillon and Muscadelle. Much is dull, especially the slightly sparkling *perlé*. Reds come from a variety of grapes: Fer, Duras, Gamay, Négrette and up to 60 percent Syrah, with smaller amounts of Cabernet Sauvignon, Cabernet Franc,

Jurançon Noir, Merlot, Portugais Bleu (the German Blauer Portugieser), and the white Mauzac. Occasional reds can be superb. Vintages: (red) '89, '90, '93, '94, '95.

Gaillac Doux Sweet white wines from Mauzac Blanc, Len de l'El, Ondenc, Sauvignon, Sémillon and Muscadelle.

Gaillac Mousseux Sparkling Gaillac made by the *méthode gaillaçoise* (involving a second fermentation in the bottle but, unlike champagne, without added sugar or yeast). Some of it can be very good. Other sparkling wines are made by the classic method. Grapes used belong to the usual Gaillac selection: Mauzac Blanc, Len de l'El, Ondenc, Sauvignon, Sémillon and Muscadelle.

Gaillac Premières Côtes Rare dry and medium-sweet white wine, higher in alcohol than simple Gaillac.

Haut Montravel Sweet white wines from the Montravel region of Bergerac. The rules are similar to Côtes de Montravel (*see* page 209). Grapes used: Sauvignon, Sémillon, Muscadelle.

Irouléguy Red, rosé and white wines from the foothills of the Pyrenees in the valley of the Nive. Most of the production is of rosé, and both rosés and reds are made from Tannat, Fer, Cabernet Sauvignon and Cabernet Franc. The small amount of white comes from Gros Manseng, Petit Manseng, Courbu, Lauzat, Baroque, Sauvignon and Sémillon.

Jurançon Sweet wines from an area southwest of the town of Pau. Grapes are Gros Manseng, the better-quality Petit Manseng and Courbu. For this increasingly rare but outstanding sweet wine, grapes are picked as raisins, with concentrated sugars giving a spicy wine with a lemony tang and golden colour. Examples, when they can be found, can be a revelation. Vintages: '86, '88, '89, '90, '94, '95.

Jurançon Sec A dry, and much duller, version of Jurançon, from the same grapes: Gros Manseng, Petit Manseng, Courbu.

Madiran Red wine from the southern edge of the Armagnac region. The principal grape is Tannat, which makes a hard, tough, tannic wine when young that has to spend 20 months in bottle. It needs at least five years before it begins to open out, with some elegance but more rough power. Other grapes used are Cabernet Sauvignon, Cabernet Franc and Fer. The more Cabernets are used, the more sophisticated (but less typical) the wine becomes. The white wine of the area is called Pacherenc du Vic-Bilh (*see* page 211). Vintages: '85, '86, '88, '89, '90, '93, '94, '95

Marcillac Sound, simple red and rosé wines produced from just north of Rodez in the Aveyron *département*. The grape varieties include both Cabernets, Gamay, Jurançon Noir and Merlot, with at least 80 percent Fer. The appellation was created in 1990.

Monbazillac A famous name in sweet wines, but one which has fallen on bad times. The wine can be as good as Sauternes but it rarely is because it is sulphured and not enough attention is paid to the degree of botrytis in the grapes. The few producers who make it well produce wines that are even richer than

Sauternes, developing faster and fading more quickly. Grapes used are Sémillon, Sauvignon and Muscadelle. Vintages: '86, '88, '89, '90, '95.

Montravel A range of white wines from dry to sweet made at the western edge of the Bergerac region, along the lower slopes bordering the road to St-Émilion. Wines are made from Sémillon, Sauvignon, Muscadelle, Ugni Blanc, Chenin Blanc and Ondenc.

Pacherenc du Vic-Bilh White wine from the same area as Madiran (*see* page 211). It can be dry or slightly sweet, but always has intense fruit and a luscious smell, sometimes likened to ripe pears. Grapes are Ruffiac (or Pacherenc), Gros Manseng, Petit Manseng, Courbu, Sauvignon and Sémillon. Production is small, and almost all of it is consumed locally.

Pécharmant The best red wines of Bergerac come from a small area on the right bank of the Dordogne River, east of the town of Bergerac. Grape varieties are Cabernets Sauvignon and Franc, Malbec and Merlot. The wines, higher in alcohol than simple Bergerac, are also aged longer in wood and mature well for five or six years. Better quality than any simple Bordeaux AC. Vintages: '86, '88, '89, '90, '93, '94, '95.

Rosette Medium-sweet wine from the slopes north of the town of Bergerac. Production is small, most of the white in the area going as Bergerac Sec. Grapes used are Sauvignon, Sémillon and Muscadelle.

Saussignac A rare white wine, normally dry, made around the village of Saussignac, west of Monbazillac. The wines need an alcohol level of 12.5 percent, making them richer and fuller than ordinary Bergerac Sec. Grapes are Sémillon, Sauvignon, Muscadelle, Ondenc and Chenin Blanc.

VDQS

Côtes du Brulhois Vineyard area just south of Buzet, on both sides of the Garonne River. Red and rosé only, made from Cabernet Sauvignon, Cabernet Franc, Merlot, Tannat and Malbec. Elevated to VDQS status from *vin de pays* in 1984.

Côtes de St-Mont Red, rosé and white wines from the south-western corner of the Armagnac region. Reds come from Tannat, with both Cabernets and Merlot, and are attractive, simple and slightly rough. Whites are from Meslier, Jurançon, Picpoul and Sauvignon. The main producer is the local Madiran cooperative.

Tursan Red, rosé and dry white wines from the eastern Landes, bordering the AC area of Madiran and Pacherenc du Vic-Bilh. The style is like a minor version of these wines. Reds and rosés are from Tannat, Cabernet Franc, Cabernet Sauvignon and Fer; whites from the local Baroque.

Vin d'Entraygues et du Fel A tiny production of red, rosé and dry whites from the southern slopes of the Massif Central. Reds and rosés from a range of grapes: both Cabernets, Jurançon Noir, Fer, Gamay, Merlot, Négrette and Pinot Noir. Whites from Chenin Blanc and Mauzac.

Vin d'Estaing Another tiny area producing no more than 1,000 bottles or so a year from the same area and grape varieties as the Vin d'Entraygues et du Fel.

Vin de Lavilledieu Almost exclusively red wines are produced from another small area on the River Garonne to the north of the Côtes du Frontonnais. Virtually every local grape variety available seems to be thrown into the vat, but the principal ones are Négrette, Fer, Gamay, Jurançon Noir, Mauzac Noir and Picpoul.

VINS DE PAYS

Regional *vin de pays*

Vin de Pays du Comté Tolosan Covering the whole of the Southwest region, from the southern borders of the Gironde *département* of Bordeaux to the Pyrenees and east to Toulouse. Like many of the regional *vins de pays*, its production is small and most wines are classified by smaller zones within it. Red wines are made from Duras, Fer-Servadou, Tannat, the Bordeaux grapes and Syrah and Gamay. Only three percent of production is white.

Departmental *vins de pays*

Vin de Pays de la Dordogne A *vin de pays* covering much the same area as the Bergerac AC. The tiny production, made from Bordeaux grapes (60 percent of which are white) comes from areas which are not covered by the AC regulations.

Vin de Pays de la Haute-Garonne South of Toulouse, this is a *vin de pays* surrounding the AC vineyards of Fronton. The grapes are typical of the Southwest: Tannat, Jurançon Noir and Négrette, plus Bordeaux varieties, Syrah and Gamay. Production is 90 percent red.

Vin de Pays du Tarn-et-Garonne Most of the tiny production is from west of Montauban, and is principally of red wines with some rosé. A melange of Southwestern grapes is employed. Whites are made from Mauzac.

Other departmental *vins de pays*:

Vin de Pays de l'Aveyron
Vin de Pays du Gers
Vin de Pays des Landes
Vin de Pays du Lot
Vin de Pays du Lot-et-Garonne
Vin de Pays des Pyrénées-Atlantiques

Zonal *vins de pays*

Vin de Pays de l'Agenais Between Agen, of crystallised prune fame, and Marmande. These wines are mainly red, with some white, and made from local grape varieties (Abouriou, Fer-Servadou for red, Gros Manseng for white) and also Bordeaux *cépages nobles*.

Vin de Pays des Charentais This *vin de pays* uses the surplus grapes grown initially for cognac production. It is not surprising then, that the wines are mainly white (Chardonnay and Chenin Blanc mingling with Bordeaux grapes, and also Ugni Blanc – the cognac grape). The smaller amount of red wine is made from Bordeaux grapes and from Gamay.

Vin de Pays des Coteaux du Quercy South of Cahors, this zone produces mostly red wines, from the local Cahors grapes (Auxerrois or Cot) and Tannat and the Bordeaux varieties.

Vin de Pays des Côtes de Gascogne One of the most familiar *vin de pays* areas, due largely to the fact that it fulfils a huge demand for white wines. Covering much of the armagnac production zone, the white wines (84 percent of production) are made from local grapes: Colombard, Ugni Blanc and Gros Manseng.

Vin de Pays des Côtes du Tarn From the region of Gaillac, around Albi, this area produces large quantities of both red and white wines, and also a small amount of rosé. Red wines are made from Bordeaux *cépages nobles* and also Gamay and local grapes; white wines are made from Len de L'El, Muscadelle and Mauzac. The latter are especially important on the export market.

Vin de Pays de St-Sardos A tiny production, mainly of red wines, from vineyards southwest of Montauban.

Vin de Pays des Terroirs Landais A small quantity of wine, produced from vineyards among the forests of the Landes. There are four different areas: in the sand-dunes along the Atlantic coast; the Coteaux du Chalosse in the south of the *département*; the Côtes de l'Adour, along the valley of that river; and Les Sables Fauves, part of the armagnac area. These are mostly white wines.

Other zonal *vins de pays*:

Vin de Pays de Bigorre
Vin de Pays des Coteaux de Glanes
Vin de Pays des Coteaux et Terrasses de Montauban
Vin de Pays des Côtes du Condomois
Vin de Pays des Côtes de Montestruc
Vin de Pays des Gorges et Côtes de Millau
Vin de Pays de Thézac-Pérricard

Southwest Producers

BÉARN AC

Les Vignerons de Bellocq
64270 Bellocq.
Vineyards owned: 150ha. 400,000 bottles. Coop (130 members).
The most important source of Béarn wine, this cooperative makes a range of rosé (the vast majority of its production), red and white wines, using controlled-temperature techniques and eschewing any use of wood. Reds include a 100 percent Cabernet Franc and Cabernet Sauvignon wine, and two top red *cuvées*, Sire d'Albert and Cuvée Henri de Navarre as well as a number of single domaine wines.
Open: Mon–Sat 9am–noon, 2–7pm; July and Aug open Mon–Sun.

BERGERAC AC

Domaine de l'Ancienne Curé
Colombier, 24560 Issigeac.
Vineyards owned: 32.5ha. 173,000 bottles. VP-R
Monsieur Christian Roche makes a range of Bergerac wines:
Monbazillac, Bergerac Sec (a blend of Sémillon and Sauvignon
Blanc), a Côtes de Bergerac Moelleux and red and rosé Bergerac.
Temperature-controlled fermentation is used for the white wines,
but reds are vinified in wood.
Open: Mon–Sat 9am–7pm; Sun by appointment only.

Château du Bloy (Guillermier Frères)
Bonneville, 24230 Vélines.
Vineyards owned: 33.5ha. 125,000 bottles. VP-R
Red wines under Côtes de Bergerac and Bergerac appellations are
the mainstay of the Guillermier brothers' estate, using Merlot,
Cabernet Franc, Cabernet Sauvignon and a little Malbec. The firm
also makes rosé Bergerac, dry white Montravel from Sauvignon
Blanc and Bergerac as well as some sweet Bergerac.
Open: Mon–Sun 9am–noon, 2–6pm.

Château la Borderie
24240 Monbazillac.
Vineyards owned: 92ha. 445,000 bottles. VP-R
Two estates make up the family property of Château la Borderie.
On the larger estate, which bears the château name, the Vidal
family makes Monbazillac, (some of which has oak-ageing), red
Côtes de Bergerac, dry white Bergerac (from 100 percent
Sauvignon) and Bergerac rosé. The smaller, ten-hectare Château
Treuil de Nailhac estate produces the Monbazillac, the red and the
dry white. *Open: Mon–Sat 8am–noon, 2–6pm.*

Comte de Bosredon (Château Belingard)
Pomport, 24240 Sigoulès.
Vineyards owned: 85ha. 550,000 bottles. VP-R
This ancient family estate is home to some Celtic remains as well
as the Bosredon family. Comte Laurent de Bosredon makes red
wines that are designed for ageing, although in some ways his
first love is sweet Monbazillac. Some of the sweeter Monbazillac
and Côtes de Bergerac is matured for a time in wood. Top *cuvées*
are Blanche de Bosredon and Cuvé Prestige. A modern-style
Bergerac Sec is attractive. *Open: Mon–Sat 8am–12.30pm, 2–7pm.*

Michel Brouilleaud
24240 Monestier. Vineyards owned: 8ha. 15,000 bottles. VP-R
Monsieur Brouilleaud's main production is of a full, rich red
Bergerac, made from 60 percent Cabernet Sauvignon and 40
percent Merlot. The firm makes much smaller quantities of
Bergerac rosé and sweet and dry Bergerac white and uses the
brand name Clos de la Croix Blanche.
Open: Mon–Sat 8am–noon, 2–7pm.

Château Champerel
Pécharmant, 24100 Bergerac.
Vineyards owned: 6ha. 44,000 bottles. VP-R
A very fine, intense, red Pécharmant, half Cabernet Sauvignon, half Merlot fermented in stainless steel and aged for at least a year in new *barriques*, is the only wine. *Open: By appointment.*

Château Court-les-Mûts
Razac de Saussignac, 24240 Sigoulès.
Vineyards owned: 56ha. VP-R
An excellent example of modern winemaking, run by oenologist Pierre-Jean Sadoux. He makes fruity red Bergerac in stainless steel and rare dry and sweet whites from the Saussignac AC. He also produces a sparkling bottle-fermented *brut*, Vin de Fête.

Domaine des Eyssards
24240 Monestier.
Vineyards owned: 40ha. VP-R
Pascal Cuisset is winemaker at this family-owned estate. Huge improvements in the vineyard will be seen in the wines from '88 onwards. Excellent wines now made include the dry white and red Bergerac Cuvée Prestige. The red, 65 percent Cabernet Franc and 35 percent Cabernet Sauvignon, is full bodied with good fruit and wood flavours. *Open: Mon–Sun.*

Château Le Fagé
Pomport, 24240 Sigoulès.
Vineyards owned: 40ha. 150,000 bottles. VP-R
A traditional estate which has been in the Gerardin family for 200 years. It makes white Bergerac Sec, Monbazillac and a Côtes de Bergerac red, which is matured in cement tanks and normally bottled in the year after the harvest. The name Château de Géraud is also used. *Open: Mon–Sun 8am–8pm.*

Domaine du Haut-Pécharmant
Pécharmant, 24100 Bergerac.
Vineyards owned: 42ha. 240,000 bottles. VP-R
The Pécharmant made on this estate, owned by the Roches family, is a blend of 40 percent Cabernet Sauvignon, 30 percent Merlot, 20 percent Cabernet Franc and ten percent Malbec. Monsieur Roches also makes a special *cuvée* which has 70 percent Cabernet Franc. *Open: Mon–Sat 8am–noon, 2–7pm; Sun 3–8pm.*

Château de la Jaubertie
Colombier, 24560 Issigeac.
Vineyards owned: 46ha. 300,000 bottles. VP-R and N
Techniques inspired by Australian winemakers have produced a range that is very successful in the UK (owner Hugh Ryman is English). His whites, especially a 100 percent Sauvignon, have excellent fruit and varietal character. Reds are also well made: the barrel-aged *réserve* is especially good. The approach may not be typical of Bergerac, but it works. *Open: Appointments necessary.*

Domaine de Libarde
Nastringues, 24230 Vélines.
Vineyards owned: 20ha. 60,000 bottles. VP-R
A traditionally run estate, right at the western end of the Bergerac region, just before it turns into Bordeaux. Bergerac Rouge, Montravel dry white and Haut-Montravel sweet white are all produced. The Haut-Montravel is especially worth seeking out.
Open: By appointment only.

Cave Coopérative de Monbazillac
Monbazillac, 24220 Sigoulès. Vineyards owned: 876ha.
5.5 million bottles. Coop (150 members).
The largest producer in Monbazillac, and owner of the showpiece Château de Monbazillac – a 20-hectare estate surrounding a superb medieval castle. It produces red and dry white Bergerac, Pécharmant and *vin de table*. Quality could be better, but the wines are reliable. The cooperative forms part of the giant Unidor group (*see* page 217). *Open: Mon–Fri 9am–noon, 2–5pm.*

René Monbouché
Gendre Marsalet, 24240 Monbazillac.
Vineyards owned: 26ha. 45,000 bottles. VP-R
The domaines of Monsieur Monbouché comprise three estates: Gendre Marsalet, which produces Côtes de Bergerac red; Grand Conseil, producing white Bergerac Sec, and Theulet et Marsalet which makes Monbazillac. The reds and the Monbazillac are matured for a time in wood. *Open: Appointments preferred.*

Château Montaigne
24230 Vélines. Vineyards owned: 15ha. VP-R
This is the country estate of the Mèhler-Besse family, part-owners of Château Palmer in the Médoc and major Bordeaux *négociants*. At this former home of the philosopher Montaigne a red Bergerac from Merlot and the Cabernets is produced.
Open: By appointment only.

Château de Panisseau
Thénac, 24240 Sigoulès.
Vineyards owned: 70ha. 465,000 bottles. VP-R
This large estate surrounds a pretty little 13th-century château. Two dry whites are made, one from 100 percent Sauvignon Blanc, the other from 80 percent Sémillon (with only a touch of Sauvignon); also a classic Bergerac *rouge*, and a rosé from 100 percent Cabernet Sauvignon. The Sémillon dry white is especially worth seeking out, as is a sweet Côtes de Bergerac. *Open: Mon–Fri 9am–noon, 2–6pm; July and Aug Mon–Sun 9am–6pm.*

Clos Peyrelevade
Pécharmant, 24100 Bergerac.
Vineyards owned: 10ha. 40,000 bottles. VP-R
Pécharmant is the only wine produced on this estate – a blend of 55 percent Merlot, 20 percent Cabernet Sauvignon, 16 percent

Cabernet Franc and nine percent Malbec. Although the wine is not matured in wood, it needs some time in bottle. Three-quarters of the production is bottled in half-bottles and magnums.
Open: Appointments preferred.

Château la Raye
24230 Vélines. Vineyards owned: 15ha. 60,000 bottles. VP-R
Jean Itey de Peironnin has a charming château and from here he produces a very fine red Bergerac (a blend of 50 percent Merlot and 50 percent Cabernets) and a sweet Côtes de Montravel.
Open: By appointment only.

Château Thénac
Thénac-le-Bourg, 24240 Sigoulès.
Vineyards owned: 15ha. 120,000 bottles. VP-R
Modern techniques are used in making a red Bergerac with 33 percent Merlot, 33 percent Cabernet Franc and 33 percent Cabernet Sauvignon (one percent Malbec), and a clean-tasting Bergerac Sec. *Open: By appointment only.*

Château de Tiregand
Creysse, 24100 Bergerac.
Vineyards owned: 40ha. 182,000 bottles. VP-R
The St-Exupéry family have owned this estate with its 17th-century château since 1830. It is the largest producer of AC Pécharmant, and this wine accounts for almost the entire production of the estate. The wine is aged in wood for anything up to two years, giving richness and concentration. A little white Bergerac Sec is also made. *Open: Mon–Sat 8am–noon, 2–6pm.*

UNIDOR
Union des Coopératives Vinicoles de la Dordogne,
24106 St-Laurent-des-Vignes. Vineyards owned: 4,009ha.
7 million bottles. Coop (15 coops as members).
This amalgamation of cooperatives controls nearly 40 percent of all Bergerac and takes in wine from Côtes de Duras and the eastern edges of the Bordeaux vineyard at Ste-Foy-le-Grande. The plant matures and bottles the wine and is run on very modern lines, but there are few excitements. Brands include Monsieur Cyrano, Domaine de la Vaure, L'Océanière, Fort Chevalier, Les Trois Clochers, Sélection Unidor and Château Septy.
Open: By appointment only.

BUZET AC

Château du Frandat
47600 Nérac. Vineyards owned: 26.5ha. 86,000 bottles. VP-R
Patrice Sterlin makes both his red and white Buzet in stainless steel, but then ages the red for up to two years in tank and between three months and a year in wood. He makes a point of not selling this wine until it is at least two years old. He is also a producer of armagnac. *Open: Mon–Sat 9am–noon, 2–6pm.*

Les Vignerons de Buzet
Buzet-sur-Baïse, 47160 Damazan. Vineyards owned: 1,700ha.
12 million bottles. Coop (270 members).
The cooperative controls most of the Buzet AC production. It uses
a number of different labels but the best wine is Baron d'Ardeuil,
a ripe, rich wine from older vines. The standard generic Buzet is
also good as an easy-to-drink wine. Other labels used are Le Lys
for red, white and rosé, Château de Gueyze for red, Carte d'Or
and Tradition. The cooperative also makes small amounts of rosé
and white. *Open: Mon–Fri 9–11am, 2–4pm, by appointment.*

CAHORS AC

Château La Caminade
Resses et Fils, 46140 Parnac.
Vineyards owned: 35ha. 256,000 bottles. VP-R
Some stainless steel is used for vinification on this family estate,
and the grapes are de-stalked before fermentation. Although
wines are aged for a year in wood, they are not austere. The top
cuvée is Clos de Commendery. *Open: Mon–Fri 8am–noon, 2–7pm.*

Château de Cayrou
46700 Puy-L'Evêque.
Vineyards owned: 40ha. 200,000 bottles. VP-R
M Jouffreau owns two estates: 16th-century Château de Cayrou
and smaller, ten-hectare Clos de Gamot. He uses organic methods
and stainless steel. His wines, austere while young, age well. He
uses the brand names Comte de Guiscard as well as the estate
name. A new wine, first made in '96 and called Le Clos St-Jean,
comes from a replanted, almost single-varietal vineyard at
Labastide-du-Vert. *Open: Appointments preferred.*

Château de Chambert
Floressas, 46700 Puy-L'Évêque.
Vineyards owned: 59ha. 330,000 bottles. VP-R
An estate restored in the 1970s by a local *négociant*, Caves St-
Antoine. The first substantial vintage was in '79. Vinification is in
stainless steel and ageing in *barriques*. As the vines mature,
quality is improving. Domaine les Hauts de Chambert is a second
wine. *Open: Mon–Sat 8am–noon, 1.30–6pm; Sun by appointment.*

Côtes d'Olt
Parnac, 46140 Luzech. Vineyards owned: 1,300ha.
8.6 million bottles. Coop (330 members).
The largest cooperative in Cahors, producing a number of brand-
named wines: Côtes d'Olt, Comte André de Monpezat, Marquis
d'Olt and the wood-aged Imperial, as well as a number of single
vineyard wines. Standards have improved considerably during
the 1980s, with the introduction of stainless steel and the use of
new wood. As a result, more of the production from here is sold
in bottle and less in bulk.
Open: Mon–Fri all year; Sat also in summer (holiday period only).

Durou et Fils (Domaine de Gaudou)
Gaudou, Vire-sur-Lot, 46700 Puy-L'Évêque.
Vineyards owned: 20ha. VP-R
As son succeeds father methods may change here, although stainless steel has been used since 1980. What may be reviewed is Durou *père*'s dislike of new wood. The vineyards are on some of appellation's best land. A little white *vin de table* is also made.

Domaine de Garriques
Vire-sur-Lot, 46700 Puy-L'Évêque.
Vineyards owned: 17ha. 100,000 bottles. VP-R
Roger Labruyère uses stainless steel and aims at a lighter style of wine with plenty of fruit. He has a little Jurançon in the blend which is typically 70 percent Malbec. *Open: Mon–Sun.*

Château de Haute-Serre
46230 Cieurac. Vineyards owned: 62ha.
372,000 bottles. VP-R and N
Georges Vigouroux, a big name in Cahors, owns the Château de Haute-Serre and the small Château de Mercues (now a four-star hotel). The Haute-Serre wine, produced in a vineyard reclaimed from scrub land in the 1970s, is rich in fruit when young, matures quickly and is fairly commercial. *Open: Mon–Sun 8am–7pm.*

Domaine de Lagrezette
46140 Caillac. Vineyards owned: 53ha. VP-R
Modern production facilities and 18 to 24 months' new-oak barrel ageing means that the Cahors produced here is anything but traditional. The blend in this, the only wine, is mainly Auxerrois plus Merlot and a little Tannat. *Open: Mon–Sun 10am–7pm.*

Domaine de Paillas
Floressas, 46700 Puy-L'Évêque.
Vineyards owned: 27ha. 180,000 bottles. VP-R
A young vineyard producing soft wines. Stainless steel is used for vinification. The Lescombes family bought the estate in 1978 and has replanted on the slopes above the valley floor. The wine can be drunk reasonably young, but does repay some ageing in bottle. *Open: Mon–Fri 8am–noon, 1.30–5.30pm.*

Château Pech de Jammes
46090 Flaujac-Poujols. Vineyards owned: 10ha. VP-R
Thanks to its American ownership, this is claimed to be the best-selling Cahors in the US. The one wine, 80 percent Auxerrois, 15 percent Merlot and a little Tannat, is aged in small *barriques* for 18 months and can be particularly intense. *Open: By appointment.*

Domaine Pineraie
Leygues, 46700 Puy-L'Évêque.
Vineyards owned: 37ha. 120,000 bottles. VP-R
Stainless-steel vinification and wood maturation produce wines with good fruit and some ageing ability. The 85 percent Auxerrois,

15 percent Merlot blend has a maceration of 15 days, which brings intense colour to the wines. *Open: Mon–Sat 8am–noon, 2–7pm.*

Château de Quattre
Bagat-en-Quercy, 46800 Montcuq.
Vineyards owned: 37ha. 246,000 bottles. VP-R
Three estates are owned by the Heilbronner family: Châteaux de Quattre (19-hectares), de Guingal (16-hectares) and de Treilles (18-hectares). Most of the wines are for drinking young, although some *cuvées* from de Treilles are aged in wood. The de Guingal wines are 100 percent Malbec (Auxerrois). *Open: Mon–Sun.*

Rigal et Fils
Parnac, 46140 Luzech. Vineyards owned: 69ha. VP-R and N
The family grew vines long before being *négociants* and has lately sold much of the *négociant* business, although it still distributes the wines of Domaines Eugénie, Le Castelas, Soullaillou and du Parc. The *négociant* blend is called Carte Noire. Wines from the family's own properties are: Château St-Didier, Prieure de Cenac and Château de Grézel. There is considerable use of new wood, especially in the prestige *cuvée* called Apogée.

Château Triguedina
46700 Puy-L'Évêque.
Vineyards owned: 50ha. 300,000 bottles. VP-R
The Baldès family has owned this large, important estate since 1830 and has invested large sums in installing stainless steel for vinification. Clos Triguedina is designed to be drunk young; Prince Probus, 100 percent Auxerrois aged in new oak, needs some bottle-age. The estate also has a fascinating museum.
Open: Mon–Fri 9am–noon, 2–6pm; Sat/Sun by appointment.

CÔTES DE DURAS AC

Domaine Amblard
St-Sernin, 47120 Duras.
Vineyards owned: 68ha. 300,000 bottles. VP-R
Guy Palivert makes mainly red and dry white wines at his large estate. Methods are modern and the resulting Sauvignon Blanc is particularly successful. *Open: Mon–Sat 8am–7pm.*

Domaine des Cours
Ste-Colombe, 47120 Duras.
Vineyards owned: 17ha. 23,000 bottles. VP-R
The Lusoli family makes an attractive, fruity white Sauvignon from free-run juice with temperature-controlled fermentation, and a more traditional red from 50 percent Merlot, 50 percent a blend of the two Cabernets. *Open: Appointments preferred.*

Domaine de Durand
47120 Duras. Vineyards owned: 21ha. 100,000 bottles. VP-R
Jean Michel Fonvielhe makes serious wines at his estate. The red

particularly, with its high proportion of Cabernet Franc and its long ageing in the cellars, repays keeping. Whites, made with Sauvignon and Sémillon, are more lightweight but there is an interesting sweet wine. *Open: Mon–Fri 9am–7pm.*

Château Lafon
Loubès-Bernac, 47120 Duras.
Vineyards owned: 12ha. 80,000 bottles. VP-R
Owned since 1989 by the Gitton family, which is more familiar in Sancerre on the Loire. This small estate has been revitalised with no expense spared and now produces top-quality whites from Sauvignon Blanc and Sémillon. Reds are also made, some of which are 100 percent Merlot, others a blend of Malbec, Cabernet Sauvignon and Merlot. *Open: By appointment only.*

Domaine de Laulam
47120 Duras. Vineyards owned: 19.5ha. 145,000 bottles. VP-R
Gilbert Geoffroy, from Burgundy, bought this estate in the 1970s. He makes a top-quality, wood-aged Sauvignon Blanc and different *cuvées* of red, the best of which is called Duc de Laulam. A small amount of rosé is also made. *Open: Mon–Sat 8am–8pm.*

SCA Les Vignerons des Coteaux de Duras
47120 Duras.
Vineyards owned: 450ha. 946,000 bottles. Coop (85 members).
As with so many of these smaller AC areas in the Southwest, it is the local cooperative that keeps the area ticking over. Production is divided equally between red and white, and includes varietal reds – Cabernet Sauvignon (designed for a little ageing), Merlot (to be drunk young) and white Sauvignon, as well as a more usual blend including Sémillon and Muscadelle with the Sauvignon. The brand name is Berticot. *Open: Mon–Fri 8am–noon, 2–6pm.*

CÔTES DU FRONTONNAIS AC

Domaine de Baudare
Campas, 82370 Labastide St-Pierre.
Vineyards owned: 27ha. 120,000 bottles. VP-R
Typically fruity Frontonnais wines are produced here: controlled fermentation brings out the colour and flavour of the Négrette in the red and rosé, both of which are bottled as Domaine de Baudare. The estate also makes Vin de Pays du Comté Tolosan – red as well as sweet and dry white. *Open: By appointment only.*

Château Bellevue la Forêt
D49, 31620 Fronton.
Vineyards owned: 115ha. 843,000 bottles. VP-R
A newly developed estate growing traditional varieties: 50 percent Négrette, Cabernets Franc and Sauvignon, plus Gamay and Syrah. The lighter of the reds is called André Daguin; Bellevue la Forêt is red or rosé, and small quantities of Cuvée Spéciale, a red aged in new wood, are also produced. *Open: Appointments preferred.*

Château Colombière
Villaudric, 31620 Fronton.
Vineyards owned: 25ha. 163,000 bottles. VP-R
Baron François de Driésen makes a range of reds and rosés at his
estate. He uses carbonic maceration for Négrette and Gamay, and
the Gamay goes into a rosé *vin gris*. The top of the range is the
Baron de D Rouge, (50 percent Negrette); the other two reds,
Réserve du Baron and Château la Colombière, are lighter and
have a higher percentage of Negrette. The style is attractively
forward and fruity. *Open: Mon–Sat 9am–noon, 2–6pm.*

Cave Coopérative Les Côtes de Fronton
31620 Fronton. Vineyards owned: 700ha. 2.7 million bottles.
Coop (300 members).
One of the biggest cooperatives in France, mainly due to its huge
production (830,000 cases) of *vin de table* and *vin de pays*. It also
makes Côtes du Frontonnais, which reaches a fair standard. The
two estate wines, Château Marcelot and Château de Cransac, are
vinified separately. *Open: Mon–Sat 8am–noon, 2–6pm.*

CÔTES DU MARMANDAIS AC

Cave Coopérative de Cocumont
Cocumont, 47250 Bouglon. Vineyards owned: 1,001ha.
1 million bottles. Coop (340 members).
This modern, well-run cooperative makes Côtes du Marmandais,
some Bordeaux AC wines and Vin de Pays de l'Agenais.
Open: Appointments preferred.

Société Coopérative Vinicole des Côtes du Marmandais
Beaupuy, 47200 Marmande. Vineyards owned: 650ha.
5.3 million bottles. Coop (280 members).
About half the production is of Côtes du Marmandais, the rest is
Vin de Pays de l'Agenais and *vin de table*. Stainless steel is used
and standards have been rising. The wine is like a sub-claret: soft,
with a good dollop of Merlot. A number of château names are
used for the Marmandais wines. This cooperative has joined that
at Buzet (*see* page 218) for sales purposes. *Open: Mon–Sat 8am–
noon, 2–6.30pm (7pm in summer); Sun by appointment.*

GAILLAC AC

Boissel-Rhodes
81600 Gaillac. Vineyards owned: 30ha. VP-R
The Boissel family also owns the Château de Rhodes. It produces
a dry sparkling bottle-fermented wine, René Rieux; reds from
Duras, Syrah, Fer and Gamay and a *primeur* from just Gamay.

Domaine des Bouscaillous
81140 Castelnau de Montmirail.
Vineyards owned: 18ha. 100,000 bottles. VP-R
Yvon Maurel makes a range of Gaillac wines. The reds include a

100 percent Gamay *primeur* as well as a wine designed for some ageing in which the Duras grape predominates. There is also a rosé – a blend of Jurançon and Gamay. Whites include a dry white with 80 percent Len de l'El and 20 percent Sauvignon, and a sweet white made from Mauzac. Mauzac is also used for a delicious low-alcohol Pétillant de Raisin. *Open: Appointments preferred.*

Vignobles Jean Cros
Mas des Vignes, 81140 Cabuzac-sur-Vère.
Vineyards owned: 48ha. 333,000 bottles. VP-R
This family concern has undergone recent changes with the death of Jean Cros, and it is to be hoped that standards can be restored: this was once the premier producer in the appellation. The firm owns two vineyards: Domaine Jean Cros and Château Larroze, from which it produces a full range, including a white from 100 percent Mauzac and reds from Duras plus Syrah and Braucol. *Open: Oct–end May Mon–Sat 9am–noon, 2–6pm; Sun afternoon only; June–end Sept Mon–Sat 9am–7pm; Sun 2–7pm.*

Domaine Delacroux
Lincarque, 81150 Cestayrols.
Vineyards owned: 35ha. 27,000 bottles. VP-R
The Derrieux family also owns Château Philippe. From these two properties a full range of Gaillac wines is made, among which the red and dry white are the most important.
Open: Mon–Sat 8am–noon, 2–6pm; appointments preferred.

Domaine de Labarthe
Castanet, 81150 Marssac.
Vineyards owned: 28ha. 238,000 bottles. VP-R
The Albert family has been making wine here since the 17th century and now produces a full range of Gaillacs. The firm makes a *primeur* from Gamay and a soft, warm *vin de garde* from the local Duras and Braucol plus the Bordeaux Cabernets and Merlot. Rosé comes from Gamay and Syrah. Len de l'El is balanced with Sauvignon in a dry white, while 100 percent Mauzac is used for the sweet white. It also makes a bottle-fermented wine from Mauzac and Len de l'El, as well as an oak-aged white called Heritage. *Open: Mon–Sat 8am–noon, 2–7pm; Sun by appointment.*

Cave de Labastide de Levis
81150 Marssac sur Tarn. Vineyards owned: 1,644ha.
7 million bottles. Coop (521 members).
The cooperative dominates the Gaillac AC area, producing wines that are mostly sold ready for drinking. The semi-sparkling Gaillac *perlé* can be quite attractive, and the Gaillac Primeur red is full of fresh fruit. It also makes a sweet, low-alcohol Pétillant de Raisin. *Open: Appointments preferred.*

Manoir de l'Emmeillé
81140 Campagnac. Vineyards owned: 38ha. 200,000 bottles. VP-R
The name means 'almond tree' in the local dialect. Here the

Poussou family makes three reds: the top *cuvée* is called Cuvée Prestige. A Gamay *primeur* and a dry and sweet white are also made. *Open: Mon–Sat 8am–noon, 2–6pm.*

Château Moussens
81150 Cestayrols. Vineyards owned: 24ha. 20,000 bottles. VP-R
Reds and whites are made in equal quantity. The red combines Fer, Duras and Merlot, and the top *cuvée*, Adrien Monestié (the name of the owner's wife), spends 12 months in wood. The whites are the stars here, a typical blend of Mauzac and Len de l'El, and there is also a rosé. *Open: By appointment only.*

Domaine de Pialentou
Brens, 81600 Gaillac.
Vineyards owned: 12ha. 25,000 bottles. VP-R
In good vintages the red has tannin enough for three or four years in bottle, but enough fruit to be drunk younger. M Ailloud also makes a dry white and a rosé. *Open: Appointments preferred.*

Mas Pignou
81600 Gaillac. Vineyards owned: 33ha. 188,000 bottles. VP-R
Dry white and red are produced at this estate, which is owned by Jacques Auque. It has a very fine view of the town of Gaillac. M Auque's red, using Braucol, Duras, Merlot and the two Cabernets, has some wood maturing which gives it good ageing ability without losing fruit. The white is a 50:50 Sauvignon and Len de l'El blend. *Open: Mon–Sat 9am–noon, 2–8pm; Sun by appointment.*

Robert Plageoles (Domaine de Très Cantous)
81600 Gaillac. Vineyards owned: 21ha. 50,000 bottles. VP-R
One of Gaillac's best producers, M Plageoles owns two estates – ten-hectare Domaine de Très Cantous and 11-hectare Domaine de Roucou Cantemerle. Some wines are a blend from both estates. Reds are made from Duras and Gamay, whites incude a sparkling Gaillac Mousseux, a delicious dry Sauvignon and a sweet white Mauzac, still wines and a rare AC Gaillac Premières Côtes (sherry-like *vin de voile* from Mauzac, which stays in cask for six years). A sweet wine, Vin d'Autanis from Ondenc, is also made: a style not seen for around a century. *Open: By appointment only.*

IROULÉGUY AC

Cave Coopérative des Vins d'Irouléguy et du Pays Basque
64430 St-Étienne-de-Baïgorry.
Vineyards owned: 131ha. 626,000 bottles. Coop (49 members).
This cooperative virtually controls the whole of Irouléguy production and has gone some way towards saving the appellation for posterity. The aim is to increase the area under vine to 200 hectares by the turn of the century. It makes a range of wines including some single-vineyard examples under domaine names of which the most important is the red Domaine Mignaberry. *Open: By appointment only.*

JURANÇON AC

Domaine Cauhapé (Henri Ramonteu)
64360 Monein. Vineyards owned: 25ha. 150,000 bottles. VP-R
One of the dynamic figures trying to revitalise the area, Henri Ramonteau is constantly experimenting with barrel-ageing for sweet wines, and barrel fermentation and the use of skin contact for dry whites to give greater intensity of flavour. He grows Petit and Gros Manseng and Courbu. For sweet wines, he leaves the grapes on the vines to increase their sweetness and concentration. He also makes Béarn red.
Open: Mon-Fri 8am-noon, 2-7pm, by appointment.

Domaine Guirouilh
Route de Belair, Lasseube, 64290 Gan.
Vineyards owned: 8ha. 50,000 bottles. VP-R
An ancient estate that has been in the Guirouilh family since the 17th century. It specialises in a traditional sweet Jurançon made from dried grapes and aged in oak. Most of the production is of a floral dry white. *Open: Appointments preferred.*

Cru Lamouroux
La Chapelle de Rousse, 64110 Jurançon.
Vineyards owned: 12ha. 35,000 bottles. VP-R
Monique and Richard Ziemek produce only Jurançon Moelleux from their vineyard. They have three parcels of land, at Cru Lamouroux, at Le Clos Mirabel and at Domaine Peyrouse. The wine, made from 60 percent Petit Manseng and 40 percent Gros Manseng, is vinified in stainless steel and matured in wood for 18 months before bottling. It is a classic sweet wine with intense flavours of pineapple and honey.
Open: Mon-Sat 9-11.30am, 2-7pm.

Caves des Producteurs de Jurançon
63 Avenue Henri-IV, 64290 Gan. Vineyards owned: 530ha.
2.8 million bottles. Coop (200 members).
Jurançon dry and sweet in different qualities are the only AC wines made here. By far the bulk is of dry Jurançon, made from Gros Manseng, in three styles: Sélection Viguerie Royale, Primeur and Millésime. The same styles apply to the sweet Jurançon. The cooperative also sells wine from three small estates: Château les Astous, Domaine des Terrasses and Domaine Lasserre.
Open: Mon-Sat 9am-noon, 2-6.30pm; Sun during summer.

Clos Uroulat
64360 Monein. Vineyards owned: 7.5ha. 30,000 bottles. VP-R
Charles Hours, the owner of this small property, makes a classic style of sweet Jurançon Moelleux, ageing the wine in *barriques* for 12 months, using 100 percent Petit Manseng. He also makes Jurançon Sec, using stainless steel for vinification and a blend of Gros Manseng and Courbu. The quality of both wines is high.
Open: By appointment only.

MADIRAN AC
PACHERENC DU VIC-BILH AC

Château d'Arricau-Bordes
Arricau-Bordes, 64350 Lembeye.
Vineyards owned: Madiran 18ha. 120,000 bottles. VP-R
An estate based around a ruined 12th-century château (associated with d'Artagnan of *The Three Musketeers*). In 1980 Tannat and the two Cabernets were planted. The wine is aged in stainless steel although there are plans to use some wood maturation in the future. At present the wines tend to lightness, but they improve with every vintage. *Open: Mon–Sun during working hours.*

Château d'Aydie
Haute Biste, Aydie, 64330 Garlin. Vineyards owned: Madiran 40ha, Pacherenc 5ha. 340,000 bottles. VP-R
Monsieur Leplace's Madiran is dominated by Tannat (up to 60 percent), with 20 percent each of the two Cabernets. It is made traditionally and aged in wood, giving initially quite a tough wine, but one that mellows with time. A new wine, 100 percent Tannat, is aged in new wood. He also makes smaller amounts of white Pacherenc du Vic-Bilh using stainless steel to give a fresh, crisp dry wine and a sweet wine. *Open: Mon–Fri, during working hours.*

Château Barréjat
Maumusson-Laguian, 32400 Riscle. Vineyards owned: Madiran 14ha, Pacherenc 2ha. 100,000 bottles. VP-R
The Capmartin family has owned this estate for three generations and owns the seven-hectare Domaine Capmartin. It makes traditional Madiran, using a slow maceration to obtain maximum colour; the wine develops relatively fast, but ages well. The blend is 50:50 Tannat and the Cabernets. The Pacherenc du Vic-Bilh is vinified in stainless steel. *Open: Mon–Sat 8am–noon, 2–7pm.*

Alain Brumont
Maumusson, 32400 Riscle.
Vineyards owned: Madiran 77ha. 500,000 bottles. VP-R
M Brumont, one of Madiran's dominant figures, owns three estates, all producing Madiran: Domaine Bouscassé (36 hectares), Château Moutus (29) and Domaine Meinjarre (12). Bouscassé spends a year in wood; for Moutus the wood is new. He also makes Rosé de Béarn and dry and sweet Pacherenc from a newly bought property. *Open: Mon–Sat 8am–8pm.*

Patrick Ducournau
Maumusson-Laguian, 32400 Riscle.
Vineyards owned: Madiran 12ha, Pacherenc 2.5ha.
93,000 bottles. VP-R
One of the rising generation of winemakers, M Ducournau makes his wines under the names of Chapelle Lenclos, (the top *cuvée*) and Château Mouréou. Chapelle Lenclos is 100 percent Tannat and regularly wins awards; Château Mouréou has 70 percent

Tannat. Petit Manseng is used to produce a sweet as well as a dry Pacherenc. *Open: Mon-Sat 8am-noon, 2-6pm, by appointment only.*

Lucien Oulie (Domaine du Crampilh)
Aurion-Idernes, 64350 Lembeye.
Vineyards owned: 20ha. 132,000 bottles. VP-R
Red Madiran and white Pacherenc du Vic-Bilh are both made here and the full range of local grapes is used. The Madiran needs four or five years' ageing; the Pacherenc should be drunk young and fresh. *Open: By appointment only.*

Château Peyros
Corbères Abères, 64350 Lembeye.
Vineyards owned: 20ha. 150,000 bottles. VP-R
Stainless steel is used for vinification in this carefully run estate which Monsieur de Robillard purchased in 1967. He makes only Madiran, using 50 percent Cabernet Franc, 45 percent Tannat and five percent Cabernet Sauvignon. There are two *cuvées*: Le Couvent which is aged in wood and Château Peyros which is aged in tank. There are plans to make Pacherenc, both dry and sweet. *Open: Appointments preferred.*

Domaine Pichard
Soublecause, 65700 Maubourguet. Vineyards owned: Madiran 12ha, Pacherenc 0.5ha. 80,000 bottles. VP-R
Monsieur Vigneau makes what is locally considered a fine Madiran using 45 percent Tannat, 40 percent Cabernet Franc and 15 percent Cabernet Sauvignon. He ages the wine in wood before bottling. His small production of Pacherenc du Vic-Bilh is bottled young. *Open: Mon-Sat 8am-7pm.*

Producteurs Plaimont
Route d'Orthez, 32400 St-Mont. Vineyards owned: 2,320ha. 11 million bottles. Coop (1,350 members).
This large cooperative brings together three smaller cooperatives to produce Madiran, Côtes de St-Mont and Vin de Pays des Côtes de Gascogne. The white *vin de pays* has been a runaway success for its clean, perfumed taste, given by the Colombard grape. Some Madiran and Côtes de St-Mont ('Collection Plaimont') are aged in new wood, while the standard range is known as Plaimont Tradition. *Open: Mon-Sat 9am-noon, 2-6pm.*

Domaine de Teston
Maumusson, 32400 Riscle.
Vineyards owned: 20ha. 157,000 bottles. VP-R
Madiran, Pacherenc du Vic-Bilh and the VDQS wines of Côtes de St-Mont are all made by Monsieur Laffitte. He uses stainless steel and modern technology but then matures the red in new wood. He says he is particularly proud of his newly acquired Côtes de St-Mont vineyard which is planted with 70 percent Tannat, 20 percent Cabernet Sauvignon and ten percent Fer Servadou. *Open: By appointment only.*

MARCILLAC AC

Pierre Lacombe
Avenue de Rodez, 12330 Marcillac.
Vineyards owned: 3ha. 8,000 bottles. VP-R
M Lacombe makes small quantities of light, fruity, and easy-to-drink red Marcillac using only Fer Servadou. He vinifies in wood.

Laurens-Teulier
Domaine du Cros, 12390 Rignac.
Vineyards owned: 5ha. 20,000 bottles. VP-R
M Teulier uses only Fer Servadou (Mancoi), no herbicides in the vineyard and egg-white for fining. Vines over 40 years old yield a deep, intense wine, aged in old wood. Domaine du Cros, matured for two years, is the best wine. *Open: Mon–Sun 9am–1pm, 2–7pm.*

Cave des Vignerons du Vallon
Valady, 12330 Marcillac.
Vineyards owned: 105ha. 400,000 bottles. Coop (60 members).
The cooperative dominates production in this small area. It makes a Cuvée Réserve and Marcillac Tradition red and rosé, all using 100 percent Fer Servadou. *Open: Mon–Sat 9am–noon, 2–6pm.*

CÔTES DU BRULHOIS VDQS

Cave Coopérative de Goulens-en-Brulhois
Goulens, 47390 Layrac. Vineyards owned: 95ha.
227,000 bottles. Coop (250 members).
Mostly Côtes du Brulhois is made, (Cuvée des Anciens Prieurés is the better of the two *cuvées*) plus Buzet and Vin de Pays de l'Agenais. *Open: Mon–Fri 8am–noon, 2–6pm; Sat 8am–noon.*

TURSAN VDQS

Les Vignerons du Tursan
40320 Geaune. Vineyards owned: 275ha. 1.3 million bottles.
Coop (230 members).
Red, rosé and white Tursan are the only wines from this cooperative, which takes the vast majority of wine from this small VDQS area. Carte Noire and Domaine de La Castèle are the better *cuvées. Open: Mon–Fri 8am–noon, 2–5.30pm; Sat 8am–noon, 2–5pm.*

VIN DE LAVILLEDIEU VDQS

Cave Coopérative La Ville Dieu du Temple
82290 La Ville Dieu du Temple.
Vineyards owned: 21ha. 190,000 bottles. Coop (16 members).
The 16 members are virtually the only producers of this VDQS (though there are plans to expand), using ten percent Negrette and 30 percent each of Gamay, Syrah and Cabernet Franc. Vin de Pays du Comte Tolosan, Coteaux de Quercy and Coteaux et Terrasses de Montauban are also made. *Open: By appointment only.*

Index

Indexers' note: The following abbreviations are used in the index: Ch (Château); Coop (Coopérative); Dom (Domaine[s]). Where names of wines and vineyards are the same they are indexed together. Personal name brands are not inverted.